How to Milk an A

Stuff an Eg

And Armor a Turnip

A Thousand Years of Recipes

by

David Friedman

and

Elizabeth Cook

© David Friedman and Elizabeth Cook,
1988, 1990, 1992, 1996, 1998, 2000, 2011
ISBN: 978-1-460-92498-3
Copies may be purchased online from
https://www.createspace.com/3565795

If you wish to reproduce or reprint anything in this book, you may do so subject to the following conditions:
1. The material should be accompanied by a credit line giving the source and author.
2. Any article or recipe that is quoted must be quoted in full, with no changes, deletions, or additions.
3. If you are making more than 100 copies, you must first get permission from the author.
4. Recipes may be quoted on web pages, provided that the source is credited. We would appreciate a link to the online version of this volume, at the URL below.

http://www.daviddfriedman.com/Medieval/To_Milk_an_Almond.pdf

To the memory of

Marion Walke

Introduction

The Society for Creative Anachronism is a group that does historical recreation from the Middle Ages and Renaissance. Some of its events are feasts. When I discovered it, about forty years ago, it struck me that medieval feasts with diners in medieval clothing ought to be have medieval food.

I found collections of English recipes from the fourteen and fifteenth centuries compiled by nineteenth century enthusiasts, along with a translation of a thirteenth century Arabic cookbook published in a scholarly journal in the nineteen thirties. Over the years since, my collection of sources has expanded, in part through translations by fellow enthusiasts, among them my wife and daughter.

Most period recipes omit inessential details such as quantities, temperatures, and times. You take some of this and enough of that, cook it until it is done, add a bit of something else and serve it forth. The problems of getting from that to something that tastes good make cooking from *Two Fifteenth Century Cookery Books* more interesting than cooking from Fanny Farmer. And you end up with a dish that, as best you can tell, nobody else has made for the past five hundred years. Think of it as experimental archaeology.

This volume contains the result of my and my wife's efforts, assisted by lots of other people, at working out period recipes. Each recipe starts with the original or a translation of the original, followed by information on how we make it. One of the things I have learned from reading secondary sources on historical cooking is that you should never trust a secondary source that does not include the primary, since you have no way of knowing what liberties the author may have taken in his "interpretation" of the recipe.

The volume also contains a number of related articles—what foodstuffs were available when, how to produce a medieval feast, and much else. It is a selection from a longer volume intended for readers active in the SCA, a Miscellany covering medieval cooking and much else that has gone through nine self-published editions and will shortly be available in a tenth. For readers unfamiliar with the organization, it is worth explaining that members adopt "personae" with period names, some of which appear here. Mine is a North African Berber named Cariadoc from about 1100 A.D.

Enjoy.

David Friedman

If you would like to discuss any of the issues raised in the articles, exchange recipes, volunteer to translate cookbooks, or correspond with us on any other subject, our address is:

David Friedman and Betty Cook
(Cariadoc and Elizabeth)
3806 Williams Rd.,
San Jose, CA 95117
ddfr@daviddfriedman.com
www.daviddfriedman.com/Medieval/
Medieval.html

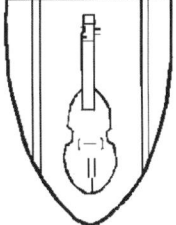

Table of Contents

Introduction — 0
Recipes — 1

Sources for Recipes — 1
Early Period — 1
English/French 13th-15th c. — 1
English 16th-17th c. — 2
German — 2
Italian, Spanish and Portuguese — 2
Islamic and Indian — 2
Chinese — 3
Other — 3

Ingredients — 4

European Dishes — 9
Bread — 9
Vegetables — 11
Seafood — 19
Soups — 22
Poultry — 25
Meat Dishes — 31
Meat, Cheese and Egg Pies — 40
Desserts, Appetizers, Etc. — 46
Drinks — 64
Sauces — 65
Pasta, Rice, etc. — 68
Miscellaneous — 72

Islamic Dishes: Middle East and al-Andalus — 75
Bread — 75
Meat with Sauce or Stew — 76
Fried Dishes — 93
Dishes with Legumes — 99
Dishes with Grains, Bread, or Pasta — 101
Oven Dishes and Roasting — 108
Relishes & Dips — 111
Deserts — 113
Drinks — 125
Odds and Ends — 125

Indian Dishes — 126

Chinese Dishes — 129

Index of Recipes — 131

Additional Material on Period Cooking — 135
Cooking from Primary Sources: Some General Comments — 135
Late Period and Out of Period Foodstuffs — 138
Scottish Oat Cakes: A Conjectural Reconstruction — 145
Hildegard von Bingen's Small Cakes — 146
To Prepare a Most Honorable Feast — 147
To Make a Feast — 150
An Islamic Dinner — 155
How to Make Arrack — 157
A Dinner at Pennsic — 158

Recipes

The sources of these recipes range, with a few exceptions, from the sixth century to the sixteenth. The original, or an English translation of the original, is given in *chancery font*, followed by a list of ingredients with quantities and, usually but not always, additional instructions. For a few of the less readable early English recipes we also give a modernized version of the original text. The only intentional modifications we have made are to modernize the spelling in some recipes and to omit the medical comments which Platina (routinely) and the authors of the Andalusian cookbook (occasionally) include in their recipes.

How well worked out the recipes are varies; some we have been doing for many years, others are the result of one or two tries. Before serving to anyone other than close friends and fellow cooking enthusiasts, try the recipe out at least once and adjust it to taste.

Sources for Recipes

Early Period

Anthimus, *De Observatio Ciborum*, translated by Shirley Howard Weber, published by E. J. Brill Ltd, Leiden 1924. This is a letter on the subject of diet, written in the sixth century by a Byzantine physician to Theoderic, King of the Franks. It includes several recipes.

Apicius, *The Roman Cookery Book*, tr. Barbara Flower and Elisabeth Rosenbaum, George G. Harrap & Co. Ltd., London, 1958. This is a recommended translation and includes the Latin original. The earlier translation by Vehling is not recomended, as he changes the recipes considerably.

English/French 13th-15th c.

Ancient Cookery from *A Collection of the Ordinances and Regulations for the Government of the Royal Household made in Divers Reigns from King Edward III to King William and Queen Mary also Receipts in Ancient Cookery,* printed for the Society of London Antiquaries by John Nichols, 1740. The recipes are from the early 15th century.

Curye on Inglysch: English Culinary Manuscripts of the Fourteenth Century (Including the Forme of Cury), edited by Constance B. Hieatt and Sharon Butler, published for the Early English Text Society by the Oxford University Press, 1985. Still in print as of 2010.

The Forme of Cury, A Roll of Ancient English Cookery, ed. S. Pegge, printed for the Society of London Antiquaries by John Nichols, 1780. This is English c. 1390; for a later edition see *Curye on Inglysch* above.

Constance B. Hieatt, *An Ordinance of Pottage,* Prospect Books, London, 1988 (15th c. English).

Constance B. Hieatt and Robin F. Jones, *Two Anglo-Norman Culinary Collections Edited from British Library Manuscripts Additional 32085 and Royal 12.C.xii, Speculum* v. 61 n. 4, pp. 859-882, 1986. Referred to below as "Anglo-Norman."

Le Menagier de Paris, 1395, tr. Janet Hinson (Lady Mairoli Bhan); also translated as *The Goodman of Paris*, Power and Coulton, tr., but with only selections from the recipes. Recipes from Power and Coulton are given as "Goodman;" recipes from Hinson are given as "Menagier." Page references are to volume II of the collection of source material we used to sell. The Hinson translation is webbed at: www.daviddfriedman.com/Medieval/Cookbooks/Menagier/Menagier_Contents.html

A Noble Boke off Cookry Ffor a Prynce Houssolde, ed. Mrs. Alexander Napier, 1882 (c. 1470).

Chiquart, *Du Fait de Cuisine,* 1420, tr. by Elizabeth from the French original published by Terence Scully in Vallesia v. 40, pp. 101-231, 1985. There is also a published translation by Scully. Elizabeth's transation is webbed at: www.daviddfriedman.com/Medieval/Cookbooks/Du_Fait_de_Cuisine/du_fait_de_c_contents.html

Pepys 1047. Published as *Stere Hit Well: Medieval recipes and remedies from Samuel Pepys's Library.* Modern English version by G.A.J. Hodgett. The modern English version is unreliable but the book includes a facsimile of the late fifteenth century original.

Two Fifteenth Century Cookery Books (1430-1450), Thomas Austin Ed., Early English Text Society, Oxford University Press, 1964.

Le Viandier (c. 1392), Taillevent. Our recipes are from a partial translation by Elizabeth Bennett [Mistress Alys Gardyner]; two complete translations have also been published.

English 16th-17th c.

Sir Kenelm Digby, *The Closet of Sir Kenelm Digby, Opened* (published posthumously in 1669). This is slightly out of period, but contains the earliest collection of fermented drink recipes that we know of. Some of this is webbed at: realbeer.com/spencer/digby.html

The English Huswife, by Gervase Markham (1615, but Mistress Marion informs us that Markham is a notorious plagiarist, so the material is probably somewhat earlier).

Sir Hugh Platt, *Delights for Ladies*, London, 1609.

A Proper Newe Booke of Cokerye, ed. Catherine Frances Frere, Cambridge, W. Heffer and sons, Ltd., 1913 (16th century).

German

Daz Buoch von Guoter Spise (between 1345 and 1354), tr. Alia Atlas. Webbed at: http://cs-people.bu.edu/akatlas/Buch/buch.html

Sabina Welser's Cookbook, tr. from *Das Kochbuch der Sabina Welserin* (c. 1553) by Valoise Armstrong, Little Rock, Arizona, 1998. Webbed at: www.daviddfriedman.com/Medieval/Cookbooks/Sabrina_Welserin.html

Italian, Spanish and Portuguese

Platina, *De Honesta Voluptate*, Venice, L. De Aguila, 1475. Translated by E. B. Andrews, Mallinkrodt 1967. (Both Platina and Kenelm Digby were published as part of the "Mallinkrodt Collection of Food Classics.") Reprinted by Falconwood Press, 1989. Page numbers given herein are from the Falconwood edition. This is the version we have worked from; a new and (I gather) inproved translation is Platina, *On Right Pleasure and Good Health,* tr. Mary Ella Milham, Medieval and Renaissance Texts and Studies, Tempe, Arizona, 1998.

Due Libre B, An Early 15th Century Recipe Collection from Southern Italy. Translated by Rebecca Friedman. Webbed at: http://www.daviddfriedman.com/Medieval/Cookbooks/Due_Libre_B/Due_Libre_B.html

Epulario, or, The Italian Banquet, London, 1598. Reprinted Falconwood Press, Albany, NY, 1990. This is a late-period English translation of an Italian cookbook with a lot of overlap with Platina, including some of the same sequences of recipes and at least one typo in common.

Messibugio, *Libro Novo* 1557. Translated by Master Basilius (Charles Potter).

Diego Granado, *Libro del arte de cozina,* 1599. A few recipes from this have been translated by Lady Brighid ni Chiarain of Tethba, Settmour Swamp (Robin Carroll-Mann).

Ruperto de Nola, *Libro de Guisados*, 1529. Translated by Lady Brighid ni Chiarain (Robin Carroll-Mann). Webbed at: http://www.florilegium.org/files/FOOD-MANUSCRIPTS/Guisados1-art.html

Um Tratado Da Cozinha Portuguesa Do Seculo XV (A Text on Portuguese Cooking from the Fifteenth Century). Translated by Jane L. Crowley with the assistance of a modern Portuguese text by Professor Antonio Gomes Filho. Referred to as "Portuguese" below.

Islamic and Indian

Ain-I-Akbari (part of the *Akbarnama*) by Abu al-Fazl ibn Mubarak, H. Blochmann tr., edited by D. C. Phillott, Calcutta 1927. An account of Mughal India, especially Akbar's court, in the late 16th century. It includes ingredient lists (with quantities but without instructions) for thirty dishes and descriptions of how to make bread and arrack. Webbed at: http://www.archive.org/details/ainiakbari00jarrgoog

Al-Baghdadi, *A Baghdad Cookery Book* (1226 A.D./623 A.H.), A.J. Arberry, tr., Islamic Culture 1939, and republished in *Medieval Arab Cookery* (see below). There is now a new and probably better translation by Charles Perry, but we have not yet used it.

An Anonymous Andalusian Cookbook of the Thirteenth Century, a translation by Charles Perry of the Arabic edition of Ambrosio Huici Miranda with the assistance of an English translation by Elise Fleming, Stephen Bloch, Habib ibn al-Andalusi and Janet Hinson of the Spanish translation by Ambrosio Huici Miranda, webbed at: http://www.daviddfriedman.com/Medieval/Cookbooks/Andalusian/andalusian_contents.htm.
Referred to below as "Andalusian." Page references are to volume II of the collection of source material we used to sell.

Annals of the Caliph's Kitchen, Ibn Sayyar al-Warraq, translated by Nawal Nasrallah. Tenth century. We also have a few recipes from the same source translated by Charles Perry.

La Cocina Arabigoandaluza, translated from Arabic into Spanish by Fernando de la Granja Santamaria and from Spanish into English by Melody Asplund-Faith. This consists of selections from a much longer Arabic original. It is referred to below as "al-Andalusi."

Medieval Arab Cookery, Essays and Translations by Maxime Rodinson, A.J. Arberry & Charles Perry, Prospect Books, 1998. Contains, along with much else, *Kitab al Tibakhah: A Fifteenth-Century Cookbook*, Charles Perry, tr., original author Ibn al-Mubarrad. Also *The Description of Familiar Foods*, a cookbook based on al-Baghdadi with additional recipes.

The Ni'matnama Manuscript of the Sultans of Mandu: The Sultan's Book of Delights, translated by Norah M. Titley, Routledge, 2005. An Indian source c. 1500.

Chinese

Paul D. Buell and Eugene N. Anderson, *A Soup for the Qan: Chinese Dietary Medicine of the Mongol Era as Seen in Hu Szu-Hui's Yin-Shan Cheng-Yao,* Kegan Paul International, London and New York, 2000. A translation of a Chinese/Mongol medical book with extensive commentary, including recipes for both food and medicinals.

Teresa Wang and E.N. Anderson, *Ni Tsan and His 'Cloud Forest Hall Collection of Rules for Drinking and Eating', Petits Propos Culinaires* #60‡, 1998. See also "Some remarks about the translation of Yun Lintang Yinshi Zhidu Ji" published in *PPC 60* by Francoise Sabban, which has corrections and alternative translations.

Other

The Domostroi: Rules for Russian Households in the Time of Ivan the Terrible, edited and translated by Carolyn Johnston Pouncy, Cornell University Press: Ithaca 1994. A Russian household management manual, most of which is probably from the 16th century, including a few recipes and a good deal of information about food.

Rudolf Grewe, "An Early XIII Century Northern-European Cookbook," in *Proceedings of A Conference on Current Research in Culinary History: Sources, Topics, and Methods*. Published by the Culinary Historians of Boston, 1986. This is an article attempting to reconstruct the lost original from which several surviving manuscripts, including the one we refer to as "A selection from *An Old Icelandic Medical Miscelleny,*" descend.

A Selection From *An Old Icelandic Medical Miscelleny,* ed. Henning Larson, Oslo, 1931. For a more recent edition, see Grewe.

‡: *Petits Propos Culinaires* is an international journal on food, food history, cookery and cookery books. See: http://rdeh.tripod.com/

Mappae Clavicula: a Little Key to the World of Medieval Techniques, tr. Cyril Stanley Smith and John G. Hawthorne, *Transactions of the American Philosophical Society*, Philadelphia, 1974. This is a collection of technical recipes which includes three candy recipes; the manuscript translated here dates to the 12th c. but there are earlier versions with fewer recipes going back to the 9th c.

Ingredients

Asafoetida: Strongly flavored spice available in Indian grocery stores, referred to as "hing" or "heeng".

Beef Broth: Canned beef broth is usually concentrated; what we use is either that, diluted in an equal quantity of water, or beef broth from beef bullion—1 cube per cup of water.

Camphor: Edible camphor can sometimes be found in Indian grocery stores; it is very strongly flavored.

Cassia, aka chinese cinnamon: Cassia is what is usually sold as cinnamon in the U.S., as distinguished from "true cinnamon," aka "ceylon cinnamon." The two spices have similar but not identical flavors.

Clarified butter, aka ghee: Available in Indian grocery stores; Indian cookbooks often have instructions for making it.

Coriander: Unless described as fresh we interpret it as meaning coriander seed, with the leaf of the same plant labelled "cilantro."

Date syrup, aka dibs: Can sometimes be found in Middle Eastern grocery stores.

Galingale: A root similar in appearance to ginger, used in Thai cooking, and sold in oriental grocery stores, fresh or ground, sometimes as "Galingas."

Ghee: Clarified Butter.

Gourd aka pumpkin: Modern squashes and pumpkins are from the New World; the problem of identifying the old world equivalent is discussed in the article "Late Period and Out of Period Foods." (p. 138). Our best guess is the opo gourd, often available in Chinese grocery stores in the U.S.

Mastic: A strongly flavored resin; I like to describe it as dehydrated turpentine. Try Middle Eastern or Indian groceries and use it in very small quantities.

Oranges/orange juice: in Europe and the Middle East before about the 16th century, this would have meant sour oranges. For more on citrus fruit, see p. 140.

Powder fort: A spice mixture mentioned in various period recipes; we have not yet been able to find a description of what spices it contains. What we use is a mixture containing, by weight: 1 part cloves, 1 part mace, 1 part cubebs, 7 parts cinnamon, 7 parts ginger, and 7 parts pepper, all ground. This is a guess, based on very limited evidence; it works for the dishes in which we have tried it.

Poudre douce: A sweet spice mixture. The composition probably varied; we usually use a mix of four parts sugar, 2 parts cinnamon, and 1 part ginger.

Samidh flour: Described in the al-Warraq translation as "the finest variety of white wheat flour." Charles Perry thinks it may be semolina, but is not sure; that is what we have used. Cake flour is one possible alternative.

Sesame Oil: In Islamic recipes, this is the clear to yellowish sesame oil sold in Middle Eastern grocery stores, which is made from untoasted sesame seeds and has only a slight flavor; something very similar can be found in health food stores. Chinese sesame oil, which is much darker, is made from toasted sesame seeds and is very strongly flavored.

Sumac: A sour red powder, found in Iranian grocery stores (and restaurants).

Tarot: A starchy root that can sometimes be found in Chinese grocery stores.

Tail: Fat from the tail of a fat-tailed sheep, used as a cooking oil in Islamic recipes. Since it is not available at the local butcher, we substitute lamb fat.

Verjuice: Sour juice, usually from unripe grapes. We use sour grape juice from Middle Eastern grocery stores. Dilute vinegar can be used as a substitute; two parts of verjuice seems to be roughly equivalent to one part of vinegar. Verjuice produced for the gourmet trade and priced accordingly has become increasingly common over the last few years.

Wheat Starch (Amidoun): Can be found in Iranian grocery stores.

Other Spices: For cubebs, grains of paradise, and long pepper try a good specialty spice store, or merchants at Pennsic; if you cannot find them, substitute pepper. Saunders is ground sandalwood root used as red food coloring. We have heard that World Spice Merchants is a good online source: wsm@worldspice.com; www.worldspice.com

Murri

Islamic recipes frequently contain an ingredient translated as "murri" or "almori." It was extensively used in early Islamic cooking, rather as soy sauce is in Chinese cooking, and vanished sometime after the fourteenth century. Al-Baghdadi gives the following recipes for making it; if you try one and it works, let me know. According to Charles Perry, the translator of the *Kitab al Tibakhah* mentioned above, the penny-royal in these recipes is a mis-translation and should be budhaj (rotted barley). He gives the following instructions for making budhaj:

"All the recipes concur that budhaj was made from barley flour (or a mixture of barley and wheat) kneaded without leaven or salt. Loaves of this dough were rotted, generally in closed containers for 40 days, and then dried and ground into flour for further rotting into the condiments."

(First recipe) *Take 5 ratls each of penny-royal and flour. Make the flour into a good dough without leaven or salt, bake, and leave until dry. Then grind up fine with the penny-royal, knead into a green trough with a third the quantity of salt, and put out into the sun for 40 days in the heat of the summer, kneading every day at dawn and evening, and sprinkling with water. When black, put into conserving jars, cover with an equal quantity of water, stirring morning and evening: then strain it into the first murri. Add cinnamon, saffron and some aromatic herbs.*

(Second recipe) *Take penny-royal and wheaten or barley flour, make into a dry dough with hot water, using no leaven or salt, and bake into a loaf with a hole in the middle. Wrap in fig leaves, stuff into a preserving-jar, and leave in the shade until fetid. Then remove and dry.*

As you can see, making murri is an elaborate process, and tasting unsuccessful experiments might be a hazardous one. Charles Perry has experimented with this, and some years ago became the first person in recent centuries, so far as we know, to make murri. He says it tastes a little like soy sauce—which contains, in addition to soy beans, fermented grains.

In addition to the surviving recipes for murri, there are also at least two surviving references to what was apparently a fake murri, a substitute made by a much simpler process. If one cannot have real murri, period fake murri seems like the next best thing. The recipe is as follows:

Byzantine Murri
Kitab Wasf, Sina'ah 52, p. 56, Sina'ah 51, p. 65: Charles Perry tr.

Description of byzantine murri [made] right away: There is taken, upon the name of God the Most High, of honey scorched in a nuqrah [perhaps this word means 'a silver vessel'], three ratls; pounded scorched oven bread, ten loaves; starch, half a ratl; roasted anise, fennel and nigella, two uqiyahs of each; byzantine saffron, an uqiya; celery seed, an uqiyah; syrian carob, half a ratl; fifty peeled walnuts, as much as half a ratl; split quinces, five; salt, half a makkūk dissolved in honey; thirty ratls water; and the rest of the ingredients are thrown on it, and it is boiled on a slow flame until a third of the water is absorbed. Then it is strained well in a clean nosebag of hair. It is taken up in a greased glass or pottery vessel with a narrow top. A little lemon from Takranjiya (? Sina'ah 51 has Bakr Fahr) is thrown on it, and if it suits that a little water is thrown on the dough and it is boiled upon it and strained, it would be a second (infusion). The weights and measurements that are given are Antiochan and Zahiri [as] in Mayyafariqin.

Note: 1 ratl=12 uqiya=1 pint;
1 Makkūk=7.5-18.8 liters dry measure. Nigella, aka kalonji or black onion seed, can be found in Indian grocery stores. The following quantities are for ⅟₃₂ of the above recipe.

3 T honey	⅔ t nigela
1 T wheat starch	¼ oz carob = 1 T
⅓ t celery seed	1 ½ oz quince
1 ½ oz bread	¼ oz walnut
½ c salt in 3 T honey	1 pint water
⅔ t fennel	lemon (¼ of one)
¼ t saffron	⅔ t anise

Cook the honey in a small frying pan on medium heat, bringing it to a boil then turning off the heat and repeating several times; it will taste scorched. The bread is sliced white bread, toasted in a toaster to be somewhat blackened, then mashed in a mortar. Toast the anise, fennel and nigela in a frying pan or roast under a broiler, then grind in a mortar with celery seed and walnuts. The quince is quartered and cored. Boil all but the lemon together for about 2 hours, then put it in a potato ricer, squeeze out the liquid and add lemon juice to it; this is the murri. The recipe generates about 1 ¼ to 1 ½ c of liquid. You can then add another ½ c of water to the residue, simmer for half an hour to an hour and squeeze out that liquid for the second infusion, which yields about ⅓ c. A third infusion using ⅓ c more water yields another ¼ c or so.

Units

Exact quantities are sometimes given in Islamic recipes; the units are: 1 ratl = 1 lb = 1 pint; 12 uqiya = 1 ratl; 10 dirham = 1 uqiya; 6 danaq = 1 dirham (information from Arberry's introduction to his translation of al-Bagdadi). So 1 dirham= ~.13 oz = ~1 ½ t of ground spice

Units used in the *Ain I Akbari* are: 1 ser = 2 lb 2 oz, 1 dam = ⁷⁄₁₀ oz, 1 misqal = ⅙ oz.

Units used in *A Soup for the Qan*:
1 chien = .011 oz, 1 liang = .11 oz, 1 chin = 16 liang = 1.8 oz.

10 ho = 1 sheng = 31.5 cubic inches = ~2 c;
1 tou = 10 shang = ~ 1 ¼ gallons.

All of these are modern values for the units; the book notes that the sheng was slightly less in the 14th century.

Other Minor Points

We usually interpret "meat" in Islamic recipes as lamb, either leg or chops. Other possibilities are mutton, veal, goat, beef and kid. Pork is forbidden by Islamic law.

The Arberry translation of al-Baghdadi uses "hour" for an Arabic term which, according to Charles Perry, actually means an indefinite length of time. We therefore have not tried to stick literally to the timing given in al-Baghdadi.

A common technique in medieval European recipes is to pass ingredients through a strainer. We generally follow the recipe the first time but thereafter, and especially when preparing large quantities, substitute a food processor. An alternative is to use a potato ricer—a sort of plunger/strainer combination.

Saffron is a common medieval ingredient. We have found that it works better if you first extract the color and flavor by crushing the saffron thoroughly into a small quantity of water, then adding the water and saffron to your dish. Cariadoc is not fond of saffron; if you are, you may want to increase our quantities. The few (Islamic) recipes which specify saffron by weight use considerably more than they would if we had written them.

So far as we can tell, the fava or broad bean is the only European/Mediterranean variety of bean commonly available other than lentils and chickpeas. It is therefore what we use in recipes that call for beans.

In interpreting recipes that contain a specific number of eggs, we usually assume that the average medieval egg is somewhat smaller than a modern large egg; we have no evidence for whether this is correct other than how the recipes come out. When we specify a number of eggs in the worked out version of a recipe, they are large eggs.

Our recipes occasionally show an

ingredient in brackets. This means either that it is described as optional in the original or that it is something, usually salt, that is not mentioned in the original but that we think should have been—one of our sources says that he doesn't mention salt because everyone knows to put it in—or, occasionally, that it is something in the recipe that we were unable to get and so omitted. Which it is should be clear from context.

In our recipes, spices such as cinnamon or cloves are ground unless stated not to be.

Some of the early English recipes use the thorn (þ), a letter that is no longer used in English. It is pronounced "th."

Pie Crust Recipes

Our only period English recipe for pie crust is late period (p. 45: "To make short paest for tarte," from *A Proper Newe Book*); it consists only of a list of ingredients, and we believe is intended as a fancy rather than plain pie crust. There is also a German recipe in Sabina Welserin. What we normally use is a simple modern recipe that contains only period ingredients and is made partly with whole wheat flour, on the guess that most period flour was coarser than ours and that the finest white flour would probably not have gone into pie crust. It is:

¾ c white flour   ⅓ c salted butter
¼ c whole wheat flour   2 ½ T water

Mix flours, cut butter finely into flour with two knives or a food processor, then mix the water into the flour-butter mixture without crushing the flour and butter together. Makes a single 9" crust.

An alternative, for recipes that specify a crust but do not say what sort, is to simply knead flour and water with a little salt. The result is much tougher than a pastry crust, which has both advantages and disadvantages. The quantities for one 9" pie are:

3 c flour   about 1 ¼ c water
¼ t salt

Sourdough

A number of our recipes use sourdough as leavening. There are recipes for making your initial batch of sourdough using wild yeast from the air, but we have never done it; we always started with a batch of sourdough from someone else.

You can keep sourdough in the refrigerator for quite a long time, but before using it you will want to spend several days getting the culture back to strength. Start by combining ¼ c sourdough with ½ c water and ½ c flour; leave it covered at room temperature for 24 hours. Take ¼ c of that, combine with ½ c water and ½ c flour, leave it covered for 12 hours. Repeat, again for 12 hours. Finally take ½ c of your now pretty lively sourdough, combine with 1 c water and 1 c flour, leave it for 6 hours, use it in your recipe. If you are going to require more than that, scale up the final stage accordingly. Put whatever sourdough is left into jars to give to all your friends so that they can use sourdough in their cooking too. Or find a good sourdough pancake recipe and use the rest for that. And remember to put some sourdough back into the refrigerator.

Almond Milk

Almond milk is an ingredient common in Medieval European recipes, particularly in Lenten dishes (milk, eggs, and meat broth all being forbidden in Lent). The recipe below is a basic one. For some recipes we make a thicker almond milk with more almonds relative to the amount of water; other recipes say "draw up a good milk of almonds with broth (or wine)," in which case the broth or wine is substituted for the water in making the almond milk.

To make almond milk: Take ¼ c (1 ¾ oz) almonds. Put them in a food processor, run it briefly. Add a little water, run it longer. Continue adding water and running the processor until you have a milky liquid. Strain through several layers of cheesecloth. Put the residue back in the food processor, add a little more water, and repeat. Continue until the residue produces almost no more milk. Throw out the residue. This should give you about 1 c of almond milk.

To Make Onion Juice

Peel your onions, cut them in pieces (8 pieces for a very large onion), put them in a food processor and reduce them to mush. Put the mush through a clean, wet dish towel (the towel will end up a bit stained). To do that, you pour the onion juice and mush into the middle of the towel, holding up the edges. When the really liquid part has gone through into the bowl underneath, you pull the edges together so that what is left is a ball of onion mush wrapped in a dish towel. Squeeze until the juice is out. You should get just over a cup of juice per pound of onion.

To Make Cilantro Juice

Take cilantro (green coriander, aka chinese parsley, as distinguished from coriander, which is the seed). Grind it in an electric spice grinder or mash it in a mortar and pestle with 2 T water per ounce of coriander; use a food processor if you are making a lot. Squeeze it through a cloth to give about 2 T of cilantro juice from each ounce of cilantro.

Andalusian Meatballs

Recipes from the Islamic cookbooks often call for meatballs or cabobs without telling you how to make them. Here are comments on meatballs from two recipes in the anonymous Andalusian cookbook, followed by one possible interpretation.

Take red, tender meat, free of tendons, and pound it as in what preceded about meatballs. Put the pounded meat on a platter and add a bit of the juice of a pounded onion, some oil, murri naqî', pepper, coriander, cumin, and saffron. Add enough egg to envelope the mixture, and knead until it is mixed, and make large meatballs like pieces of meat, then set it aside.

Pound well meat from the two legs, the shoulder and the like. Throw in some sifted flour, a head of garlic peeled and pounded with salt, pepper, cumin, coriander and caraway, and let the pepper predominate, and some good murri, and beat all this well with five eggs or as many as it will bear. Then take coarse fat, as much of this as of the pounded meat or more, and cut up fine and mix with the pounded meat. And if rue is cut into it, good. Then make it into meatballs and fry it; ...

1 lb ground meat	¼ t coriander
6 T flour	1 T murri (p. 5)
1 clove garlic	2 eggs
½ t salt	4 T olive oil or meat fat
½ t pepper	1 t rue
¼ t cumin	

Chop the garlic. Combine all of the ingredients and form into balls about 1" to 1 ½" across; makes roughly 40 of them. Fry until brown on both sides in another 4 T of oil over medium heat, about 5 to 10 minutes. Note that this is only one of many possible variations; feel free to try your own.

Final Advice

The authors of the original recipes knew more about their cuisine than we ever will. If our worked out version appears to disagree with the original, that might mean that we know something about interpreting the original—for instance that an Islamic pound has twelve ounces, not sixteen—that you do not. But it is more likely that we either have made a mistake or were for some reason unable to follow the original. If in doubt, trust the original over our version.

European Dishes
Bread

Brazzatelle of Milk and Sugar
Messibugio, *Libro Novo* 1557

To make fifty brazzatelle of four ounces each you will take fifteen pounds of best flour, three ounces of rose water, three pounds of milk, two pounds of white sugar, 25 eggs, four ounces of butter, and you will knead these things together very well.

Then you will make your brazzatelle according to the method you want to use, and then you will let rise with careful attention, and after it has risen you will boil your water, and then you will place inside the above-mentioned brazzatelle to cook, and when they come to the top you will take out, and then you will put in fresh water, and when you have removed them from within you will put them to cook in the oven, and if you want to put inside anise it is a good deed.

[The recipe does not say what shape to make them in; I think they are probably sweet bagels, but they could be pretzels. This is one sixth of the recipe, using our ounce for the ounce and assuming a twelve ounce pound in order to make the final weight come out right]

7 c flour	1 T rose water
½ c sugar	¾ c milk
[2 ½ T aniseed]	½ lb sourdough (~1 c)
⁴⁄₃ T butter	3 eggs

Combine flour, sugar, and (optional) aniseeds; cut in the butter. Combine the liquid ingredients, including the sourdough, mix, add to the dry ingredients and knead until you have a smooth dough. Cover with a damp towel, let rise two hours. Divide into 10 equal portions.

Roll each into a cylinder about 10"-12" long, join the ends to form a torus (bagel).

or

Roll each into a cylinder about 18" -24" long, make into a pretzel shape.

Leave it to rise 1 hr 45 minutes or so at room temperature.

Fill a pot at least three inches deep with water. Bring the water to a boil. Put in as many of the *brazzatelle* as you can manage without their sticking together. Boil until they rise to the top, which should start happening in a minute or so; if they are sticking to the bottom, loosen with a spatula (pancake turner). When each *brazzatella* floats to the top take it out, dunk it briefly in a bowl of water, drain. Bake in a 425° oven until brown—about 25 minutes.

(I use sourdough but you could also try it with yeast.)

Rastons
Two Fifteenth Century p. 52

Take fayre Flowre, and þe whyte of Eyroun, and þe yolk, a lytel; þan take Warme Berme, and putte al þes to-gederys, and bete hem to-gederys with þin hond tyl it be schort and þikke y-now, and caste Sugre y-now þer-to, and þenne lat reste a whyle; þan kaste in a fayre place in þe oven, and late bake y-now; and þen with a knyf cutte yt round a-boue in maner of a crowne, and kepe þe crust þat þou kyttyst; and þan pyke al þe cromys with-ynne to-gederys, an pike hem smal with þyn knyf, and saue þe sydys and al þe cruste hole with-owte; and þan caste þer-in clarifiyd Botor, and mille þe cromes and þe botor to-gederes, and keuere it a-gen with þe cruste, þat þou kyttest a-way; þan putte it in þe ovyn agen a lytil tyme; and þan take it out, and serue it forth.

2 ¼ c flour	½ c sugar
2 egg whites	1 egg yolk
½ T dried yeast	1 c butter
(mixed with ½ c water)	

After mixing all ingredients except for butter, let the dough rise 45 minutes to an hour. Mold the dough on a greased cookie sheet, let rise a little more. Bake at 350° about 1 hour. Cut off top as described, mix insides of loaf with melted butter, and replace top. Second baking is about 5 minutes at the same temperature.

Para Hazer Tortillon Relleno: To Make a Stuffed Tortillon
Libro del arte de cozina

Knead two pounds of the flower of the flour with six yolks of fresh eggs, and two ounces of rosewater, and one ounce of leaven diluted with tepid water, and four ounces of fresh cow's butter, or pork lard which has no bad odor, and salt, and be stirring said dough for the space of half an hour, and make a thin leaf or pastry and anoint it with melted fat which should not be very hot, and cut the edges around, sprinkle the pastry with four ounces of sugar, and one ounce of cinnamon, and then have a pound of small raisins of Corinth, which have been given a boil in wine, and a pound of dates cooked in the same wine, and cut small, and all of the said things should be mixed together with sugar, cinnamon, and cloves, and nutmeg, and put the said mixture spread over the pastry with some morsels of cow's butter, and beginning with the long end of the pastry, roll it upwards, taking care not to break the dough, and this tortillon or roll must not be rolled more than three turns, so that it will cook better, and it does not have to go very tight. Anoint it on top with fat, not very hot. It will begin to twist by itself at one end which is not very closed, in such a manner that it becomes like a snail. Have the pie pan ready with a pastry of the same dough, somewhat fatty, anointed with melted fat, and put the tortillon lightly upon it without pressing it, and make it cook in the oven, or under a large earthen pot with temperate fire, tending it from time to time by anointing it with melted cow's butter, and being almost cooked, put sugar on top, and rosewater, and serve it hot. The pie pan in which you cook the tortillones must be wide, and must have very low edges.

(Translator's notes: All of the recipes which bear the name "tortillon" have a rolled-up pastry with some kind of filling. If I had to translate the Spanish, I would render it as something like "roll-pastry". The noun "manteca" can mean either butter or lard. I have translated "manteca de vaca" as cow's butter, "manteca de puerco" as pork lard, and undifferentiated "manteca" as fat.)

dough:
2 lb = 7 c flour
½ c butter
6 egg yolks
4 T rose water
2 T dried yeast
1 ¼ c water
2 t salt

filling:
1 lb = 3 ½ c currants
1 lb = 3 ½ c chopped dates
3 c wine
¼ c sugar
½ t cinnamon
¼+ t nutmeg
⅛ t cloves

to use in making loaf:
½ c sugar
3 ½ T cinnamon
2 T butter
~3 T melted butter
1 t rosewater
1 T sugar

Mix flour and salt in a large bowl; mix yeast with warm water, beat egg yolks with rosewater, melt ¼ c butter. Make a well in the center of the flour and pour the liquids into it, stir together with a wooden spoon, then knead for 10-15 minutes until smooth. (The original says half an hour, but the extra quarter hour doesn't seem to make much difference.) Let rise an hour and 20 minutes. To prepare filling, bring wine to a boil, add currants and dates and let boil two minutes; drain and add sugar and spices. When dough has risen, pinch off about an eighth of it and spread it out flat in the bottom of a greased 11" pie pan; spread 1 t melted butter over it. Roll the rest of the dough out on a floured board to a rectangle ~21"x18", spread with 2 t melted butter, and sprinkle on ¼ c sugar and 1 oz (3 T) of cinnamon. Spread the filling on top of that; dot with 2 T of butter in pieces. Roll up from the long side and pinch together to seal, so that the filling won't all ooze out. Coil on top of the piece of dough in the pan and spread another 2 t of melted butter over the top. Let rise another 10 minutes or so and put in a pre-heated oven at 350°. Bake 50 minutes or so, taking out once or twice to spread with more melted butter. After 45 minutes baking, sprinkle with rosewater and sugar, then put back in oven for another 5 minutes.

On Bread
Platina pp. 13-14 (Book 1)

... Therefore I recommend to anyone who is a baker that he use flour from wheat meal, well ground and then passed through a fine seive to sift it; then put it in a bread pan with warm water, to which has been added salt, after the manner of the people of Ferrari in Italy. After adding the right amount of leaven, keep it in a damp place if you can and let it rise. ... The bread should be well baked in an oven, and not on the same day; bread from fresh flour is most nourishing of all, and should be baked slowly.

¾ c sourdough	5 c white flour
2 c warm water	1 T salt
1 c whole wheat	

Mix sourdough with warm (not hot!) water and salt. Mix the flours, stir in the liquid, knead it smooth. Form into two or three round loaves and let rise overnight (8-10 hours). Bake at 350° about 50 minutes. Makes 2 loaves, about 8" across, 3"-4" thick, about 1.5 lb, or three smaller loaves. If you prefer a more sour loaf, use more sourdough and/or a longer rising time.

Vegetables

Armored Turnips
Platina p. 147 (Book 8)

Cut up turnips that have been either boiled or cooked under the ashes. Likewise do the same with rich cheese, not too ripe. These should be smaller morsels than the turnips, though. In a pan greased with butter or liquamen, make a layer of cheese first, then a layer of turnips, and so on, all the while pouring in spice and some butter, from time to time. This dish is quickly cooked and should be eaten quickly, too.

1 lb turnips	¼ t ginger
10 oz cheddar cheese	¼ t pepper
2 T butter	1 t sugar
½ t cinnamon	

Boil turnips about 30 minutes, peel and slice. Slice cheese thinner than turnips, with slices about the same size. Layer turnips, sliced cheese and spices in 9"x5" baking pan, and bake 20 minutes at 350°.

We have modified this recipe in accordance with the more detailed version in Martino's cookbook, which calls for "some sugar, some pepper and some sweet spices." Martino was apparently the source for many of Platina's recipes.

On Preparing Carrots and Parsnips
Platina p. 68 (Book 4)

... The parsnip should be boiled twice, the first liquid thrown away and cooked the second time with lettuce. Then it is put on a plate and dressed with salt, vinegar, coriander, and pepper, and is very fit to serve. ... The carrot is prepared in the same way as the parsnip, but is considered more pleasant when cooked under warm ashes and coals...

1 lb carrots	4 t vinegar
⅔ lb lettuce	½ t coriander
½ t salt	½ t pepper

Wash carrots, wash and tear up lettuce. Put carrots in boiling water, boil 12 minutes. Drain them. Put carrots and lettuce in boiling water for another 6 minutes. Drain them. Add the rest of the ingredients and mix thoroughly.

Mustard Greens
Anthimus p. 37

Mustard greens are good, boiled in salt and oil. They should be eaten either cooked on the coals or with bacon, and vinegar to suit the taste should be put in while they are cooking.

1 ¼ lb mustard greens	1 t salt
3 T oil	4 slices bacon
4 t vinegar	

Wash mustard greens. Boil stems 2 minutes, then add leaves, boil 6 more minutes and drain. Fry bacon or cook 6 minutes in microwave. Heat oil, add greens and stir, then add salt and cook 5 minutes. Crumble bacon and put over greens with vinegar. Stir it all up and cook another 3 minutes.

Russian Cabbage and Greens
Domostroi pp. 162-3

Chop cabbage, greens, or a mixture of both very fine, then wash them well. Boil or steam them for a long time. On meat days, put in red meat, ham, or a little pork fat; add cream or egg whites and warm the mixture. During a fast, saturate the greens with a little broth, or add some fat and steam it well. Add some groats, salt, and sour cabbage soup; then heat it. Cook kasha the same way: steam it well with lard, oil, or herring in a broth.

Note: the ingredient translated as "sour cabbage soup" turns up elsewhere in the Domostroi in lists of things to brew: "For brewing beer, ale, or sour cabbage soup, take malt or meal and hops. Beer from the first grade makes good sour cabbage soup. You can make vinegar, too, from a good mash." This suggests that it may really be something like alegar (beer vinegar). We therefore substitute malt vinegar.

Version 1
2 ¾ lb green cabbage (1 head)
¾ lb turnip greens
3 c water
1 ½ lb beef or lamb
6 egg whites
1 c dry buckwheat groats (kasha)
"sour cabbage soup": 1 T malt vinegar
2 t salt
"sour cabbage soup": 4 t malt vinegar

Version 2
2 lb green cabbage (1 head)
⅝ lb mustard greens
2 ½ c water
1 ¼ lb pork butt roast
½ c cream
⅔ c dry buckwheat groats (kasha)
1 ½ t salt
"sour cabbage soup": 1 T malt vinegar

Chop cabbage and greens very fine. Bring water to a boil, add cabbage and greens and simmer 30-40 minutes covered. Cut meat into bite-sized chunks. Add meat and simmer another 25 minutes (the time probably depends on the cut of meat). Add groats, salt and vinegar, and cook another 15 minutes uncovered on moderate heat, until the liquid is almost absorbed. Stir in egg whites or cream, heat for a minute or two, and remove from heat.

These are two possible interpretations of a recipe with lots of alternatives. In particular, it is not clear whether the groats, salt, and "sour cabbage soup" belong only to the fast-day version or to both meat-day and fast-day versions; we have assumed the latter.

Chebolace
Curye on Inglysch p. 99
(*Forme of Cury* no. 9)

Take oynouns and erbes and hewe hem small, and do þerto gode broth; and aray it as þou didest caboches ["seeth...and do þerto safroun & salt, and force it with powdour douce"]. If þey be in fyssh day, make on the same manere with water and oyle, and if it be not in lent, alye it with yolkes of eyren; and dresse it forth, and cast þerto powdour douce.

Note: "chibolles" are green onions, so from the title, onions should be a major ingredient.

½ lb onions   1 c beef broth *or*
greens: 1 c water + 2 T oil
½ oz parsley   10 threads saffron
4 oz mustard greens   ½ t salt
4 oz kale   3 egg yolks
4 oz spinach   ½ t poudre douce (p. 4)

Cut up onions and greens, mix with broth (or, for the fish day version, water and oil) and saffron and salt, bring to boil and cook uncovered 20 minutes on medium, until most of the broth is boiled away. Separate eggs, mix yolks with some of the broth out of the pot, and add to onions and greens. Heat for a couple minutes. Sprinkle on poudre douce and serve.

Caboges
Two Fifteenth Century p. 6 (Good–and easy)

Take fayre caboges, an cutte hem, an pike hem clene and clene washe hem, an parboyle hem in fayre water, an thanne presse hem on a fayre bord; an than choppe hem, and caste hem in a fayre pot with goode fresshe broth, an wyth merybonys, and let it boyle: thanne grate fayre brede and caste ther-to, an caste ther-to Safron an salt; or ellys take gode grwel y-mad of freys flesshe, y-draw thorw a straynour, and caste ther-to. An whan thou seruyst yt inne, knocke owt the marw of the bonys, an ley the marwe ij gobettys or iij in a dysshe, as the semyth best, and serue forth.

1 medium head cabbage	6 threads saffron
4 c beef broth	1 T salt
4 lb marrow bones	~ 2 c breadcrumbs

Wash cabbage. Cut it in fourths. Parboil it (i.e. dump into boiling water, leave there a few minutes). Drain. Chop. Squeeze out the water. Put it in a pot with beef broth and marrow bones. Simmer until soft, stirring often enough to keep it from sticking (about 20 minutes). Add saffron, salt, enough bread crumbs to make it very thick. Simmer ten minutes more. Serve.

Cress in Lent with Milk of Almonds
Menagier p. M14

Take your cress and parboil it with a handful of chopped beet leaves, and fry them in oil, then put to boil in milk of almonds; and when it is not Lent, fry in lard and butter until cooked, then moisten with meat stock; or with cheese, and adjust it carefully, for it will brown. Anyway, if you add parsley, it does not have to be blanched.

Lenten version

2 c cress = ⅓ lb	½ c almond milk (p. 7)
½ c beet leaves	¼ c parsley = ½ oz
1 T olive oil	pinch salt

Fish-day version

2 ¼ c cress = 6 oz	1 ½ oz brick cheese
1 ½ c beet leaves	[3 sprigs parsley]
2 T butter	[⅛ t salt]

Meat-day version

2 ¼ c cress = 6 oz	½ c meat stock
1 ½ c (2 oz) beet leaves	[3 sprigs parsley]
2 T lard and/or butter	[⅛ t salt]

Chop the cress and beet leaves. Dump them into boiling water, let the water come back to a boil, then drain them (about 2 minutes total in water). Heat oil or lard or butter in a skillet, add drained greens (and chopped parsley if you are using parsley). Stir fry for about 3 minutes. For Lenten version, add almond milk, let boil with greens about a minute. For fish-day version, add cheese, chopped up, and stir until cheese is melted into the greens. For meat-day version, add meat stock and cook down 2-3 minutes. Add salt, serve.

Notes: Measure greens pressed down in the measuring cup. Use a mild cheese such as brick cheese. Substitute spinach for beet leaves if necessary; the Menagier regards spinach as a kind of beet leaf. We have tried several ratios of cress to beet leaves; all seem to work reasonably well.

Lenten Foyles
Ordinance of Potage p. 38 (no. 9)

Take the same maner of herbes as thu dost to jowtys, and onyons clene paryd. Perboyle hem; presse out the watyr. Do hem yn a potte. Frye reysons in clere oyle that have be fryed yn before, and do therto with a perty of the oyle, and boyle hit up with the mylke of almondys; and put therto sugure & salte.

Note: "jowtys" is another recipe for cooked greens; the one in this cookbook calls for "kawlys [cabbage-type vegetables] & percellye and othir good herbes."

¼ head cabbage = ⅜ lb	⅓ c raisins
1 bunch parsley = 1 ½ oz	1 T oil
¼ lb spinach	2 c almond milk
2 oz turnip greens	(p. 7)
1 oz collard green	1 t sugar
6 oz onions	½ t salt

Wash greens, remove stems, cut up cabbage and onion. Make almond milk. Parboil vegetables 2-3 minutes, drain. Fry raisins in oil until they puff up and turn light brown (a few minutes). Put greens back in pot with raisins, add almond milk. Simmer 10-15 minutes, adding sugar and salt near the end.

Gourd in Juice
Platina p. 123 (Book 7)

Cook a gourd in juice or in water with a few little onions and after it is cut up, pass it through a perforated spoon into a kettle in which there is rich juice, a little verjuice and saffron. Take it from the hearth when it has boiled a little. After it has been set aside and cooled a little, put in a little aged cheese ground up and softened with two egg yolks; or keep stirring it with a spoon so that lumps do not spoil it. After you have put it into saucers, sprinkle with spices.

2 ¾ lb zucchini squash	5 oz parmesan
4 T verjuice	*spices* (cinnamon,
or 2 T wine vinegar	ginger or nutmeg)
½ c beef or chicken broth	2 egg yolks
7 threads saffron	½-¾ lb onions

Peel squash, remove seeds, slice; coarsely chop onions. Cook 10 minutes in water to cover. Drain and mash. Mix broth, verjuice, and saffron and add mashed squash. Heat, then add egg yolks and cheese. Sprinkle with one of the spices: cinnamon was considered best.

We have also made this using opo gourds from a Chinese grocery store which we believe were bottle gourds (*Lagenaria siceraria*), our best guess at the gourd used in period; see the discussion at p. 143 below. The recipe we worked out is: Double the quantity of onions and beef broth, keeping the other proportions as in the version with squash. Peel the gourd, boil it with whole small onions for an hour, then discard the onions (which seems to be what the original recipe implies). Slice gourd, mash through strainer (or use a potato ricer). Add beef broth and verjuice, heat 15 minutes on low, let cool 10 minutes, add grated cheese and egg yolks. Sprinkle with cinnamon and serve.

Fried Gourd
Platina p. 119 (Book 7)

Scrape off the skin from the gourd and cut it sideways in thin slices. When it is boiled once transfer it from the pot onto the board and leave it there till it has dried out a little. Then roll it in salt and good white flour and fry it in oil; when it is done and put on a platter, pour a garlic sauce over it, with fennel blossoms and breadcrumbs so dissolved in verjuice that it looks thin rather than thick. It would not be amiss to pass this sauce through a strainer. There are those, too, who use only verjuice and fennel bloom. If you like saffron, add saffron.

1 ⅛ lbs gourd (p. 4)	1 t salt
1 c flour	olive oil

Peel gourd and slice very thin, boil in water 7 minutes, spread out and let dry for 40 minutes. Mix flour and salt, dip gourd in it, and fry for ~4 minutes per batch in a pan with at least ¼" hot olive oil. See under sauces for Platina's garlic sauce (p. 66).

On Preparing Lettuce
Platina p. 61

.... Sprinkle them with ground salt and a little oil and pour a little more vinegar, and eat it right away. There are those who add a little mint and parsley to this preparation, so that it does not seem too bland; and so that there is not too much chill from the lettuce to harm the stomach, put cooked lettuce, with the water squeezed out, in a dish when you have dressed it with salt and oil and vinegar, and serve it to your guests. There are those who add a bit of cinnamon or pepper well-ground and sifted.

Raw Lettuce

2 c lettuce
1 t salt
1 T oil
2 T vinegar
1 T chopped mint
1 T parsley

Chop up mint and parsley. Put everything together and toss.

Cooked Lettuce

2 c lettuce
1 t salt
¾ T oil
¾ T vinegar
1 t cinnamon or pepper

Chop the lettuce, dump it in boiling water for two minutes, drain it very thoroughly squeezing out the water, add the other ingredients, serve it.

Moorish Eggplant
(*Berenjenas a la Morisca*)
De Nola no. 52

Peel the eggplants and quarter them, and their skins having been peeled, set them to cook; and when they are well-cooked, remove them from the fire, and then squeeze them between two wooden chopping blocks, so they do not retain water. And then chop them with a knife. And let them go to the pot and let them be gently fried, very well, with good bacon or with sweet oil, because the Moors do not eat bacon. And when they are gently fried, set them to cook in a pot and cast in good fatty broth, and the fat of meat, and grated cheese which is fine, and above all, ground coriander; and then stir it with a haravillo like gourds; and when they are nearly cooked, put in egg yolks beaten with verjuice, as if they were gourds.

2 ¼ lb eggplants
2 slices bacon = 3 oz
  or oil
2 oz lamb fat
2 oz parmesan
1 ½ c meat broth
1 ½ t coriander
3 egg yolks
1 T verjuice

Peel and quarter eggplants, put in boiling water, bring back to a boil and simmer for 20 minutes. Remove eggplant from water, press between two cutting boards to remove surplus water, and chop. Fry bacon about 10 minutes, add chopped eggplants, and cook 25 minutes over moderate heat. Chop lamb fat finely and grate cheese; add to eggplant with broth and coriander and cook 10 minutes, stirring frequently. Add egg yolks with verjuice and cook a minute or two until egg yolk is cooked.

Longe Wortes de Pesone
Two Fifteenth Century p. 89

Take grene pesyn, and wassh hem clene, And cast hem in a potte, and boyle hem til they breke; and then take hem vppe fro the fire, and putte hem in the broth in an other vessell; And lete hem kele; And drawe hem thorgh a Streynour into a faire potte. And then take oynones in ij. or iij. peces; And take hole wortes, and boyle hem in fayre water; And then take hem vppe, And ley hem on the faire borde, And kutte hem in .iij. or in .iiij. peces; And caste hem and the oynons into þat potte with the drawen pesen, and late hem boile togidre til they be all tendur, And then take faire oile and fray, or elles fressh broth of some maner fissh, (if þou maist, oyle a quantite), And caste thereto saffron, and salt a quantite. And lete hem boyle wel togidre til they ben ynogh; and stere hem well euermore, And serue hem forthe.

1 c split peas
1 whole onion = ⅝ lb
wortes: ½ lb chard
¼ c olive oil
(*or* fish broth)
8 threads saffron
½ t salt

Wash peas, put in 4 c of water, simmer 50 minutes covered, squash the peas with their liquid through a potato ricer, let cool. Cut up the onion into eighths. Simmer onions covered in 3 c water for 20 minutes. Add chard, cover again, cook 10 minutes more. Remove chard, cut in quarters, combine everything with peas. Add salt, saffron. Bring to simmer and add oil, simmer, stirring constantly, another 10 minutes.

Perre
Two Fifteenth Century p. 83

Take grene pesyn, and boile hem in a potte; And whan they ben y-broke, drawe the broth a good quantite thorgh a streynour into a potte, And sitte hit on the fire; and take oynons and parcelly, and hewe hem small togidre, And caste hem thereto; And take pouder of Canell and peper, and caste thereto, and lete boile; And take vynegur and pouder of ginger, and caste thereto; And then take Saffron and salte, a litull quantite, and caste thereto; And take faire peces of paynmain, or elles of such tendur brede, and kutte hit yn fere mosselles, and caste there-to; And then serue hit so forth.

1 lb peas	1 T vinegar
2 ½ c water	¼ t ginger
4 oz onions	3 threads saffron
2 T parsley	¾ t salt
½ t cinnamon	2 slices bread (~ 2 oz)
¼ t pepper	

Simmer peas in water for about 40 minutes. Mash the peas and the broth through a strainer. Add chopped onions, parsley, cinnamon, pepper. Boil for ten minutes. Add vinegar and ginger, salt and saffron. Chop up bread, put it in, boil briefly, serve.

On a more literal reading of the recipe, the peas are being discarded, perhaps to go into some other dish, and only the broth is being used; we have not yet tried it that way.

Grene Pesen Reale
Ancient Cookery p. 470

Take grene peas clene washen and let hom boyle awhile over the fire, and then poure away al the brothe, and bray a few of hom with parcel and myntes, and in the brayinge alay it with almonde mylke, and draw hit up with the same mylk, and put in the same pot, and let hit boil with hole pesen, and cast thereto sugre and saffron, and in the settynge doune of the pot, if hit be a pot of two galons, take 12 zolkes of eyren and bete hom, and streyne hom, and cast hom into the pot, and stere hit wel, and loke the potage be rennynge; and when it is dressed, straw suger above, and serve hit forthe.

almond milk: (p. 7)	1 T sugar
¼ c almonds	6 threads saffron
½ c water	2 beaten egg yolks
1 lb green fresh peas	[⅛ t salt]
2 t fresh parsley	2 T sugar
1 t fresh mint	

Make almond milk and boil peas. When the peas are boiled, mash ½ c of the peas with the parsley and mint, and add almond milk gradually. Put back with peas, add 1 T sugar and saffron, and heat; add egg yolks and salt and remove from heat; sprinkle on 2 T sugar before serving.

Lange Wortys de Chare
Two Fifteenth Century p. 5

Take beeff and merybonys, and boyle yt in fayre water; þan take fayre wortys and wassche hem clene in water, and parboyle hem in clene water; þan take hem vp of þe water after þe fyrst boylyng, an cut þe leuys a-to or a þre, and caste hem in-to þe beef and boylle to gederys; þan take a lof of whyte brede and grate yt, an caste it on þe pot, an safron & salt, & let it boyle y-now, and serue forth.

1 ½ lb beef shank	1 ⅜ lb kale
(meat and bones)	1 t salt
3 c water	12 threads saffron
⅞ lb mustard greens	¾ c breadcrumbs

Cut meat from bones, trimming off connective tissue and cutting to bite-sized pieces, put in water, bring to a boil and simmer 1 hour and 10 minutes. Wash greens; fill a large pot half full of water, bring to a boil, and parboil greens about 3 minutes. Drain and cut in thirds. Add to meat, bring back to a boil, and cook 20 minutes. Crush saffron into a little of the broth; add bread crumbs, salt and saffron, stir until thickened (another five minutes), and serve.

Note: This is the meat-day version of the recipe; the fish-day version is longe wortys de pesone on page 15.

Fried Broad Beans
Platina p. 115 (book 7)

Put broad beans that have been cooked and softened into a frying pan with soft fat, onions, figs, sage, and several pot herbs, or else fry them well rubbed with oil and, on a wooden tablet or a flat surface, spread this into the form of a cake and sprinkle spices over it.

1 c dried fava beans	1 ½ c spinach
6-8 T lard	1 ½ c parsley
⅔ c figs	1 ½ c mustard greens
½ t salt	*For sprinkling on top:*
½ t sage	¼ t ginger
½ c+ onions	½ t cinnamon
1 ½ c turnip greens	¼ t pepper

(Greens are measured packed)

Cut the figs in about 8 pieces each. Bring beans to a boil in 2 ½ c water, leave to soak about ½ hour, then simmer another hour until soft. Drain the beans, mix the whole mess together and fry it in the lard for 10 minutes, then serve it forth with spices sprinkled on it. This is also good with substantially less greens.

Makke
Curye on Inglysch p. 115
(*Forme of Cury* no. 76)

Take groundon benes and seeþ hem wel; take hem vp of the water and cast hem in a morter. Grynde hem al to doust til þei be white as eny mylke. Chawf a litell rede wyne; cast þeramong in þe gryndyng. Do þerto salt. Leshe it in disshes, þanne take oynouns and mynce hem smale and seeþ hem in oile til þey be al broun, and florissh the disshes þerwith, and serue it forth.

1 cup dried beans	1 t salt
½ c red wine	2 large onions
enough oil to fry the onions	

Soak the beans overnight then simmer 4-6 hours until tender. Chop up the onions fairly fine. Drain the beans, use a food processor to puree. Heat the wine and add it. Put the beans in each dish, fry the onions and add. Broad beans (fava beans) would be more authentic than pea beans, but we have not yet tried them in this recipe.

Funges
Curye on Inglysch p. 100
(*Forme of Cury* no. 12)

Take funges and pare hem clene and dyce hem; take leke and shrede hym small and do hym to seeþ in gode broth. Colour it with safroun, and do þerinne powdour fort.

½ lb mushrooms	6 threads saffron
1 leek	¼ t powder fort (p. 4)
1 c beef broth	¼ t salt
or chicken broth	

Wash the vegetables; slice the leek finely and dice the mushrooms. Add saffron to the broth and bring it to a boil. Add the leek, mushrooms, and powder fort to the broth, simmer 3-4 minutes, remove from the heat, and serve.

We prefer to use beef broth, but it is also good with chicken.

To Make a Tarte of Spinage
Proper Newe Booke, p. 41

Take Spynage and perboyle it tender, then take it up and wrynge oute the water cleane, and chop it very small, and set it uppon the fyre wyth swete butter in a frying panne and season it, and set it in a platter to coole then fyll your tart and so bake it.

20 oz spinach	¼ t salt
¼ lb butter	9" pastry shell
1 t cinnamon	1 T sugar
¼ t mace	

Note: recipes for other pies in this book say "season it up with sugar and cinnamon and sweet butter" or also with mace or just with sugar and butter.

Parboil spinach 3 minutes, rinse in cold water, wring it dry. Fry 2-3 minutes in butter with spices. Cool. Fill shell and bake at 350° for 40 minutes.

Potage of Onions Which They Call "Cebollada"
De Nola no. 46

Take peeled onions which are well washed and clean and cut them in thick slices, and cast them in a pot of boiling water, and then having let them come to a boil once or twice, take them out of the pot and press them between two wooden chopping boards and them fry them gently with good lard or with bacon grease, stirring with a little shovel and moving it about in the frying pan with the aforementioned little shovel which should be of wood. And if the onions dry up, cast in some good fatty mutton broth until the onions are well cooked. And then take almonds which are well peeled and white and grind them well in a mortar and then dissolve them in good mutton broth and pass them through a woolen strainer and then cast the almond milk in the pot with the onions and mix it well, and cook them well until the onions are cooked in the almond milk, and cast good grated cheese from Aragon in the pot, and stir well with a stirrer as if they were gourds, and when they are well mixed with the cheese and you see that it is cooked, prepare dishes, first casting into the pot a pair of egg yolks for each dish, and upon the dishes cast sugar and cinnamon if you wish; and it is good.

2 ½ c lamb broth	2 ½ oz parmesan
½ c almonds	4 egg yolks
1 lb 10 oz onions	1 t sugar
1 T bacon fat or lard	⅛ t cinnamon

To make the broth, put a quarter to half a pound of lamb trimmings in 4 c water and simmer an hour or so. Blanch almonds. Peel and slice onions. Grate cheese. Separate eggs. Grind almonds fine and use 2 c of the lamb broth to make almond milk from them (p. 7), straining through cheesecloth. Bring 4 c of water to a boil; add sliced onions, bring back to a boil, let boil a minute or two and then remove from heat and drain. Squeeze the onions between two wooden boards and drain off the juice. Heat bacon fat, add onions and fry for 10 minutes; add ½ c broth and cook another 5-10 minutes. Add almond milk, simmer about another 10 minutes. Stir in grated cheese; as soon as it is melted, add egg yolks, stir them in and remove from heat. Put into serving bowl, mix cinnamon and sugar and sprinkle over the top.

Benes Yfryed
Curye on Inglysch p. 141
(*Forme of Cury* no. 189)

Take benes and seeþ hem almost til þey bersten. Take and wryng out the water clene. Do þerto oynouns ysode and ymynced, and garlec þerwith; frye hem in oile oþer in grece, & do þerto powdour douce, & serue it forth.

30 oz fava beans	3 t poudre douce (p. 4)
1 small onion	3 cloves garlic (1 oz)
3 T olive oil	

Drain and wash the beans well, draining thoroughly. Chop onion, crush and mince garlic. Simmer onions and garlic in ½ c water for 3 minutes, drain. Heat the frying pan with oil at medium heat, add onions and garlic and beans (will splatter—be careful), cook, stirring frequently, 10 minutes. Then add poudre douce, mix well, cook 2 more minutes, and serve. Remember to keep stirring.

An Excellent Boiled Salad
English Huswife book 2, p. 40

To make an excellent compound boil'd Sallat: take of Spinage well washt two or three handfuls, and put it into faire water and boile it till it bee exceeding soft and tender as pappe; then put it into a Cullander and draine the water from it, which done, with the backside of your Chopping-knife chop it and bruise it as small as may bee: then put it into a Pipkin with a good lump of sweet butter and boile it over again; then take a good handfull of Currants cleane washt and put to it, and stirre them well together, then put to as much Vinegar as will make it reasonable tart, and then with sugar season it according to the taste of the Master of the house, and so serve it upon sippets.

10 oz spinach	4 T sugar
2 T butter	3 T wine vinegar
⅝ c currants	1 lb of bread to toast

Boil about 4 c water, add spinach, boil about 10 minutes. Remove and drain. Spread the spinach on a cutting board, chop and mash it by striking with the back edge of a large kitchen knife. Put it in a pot with the butter, cook about five minutes, add currants, vinegar, and sugar. Cook a few minutes longer. Serve on slices of toast.

Leek Pottage *(Potaje de Porrada)*
De Nola no. 105

You must take leeks, well-peeled, and washed and cleaned the night before, set them to soak in an earthen bowl filled with water, in the night air; and let them be this way all night until the morning; and then give them a boil, moderately, because they are very difficult to cook; and when they are well-boiled, press them a great deal between two chopping blocks, and gently fry them with the fat of good bacon; and do not cast salt upon them; and when they are well gently fried, set them to cook in a little good broth which is fatty; and then take almond milk and cast it in the pot and cook it until it is quite thick; and when it is thick, taste it for salt, and if it lacks salt cast it in; and then prepare dishes, and [cast] upon them sugar and cinnamon.

3 medium leeks (1 ¼ lb)	⅛ t salt
½ c chicken or beef broth	1 t sugar
2 slices bacon (~ 2 oz)	⅛ c almonds
¼ t cinnamon	⅜ c water

Trim roots and green part from leeks, wash and put to soak overnight.

Make almond milk (p. 7). Cut leeks into 1" pieces. Put into boiling water and cook 15 minutes. Fry bacon in a large frying pan until crisp and remove bacon, leaving fat in pan. Drain leeks and press between two cutting boards to force out the water. Fry the leeks 3 or 4 minutes at medium heat in the bacon fat. Put the broth and the leeks into a pot and bring to a boil, then add the almond milk. Cook 5 minutes. Mix cinnamon and sugar and sprinkle on top before serving.

A Puree with Leeks
Buoch von Guoter Spise # 64

A puree with leeks. Take white leek and cut small and mix well with good almond milk and with rice meal and boil that well and do not oversalt.

3 medium leeks	1 ⅛ c water
1 T rice flour	¼ t salt
¼ c almonds	

Make 1 c almond milk (p. 7). Chop white and pale green parts of the leeks and put in a pot with almond milk and rice flour. Cook, stirring often, 18-20 minutes over medium heat. Add salt and serve.

Seafood

Salmon Casserole *(Cazuela de Salmon)*
De Nola no. 182 [Good]

You must take the clean and well-washed salmon; and put it in a casserole with your spices which are: galingale, and a little pepper and ginger and saffron; and all of this well ground, and cast upon the fish with salt, and a little verjuice or orange juice, and let it go to the fire of embers; and then take blanched almonds and raisins and pine nuts and all herbs. That is, moraduj, which is called marjoram, and parsley, and mint; and when the casserole is nearly half-cooked cast all this inside.

2 lb salmon	¼ c blanched almonds
½ t galingale	1 T pine nuts
⅛ t pepper	¼ t ginger
3 T verjuice *or*	1 T fresh parsley
sour orange juice	1 t fresh mint
¼ t salt	3 T raisins
1 t fresh marjoram	15 threads saffron

Put salmon fillets in heavy pot and sprinkle on spices and verjuice. Cover and put on stove on medium low; as soon as it is at a simmer, turn down to very low heat. Chop the herbs very fine and get the nuts and raisins ready. After 15 minutes, add the remaining ingredients, and cook another 10 minutes. Serve.

Salmon Roste in Sauce
Two Fifteenth Century p. 102

Take a Salmond, and cut him rounde, chyne and all, and rost the peces on a gredire; And take wyne, and pouder of Canell, and drawe it þorgh a streynour; And take smale myced oynons, and caste þere-to, and lete hem boyle; And þen take vynegre, or vergeous, and pouder ginger, and cast there-to; and þen ley the samon in a dissh, and cast þe sirip þeron al hote, & serue it forth.

1 ¾ lb salmon	1 medium onion, 6 oz
¾ c white wine	¼ c red wine vinegar
¾ t cinnamon	¼ t ginger

Chop onion; put onion, wine, and cinnamon in small pot, cook on medium about 20 minutes. Add ginger and vinegar. Simmer. Meanwhile, take salmon steaks, cut into serving sized pieces, place on ungreased baking pan or cookie sheet. Broil for 10 minutes until lightly browned. Turn salmon, making certain pieces are separated, cook another 4 minutes or until done. Serve immediately with sauce over it.

Sturgeon pour Porpeys
Two Fifteenth Century p. 105

Take a sturgeon, turbot or porpoise, and cut it in fair pieces to bake; and then make fair cakes of fair paste, and take powder of pepper, powder of ginger, canel, and salt, and medle these powders and salt together; and take and lay a piece of the fish on a cake and lay the powders underneath the fish, and above enough; and then wet the sides of the paste with fair cold water, and close the sides together, and set him in an oven, and bake him enough.

1 lb 1 oz filleted fish	½ t pepper
2 c white flour	½ t ginger
1 c whole wheat flour	1 t cinnamon
~ 1 c water	½ T salt

Mix flour together, stir in water, knead to a smooth dough. Divide in 24 portions. Roll out each portion into an oval about 4"x5 ½". Cut a piece of fish about 1 ½"x3"x⅜". Mix ginger, cinnamon, and salt. Take ⅛ t of the mixture, put about half of it on one end of the rolled out piece of dough, put on the piece of fish, put the rest of the spice mixture on the fish. Fold over the other half of the dough and seal the edges, using a wet finger if necessary; it should look like a big ravioli. Put on a baking sheet and bake 20-30 minutes at 325°. Eat.

Variants: Make smaller or larger pasties, as you like; what I describe is simply one way that works. As an alternative to the ravioli shape, roll out the dough in a roughly circular shape, put the fish in the middle, pull the dough up at the edges and join it on top—sort of like a shu mai.

Note: Turbot is a delicate flat fish, related to halibut. We were told that Orange Roughy or Taliapia is similar, that it is not fat and does not taste very fishy. Flesh is "white, firm, flaky and savoury". The porpoise (mammal) is said to be oily.

Chisan
Ancient Cookery p. 448

Take hole roches, or tenchys, or plays, but choppe hem on peces, and frie hem in oyle; and take crusts of bredde, and draw hem with wyn, and vynegur, and bray fygges, and draw hem therwith; and mynce onyons, and frie hem, and do therto, and blaunched almonds fried, and raisinges of corance, and pouder of clowes, and of ginger, and of canell, and let hit boyle, then do thi fissh in a faire vessell, and poure thi sewe above, and serve hit forthe colde.

1 lb fish	pinch ground cloves
1 slice bread	⅛ t ginger
3 T wine	½ t cinnamon
2 T figs	3 T vinegar
1 T minced onion	2 T currants
2 T blanched almonds	

Cut up the fish and fry in oil. Mix bread, wine, vinegar, and chopped or ground figs. Fry minced onion and almonds; add to the sauce, along with remaining ingredients. Put the fish in a dish, cover with the sauce, and serve cold.

To Make Blamaunger in Lenten
Curye on Inglysch p. 89
(*Utilis Coquinario* no. 30)

Tak almound melk & do it in a pot, & tak floure of rys aftere þat þe quantite is of þe melk, or hol rys. & take of þe perche or of a luce & hew it as þou woldest do braun, & if þou fayle þerof tak newe ray &alye it up, & do þerto sugre & oyl of almoundes, or elles oyle dolyf þat is newe, or elles þe gres of a brem; & whan it is soþe, do þe oyle þerto & tak almoundes koruen on foure ifried in oyle & sette in þe disches whan it is dressed, & strew sugre aboue manerlych.

2 c almond milk: (p. 7)	1 T sugar
½ c almonds	1 T almond oil
2 c water	or olive oil
4 T rice flour (or rice)	1 c almonds
1 lb perch	1 T sugar

Make almond milk. Put in a pot, add rice flour and fish, cut up into small cubes. Cook until fish is done, about 10 minutes, add 1 T sugar and oil, cook another minute. Cut almonds in four pieces each and fry. Serve with fried almonds and second T of sugar on top.

Vyaunde de Cyprys in Lent
Two Fifteenth Century p. 28

Take good thick milk of almonds, and do it on a pot; nym the flesh of good crabs, and good salmon, and bray it small, and temper it up with the foresaid milk; boil it, and lye it with flour of rice or amyndoun, and make it chargeaunt; when it is yboiled, do thereto white sugar, a gode quantitie of white vernage pimes [apparently a wine like muscadine] *with the wine, pomegranate. When it is ydressed, strew above the grains of pomegranate.*

2 oz almonds	3 T sugar
1 c water	4 t Rhine wine
7 oz crabmeat	2 T pomegranate juice
7 oz salmon	pomegranate seeds
2 T rice flour	

Make almond milk (p. 7). Remove skin and bones from salmon, cut salmon and crab into cubes and shred it. Mix fish and almond milk and cook over medium heat; add sugar, wine, and pomegranate juice after 5 minutes; add rice flour after 10 minutes, cook, stirring, another minute, remove from heat and keep stirring another half minute. Garnish with pomegranate seeds.

Galantine for Carp
Goodman p. 289

Bray saffron, ginger, clove, grains of paradise, long pepper and nutmegs, and moisten with the greasy sewe in which the carp has been cooked, and add thereto verjuice, wine and vinegar and let it be thickened with a little toasted bread, well brayed and colorless (natheless strained bread maketh the best sauce) and let it all be boiled and poured over the cooked fish, then put onto plates.

1 ½ lb catfish or carp	¼ t cloves
5 threads saffron	2 T broth from fish
¼ t ginger	1 ½ c verjuice
¼ t pepper	2 t red wine
½ t nutmeg	4 T wine vinegar
⅛ t grains of paradise	3 T bread crumbs

Oysters in Bruette
Two Fifteenth Century p. 23

Take an schene oystrys, an kepe þe water þat cometh of hem, an strayne it, and put it in a potte, & Ale þer-to, an a lytil brede þer-to; put Gyngere, Canel, Pouder of Pepir þer-to, Safroun an Salt; an whan it is y-now al-moste, putte on þin Oystrys: loke þat þey ben wyl y-wasshe for þe schullys: & þan serue forth.

2 slices bread	⅛ t pepper
¾ c liquid from oysters	8 threads of saffron
¾ c ale	¼ t salt
3/16 t ginger	1 ¼ c oysters
⅛ t cinnamon	

Mix bread, torn up small, with liquids and heat; add seasonings and simmer until the bread has come apart and the sauce is fairly thick. Add oysters, let simmer until the oysters are done and serve forth.

Soups

A Potage with Turnips
Platina pp. 117-118 (book 7)

Turnips that have been well washed and cut up into nice bits, you cook down in some rich juice. When they have cooked and been mashed, put them near the fire again, in more rich juice, even better than before, if possible; and put in little pieces of salt pork, pepper and saffron. When it has boiled once, then take it and serve it to your guests.

3 lb turnips	1/16 -1/8 t pepper
5 c beef broth	24 threads saffron
6 oz salt pork	

Wash turnips and cut off ends and slice ¼"-½" thick. Combine 2 ½ c of the beef broth with 5 c water, heat it to a boil, then add turnips. Simmer 20 minutes, remove turnips and get rid of broth. Cut salt pork into small pieces, cutting off rind, and fry it until lightly browned, about 8 minutes. Drain. Mash turnips with a potato masher, return to pot with another 2 ½ c of beef broth, salt pork, pepper and saffron; bring to a boil, boil briefly and remove from heat. Produces about 9 c of pottage.

Note: a recipe for potage of peas earlier in the same chapter says to fry morsels of salt flesh, so we do so with the salt pork here.

Rapes in Potage [or Carrots or Parsnips]
Curye on Inglysch p. 99
(*Forme of Cury* no. 7)

Take rapus and make hem clene, and waissh hem clene; quarter hem; perboile hem, take hem vp. Cast hem in a gode broth and seeþ hem; mynce oynouns and cast þerto safroun and salt, and messe it forth with powdour douce. In the self wise make of pastunakes and skyrwittes.

Note: rapes are turnips; pasternakes are either parsnips or carrots; skirrets are, according to the OED, "a species of water parsnip, formerly much cultivated in Europe for its esculent tubers." We have never found them available in the market.

1 lb turnips, carrots, or parsnips	6 threads saffron
½ lb onions	¾ t salt
2 c chicken broth	3 t poudre douce (p. 4)

Wash, peel, and quarter turnips (or cut into eighths if they are large), cover with boiling water and parboil for 15 minutes. If you are using carrots or parsnips, clean them and cut them up into large bite-sized pieces and parboil 10 minutes. Mince onions. Drain turnips, carrots, or parsnips, and put them with onions and chicken broth in a pot and bring to a boil. Crush saffron into about 1 t of the broth and add that and the salt to the potage. Cook another 15-20 minutes, until turnips or carrots are soft to a fork and some of the liquid is boiled down. Sprinkle on the poudre douce and serve.

Potage from Meat
Platina p. 116 (book 7) (Good)

Take lean meat and let it boil, then cut it up finely and cook it again for half an hour in rich juice, having first added bread crumbs. Add a little pepper and saffron.

When it has cooled a little, add beaten eggs, grated cheese, parsley, marjoram, finely chopped mint with a little verjuice. Blend them all together in a pot, stirring them slowly with a spoon so that they do not form a ball. The same may be done with livers and lungs.

2 ⅓ lb stewbeef	1 ½ c grated cheese
4 c water	⅜ c parsley
2 ½ c beef broth	1 t fresh marjoram
1 ½ c bread crumbs	1 ½ T fresh mint
¾ t pepper	6 T verjuice
8 threads saffron	[1 t salt (to taste)]
5 eggs	

Bring meat and water to a boil and cook 10 minutes; take meat out and cut up small; put back in water with broth, bread crumbs, pepper, and saffron. Simmer ½ hour over low flame, being careful that it does not stick. Mix in remaining ingredients; the herbs should be chopped. Cook, stirring frequently, for about

5 minutes. This makes about 10 cups.

This is a rather meat-rich version; it also works with as little as half this much meat.

The Soup Called Menjoire
Taillevent p. 112

First you need the necessary meat–Peachicks, pheasants or partridges and if you can't get those, plovers, cranes or larks or other small birds; and roast the poultry on a spit and when it is almost cooked, especially for large birds like peachicks, pheasants or partridges, cut them into pieces and fry them in lard in an iron pan and then put them in the soup pot. And to make the soup you need beef stock from a leg of beef, and white bread toasted on a grill, and put the bread to soak and skim the broth and strain through a sieve and then you need cinnamon, ginger, a little cloves, long pepper and grains of paradise and hippocras according to the amount of soup you want to make, and mix the spices and the hippocras together and put in the pot with the poultry and the broth and boil everything together and add a very little vinegar, taking care that it just simmers and add sugar to taste and serve over the toasted crackers with white anise or red or pomegranate powder.

2 lbs chicken pieces	¼ t long pepper
lard to fry in	¼ t grains of paradise
~3 c beef broth	½ c hippocras (p. 64)
4 slices white bread	1 T vinegar
¼ t cinnamon	1 T sugar
⅛ t ginger	¼ t ground aniseed
3 whole cloves	

Bake chicken pieces 45 minutes at 350°. You may wish to debone them after they have cooled enough to handle before frying them in lard. Bread is toasted and then soaked until soft, then beaten into the soup along with the spices and hippocras. Add vinegar and sugar. Simmer soup about 45 minutes. Serve over toasted crackers with aniseed sprinkled on.

The hippocras in the recipe might be the spice mixture hippocras is made from rather than hippocras itself, in which case you would use a teaspoon or so—we have not tried that interpretation.

Saffron Broth
Platina p. 103 (book 6)

Put thirty egg yolks, verjuice, the juice of veal or capon, saffron, a little cinnamon together into a bowl and blend. Pass them through a strainer into a pot. Cook it down slowly and stir it continuously with a spoon until it begins to thicken. For then it is taken from the hearth and served to ten guests. While in the dishes, sprinkle with spices.

7 egg yolks	½ t cinnamon
2 T verjuice	⅛ t nutmeg
21 oz chicken broth	¼ t black pepper
10 threads saffron	

Zanzarella
Platina p. 104 (book 6)

Take seven eggs, half a pound of grated cheese, and ground bread all blended together. Put this into the pot where the saffron broth is made, when it begins to boil. When you have stirred it two or three times with a spoon, compose your dishes, for it is quickly done.

Saffron broth (one recipe)	4 eggs
3 cups ground mozzarella	3 slices bread

Variants on Platina Soups
Platina p. 104 (book 6)

Green Broth: Take all that was contained in the first broth [Saffron Broth] except for the saffron and to these things add orach and a little parsley and a few ground sprouts of wheat if there are any green ones at the time. Pass this through a strainer and cook it in the same way as above.

½ c orage	2 T wheat sprouts.
2 T parsley	

Grind them up in a mortar to get the green color. You can use spinach to substitute for the orage.

Green Pottage: You prepare green potage in the same way as described above [Zanzarella], but instead of saffron, put in herbs which I noted with the green broth.

Cretonnée of New Peas
Menagier p. M-19

Cook them almost to a puree then remove from the liquid and take fresh cow's milk. And first boil this milk before you put anything in it for it still could turn then first grind ginger to give appetite and saffron to yellow: it is said that if you want to make a liaison with egg yolks pour gently in from above these yolks will yellow it enough and also make the liaison but milk curdles quicker with egg yolks than with a liaison of bread and with saffron to color it. And for this purpose if you use bread it should be white unleavened bread and moisten it in a bowl with milk or meat stock then grind and put it through a sieve and when your bread is sieved and your spices have not been sieved put it all to boil with your peas and when it is all cooked then add your milk and saffron. You can make still another liaison, with the same peas or beans ground then strained; use whichever you please. As for liaison with egg yolks, they must be beaten, strained through a sieve, and poured slowly from above into the milk, after it has boiled well and has been drawn to the back of the fire with the new peas and spices. The surest way is to take a little of the milk and mix with the eggs in the bowl, and then a little more, and again, until the yolks are well mixed with a spoon and plenty of milk, then put into the pot which is away from the fire, and the soup will not curdle. And if the soup is thick, thin with a little meat stock. This done, you should have quartered chicks, veal, or small goose cooked then fried, and in each bowl put two or three morsels and the soup over them.

1 lb = 4 c peas	4 egg yolks
[meat stock]	*or* bread and saffron
1 c milk	2 chicken legs
½ t ginger	*or* veal or goose

Note: Save the water in which you cook the peas—it is useful for making other soups.

Boil peas 10 minutes. Mix 1 c warm milk with 4 egg yolks. Add ginger and salt to the peas, then milk and eggs; thin with meat stock if it is thicker than you want. Makes about 6 cups.

Potage of Beans Boiled
Curye on Inglysch p. 77
(*Diuersa Servicia* no. 81)

For to make a potage fene boiles, tak wite benes & seþ hem in water, & bray þe benys in a mortar al to noght; & lat þem seþe in almond mylk & do þerin wyn & hony. & seþ reysouns in wyn & do þerto & after dresse yt forth.

1 c dried fava beans	1 ½ T honey
1 c (5 oz) almonds	¼ c raisins
1 ½ c water	¼ c more wine
⅛ c wine	[½ t salt]

Soak beans overnight in 2 c water, drain. Boil them for 40 minutes in 2 c of water. Drain them, mush them in a mortar. Make 1 c almond milk (p. 7) with almonds and 1 ½ c water and set to boil; throw beans into boiling almond milk, add ⅛ c wine and honey, simmer 1 hour. Simmer the raisins in ¼ c wine for about ten minutes, add them to the pottage a few minutes before it finishes cooking.

Green Broth of Eggs and Cheese
Menagier p. M-22

Take parsley and a little cheese and sage and a very small amount of saffron, moistened bread, and mix with water left from cooking peas, or stock, grind and strain: And have ground ginger mixed with wine, and put on to boil; then add cheese and eggs poached in water, and let it be a bright green. Item, some do not add bread, but instead of bread use bacon.

3 T parsley	2 c pea stock
½ oz grated cheese	*or* chicken stock
3 small leaves fresh sage	⅛ t ginger
5 threads saffron	1 T white wine
2 thin slices white bread	1 ¾ oz cheese,
or bacon	3 eggs

Grate bread and soak it in stock (either water left from cooking peas or ½ c canned chicken broth + 1 ½ c water). Grind parsley, sage, and saffron in a mortar thoroughly; add

½ oz cheese and soaked bread and grind together. Strain through a strainer; if necessary, put back in mortar what didn't go through, grind again, and strain again. Mix wine and ginger, add to mixture, and bring to a boil over moderate heat; be careful that it does not stick to the bottom. Stir in the rest of the cheese; break eggs into soup, and continue to simmer until eggs are poached.

Note: We have used both Gouda and cheddar cheese; both are good.

Poultry

Icelandic Chicken
Icelandic p. 218 (Good)

One shall cut a young chicken in two and wrap about it whole leaves of salvia, and cut up in it bacon and add salt to suit the taste. Then cover that with dough and bake like bread in the oven.

5 c flour	½ lb bacon
about 1 ¾ c water	3 lb chicken
fresh sage leaves to cover	
(*or* 3 T dried sage)	

Make a stiff dough by kneading together flour and water. Roll it out. Cover the dough with sage leaves and the sage leaves with strips of bacon. Cut chicken in half and wrap each half chicken in the dough, sealing it. You now have two packages which contain, starting at the outside, dough, sage, bacon, chicken. Put them in the oven and bake like bread (325° for 2 hours). We find the bacon adds salt enough.

The part of the bread at the bottom is particularly good, because of the bacon fat and chicken fat. You may want to turn the loaves once or twice, or baste the top with the drippings.

Roast Chicken
Platina p. 94 (book 6)

You will roast a chicken after it has been well plucked, cleaned and washed; and after roasting it, put it into a dish before it cools off and pour over it either orange juice or verjuice with rosewater, sugar and well-ground cinnamon, and serve it to your guests.

large chicken	2 T sugar
1 ½ T sour orange juice	½ t cinnamon
2 t rosewater	

Note that orange juice at this period would have been from sour oranges.

Chykens in Hocchee
Curye on Inglysch p. 105
(*Forme of Cury* no. 36)

Take chykens and scald hem. Take persel and sawge, with oper erbes; take garlec & grapes, and stoppe the chikenus ful, and seeþ hem in gode broth, so þat þey may esely be boyled þerinne. Messe hem & cast þerto powdour dowce.

3 ½ lb chicken	¾ oz = ~10 cloves garlic
4 T fresh parsley	½ lb red grapes
1 ½ t fresh sage	5 c chicken broth
1 t fresh marjoram	1 ½ t poudre douce (p. 4)
1 ¾ t fresh thyme	

Clean the chicken, chop parsley and sage fine then mix with herbs in a bowl. Herbs are fresh, measured chopped and packed down. Take leaves off the fresh marjoram and thyme and throw out the stems, remove as much stem from parsley as practical. Add garlic cloves whole. Add grapes, and thoroughly but gently mix with the herbs. Stuff the chicken with the herbs, garlic and grapes. Close the bird with a few toothpicks. Place chicken in pot with broth and cook on stove top over moderate heat ½ hour, turn over, another ¼ hour (in covered pot). Serve on platter with poudre douce sprinkled over.

Capons Stwed
Two Fifteenth Century p. 72 (Good)

Take parcelly, Sauge, Isoppe, Rose Mary, and tyme, and breke hit bitwen thi hondes, and stoppe the Capon there-with; colour hym with Safferon, and couche him in a erthen potte, or of brasse, and ley splentes underneth and al about the sides, that the Capon touche no thinge of the potte; strawe good herbes in the potte, and put thereto a pottel of the best wyn that thou may gete, and none other licour; hele the potte with a close led, and stoppe hit aboute with dogh or bater, that no eier come oute; And set hit on the faire charcole, and lete it seeth easly and longe till hit be ynowe. And if hit be an erthen potte, then set hit on the fire whan thou takest hit downe, and lete hit not touche the grounde for breking; And whan the hete is ouer past, take oute the Capon with a prik; then make a sirippe of wyne, Reysons of corance, sugur and safferon, And boile hit a litull; medel pouder of Ginger with a litul of the same wyn, and do thereto; then do awey the fatte of the sewe of the Capon, And do the Siryppe to the sewe, and powre hit on the capon, and serue it forth.

3 lb chicken   6 threads saffron + 1 t water
First batch of herbs: *Second batch of herbs*:

⅓ c fresh parsley	2 T parsley
1 T dried sage	½ t sage
1 t dried rosemary	½ t rosemary
1 t thyme, ground	½ t thyme
2 T hyssop, dried	about ½ c flour
1 ½ c wine	enough water to make a stiff dough

Sauce:

½ c wine	10 threads saffron
½ c sugar	¼ c wine
½ c currants	1 t powdered ginger

Mix first batch of herbs and stuff chicken with them. Put chicken and wine in a pot with a lid; if you are using a stove top rather than an oven, you may want to put wood pieces or something under the chicken to keep it from sticking. Paint the chicken with water with saffron crushed into it. Sprinkle on second batch of herbs. Mix flour and water into a stiff dough, roll it out into a string, and use it between pot and lid as a seal. Bake at 350° or simmer on stove top about 1 ½ hours. Take out, drain, separate out some of the liquid without the fat. Make a thick syrup of wine, sugar, currants, and a pinch of saffron. Boil briefly. Mix another ¼ c wine with powdered ginger. Combine. Add ½ c of the liquid from the chicken to this, heat, pour over capon, serve.

Creteyney
Ordinance of Potage no. 38

Take capons and othir fowlys. Perboile hem; dyse hem. Cast hem yn a pott with cowe mylke & boyle hit therwithe. Draw payndmayne with som of the mylke and put togedyr. Take sodyn eyron; hew the white & caste therto. Sesyn hit up with poudyr, sigure, & safferyn & salt, and aley hit up with yolkes of eyron sodyn hard, & frye hem a lytyll. Ley hem in disches; poure the sewe abovyn and floresch hit with anneys in comfite.

5 ½ lb chicken	"powder":
4 c milk	1 t pepper
5 slices white bread	1 t cinnamon
5 hard-boiled eggs	1 t ginger
1 T lard or oil	½ t salt
1 T sugar	10 threads saffron
candied anise seed	

Quarter chicken, put it in boiling water for 5 to 10 minutes. Drain. Debone and dice the meat. Put it in the milk, simmer 20 minutes until the meat is well cooked. Remove from heat. Cut the bread into small pieces, combine with 1 ¼ c of the milk. Chop egg whites, fry the egg yolks in lard or oil for about 5 minutes. Mush the bread, add egg whites, egg yolk, spices including sugar and salt, using a little milk to extract color and flavor from the saffron, simmer together for about 5 minutes. Serve the chicken with the sauce over it, sprinkling candied anise over that.

Veal, Kid, or Hen in Bokenade
Two Fifteenth Century p. 13

Take Vele, Kyde, or Henne, an boyle hem in fayre Water, or ellys in fresshe brothe, an smyte hem in pecys, an pyke hem clene; an than draw the same brothe thorwe a straynoure, an caste ther-to Percely, Sawge, Ysope, Maces, Clowys, an let boyle tyl the flesshe be y-now; than sette it from the fyre, and a-lye it vp with raw yolkys of eyroun, and caste ther-to pouder Gyngere, Verjows, Safroun, and Salt, and thanne serue it forth for a gode mete.

meat (½ chicken)	8 egg yolks
2 T fresh parsley	1 t powdered ginger
3 leaves of sage	3 T vinegar
½ T hyssop	5 threads saffron
⅛ t mace	½ t salt
⅛ t cloves	

Boil meat 20 minutes before "smiting in pieces", another 20 minutes after adding parsley, etc.

Cinnamon Bruet
Menagier p. M-19

Cut up your poultry or other meat, then cook in water and add wine, and fry; then take raw almonds with the skin on, unpeeled, and a great quantity of cinnamon, and grind up well, and mix with your stock or with beef stock, and put to boil with your meat: then grind ginger, clove, and grain, etc., and let it be thick and yellow-brown.

3 ¼ lb chicken	½ t cloves
6 c water	1 t grains of Paradise
1 ½ c wine	½ t ginger
2 c almonds	[½ t salt]
8 t cinnamon	

Mix wine and water, put in the cut up chicken, bring to a boil, cook half an hour. Remove chicken and fry for about 10 minutes. Grind almonds fine. Add almonds, cinnamon, ginger, cloves and grains to the pot of broth from boiling the chicken, put the pieces of chicken back in, simmer 20 minutes. Remove and bone chicken, return almonds, chicken, liquid to pot, simmer another ½ hour. Add salt to taste.

Maumenye Ryalle
Two Fifteenth Century p. 22 (closely related recipe on p. 88)

Take Vernage, oþer strong Wyne of þe beste þat a man may fynde, an putte it on a potte, and caste þer-to a gode quantyte of pouder Canelle, and sette it on þe fyre, an gif it an hete; and þanne wrynge it soft þorw a straynour, þat þe draf go nowt owte, and put on a fayre potte, and pyke fayre newe pynys, and wasshe hem clene in Wyn, and caste a gode quantyte þer-to, and take whyte Sugre þer-to, as moche as þe lycoure is, and caste þer-to; and draw a few Sawnderys wyth strong wyne þorwe a straynoure, an caste þer-to, and put alle on one potte, and caste þer-to Clowes, a gode quantyte, and sette it on þe fyre, and gif it a boyle; þen take Almaundys, and draw them with mythty Wyne; and at þe firste boyle ly it vppe with Ale, and gif it a boyle, and sette it on þe fyre, and caste þer-to tesyd brawn, (of defaute of Pertrich or Capoun) a gode quantyte of tryid Gyngere perase, and sesyn it vppe with pouder Gyngere, and Salt and Safroun; and if it is to stonding, a-ly it with Vernage or swete Wyne, and dresse it Flat with þe backe of a Sawcere in þe Vernage or mygthty Wyne, and loke þat þou haue Sugre y-nowe, and serue forth hote.

3 lb chicken	1 c sugar
1 c vernage	10 T ground almonds
1 T cinnamon	½ c ale
½ t saunders	1 T fresh ginger
½ c more wine	¼ t powdered ginger
¼ c pine nuts	¼ t salt
½ t cloves	6 threads saffron

Microwave (or boil in very little water) chicken 6 minutes initially to make it easier to bone. Chicken should be boned, skinned, and shredded. Put vernage (or other sweet white wine) and cinnamon into the pot and boil; mix saunders with extra wine and add that and pine nuts, cloves, and sugar to pot; add almonds, let cook while chopping ginger, and add everything else, then boil about 30 minutes uncovered.

Moorish Chicken
Portuguese p. P-3

Cut up a fat hen and cook on a mild flame, with 2 spoons of fat, some bacon slices, lots of coriander, a pinch of parsley, some mint leaves, salt and a large onion.

Cover and let it get golden brown, stirring once in a while. Then cover hen with water and let boil, and season with salt, vinegar, cloves, saffron, black pepper and ginger. When chicken is cooked, pour in 4 beaten yolks. Then take a deep dish, lined with slices of bread, and pour chicken on top.

4 lbs chicken	½ t salt
10 oz onion	2 T vinegar
1 t parsley	¼ t cloves
½ T mint	8 threads saffron
⅓ c cilantro	½ t ginger
2 T lard	½ t pepper
5 strips bacon	4 egg yolks
2 ½ c water	6 slices bread

Dismember chicken (thighs, legs, wings in two pieces, etc.), slice onion, wash and coarsely chop parsley, mint, and cilantro. Melt fat, fry bacon a couple of minutes, put chicken, herbs, salt, and onion into pot and fry uncovered about 10 minutes, cover and cook covered another 20 minutes. Add water, vinegar, additional spices, bring to a boil and cook 45 minutes. Toast bread, arrange toast in bowl. Break egg yolks, stir them in and remove pot from heat, and pour into bowl with toast.

Note that this is a 15th-century Portuguese idea of an Islamic dish: a real Islamic dish would not include bacon!

How You Want to Make a Food of Hens
Daz Buoch von Guoter Spise p. B-7 (#28)

This is called King's Hens. Take young roasted hens. Cut them in small pieces. Take fresh eggs and beat them. Mix thereto pounded ginger and a little anise. Pour that in a strong pot, which will be hot. With the same herbs, which you add to the eggs, sprinkle therewith the hens and put the hens in the pot. And do thereto saffron and salt to mass. And put them to the fire and let them bake [at the] same heat with a little fat. Give them out whole. That is called King's Hens.

3 lb chicken	¼ t anise on chicken
2 T fresh ginger	12 threads saffron
¾ t anise	1 t salt
5 eggs	7 T chicken fat
2 t fresh ginger	

Put whole chicken in oven at 350°, bake 1 hour. Let cool, cut into pieces, partially deboning. Cut 2 T ginger up fine and pound with ¾ t anise in mortar. Take a bowl, beat eggs, add ginger, anise, beat together. Heat a pot on the stove, add egg mixture. Put cut up chicken on the egg mixture. Sprinkle chicken with another 2 t ginger and ¼ t anise. Crush saffron into 1 t water, sprinkle saffron and salt over pot. Sprinkle chicken fat (drippings from baking the chicken) overall. Put in oven, bake 30 minutes at 350°.

Mirause of Catelonia
Platina p. 92 (book 6) (Good)

The Catelans are a refined people who in character and customs are hardly unlike the Italians and skillful with food; they have a dish which they call mirause and prepare it thus: capons or pullets or pigeons well cleaned and washed they put together on a spit and turn over the hearth until they are half cooked. Then they remove them and cut them in pieces and put them in a pot. Then they chop almonds that have been toasted under warm ashes and cleaned with some cloth. To this they add some bread crumbs lightly toasted with vinegar and juice and pass all this through a strainer. This is all put in the same pot with cinnamon and ginger and a good amount of sugar and left to boil on the coals with a slow fire until it is done, all the time being stirred with a spoon so that it does not stick to the pot.

3 ¼ lb chicken	½ t ginger
¾ c roasted almonds	1 T sugar
¼ c breadcrumbs	10.5 oz concentrated
1 T vinegar	chicken broth
½ t cinnamon	

Preheat oven to 450°. Put in chicken, reduce temperature to 350°, bake about 45 minutes. Chop almonds fine, mix chopped almonds, breadcrumbs, vinegar, and a little of the chicken broth and run through a food processor until smooth (or squish through a strainer, grind the residue with a mortar and pestle, and then put it through the strainer). Cut up chicken into large pieces, put in pot with sauce, spices, sugar, the juice from roasting the chicken and the rest of the chicken broth and cook about 15 minutes, stirring almost constantly.

Bruette Saake
Two Fifteenth Century p. 27

Take Capoun, skalde hem, draw hem, smyte hem to gobettys, Waysshe hem, do hem in a potte; þenne caste owt þe potte, waysshe hem a-gen on þe potte, and caste þer-to half wyne half Broþe; take Percely, Isope, Waysshe hem, and hew hem smal, and putte on þe potte þer þe Fleysshe is; caste þer-to Clowys, quybibes, Maces, Datys y-tallyd, hol Safroune; do it ouer þe fyre; take Canelle, Gyngere, tempere þin powajes with wyne; caste in-to þe potte Salt þer-to, hele it, and whan it is y-now, serue it forth.

3 lbs frying chicken	½ t mace
2 c broth	¼ c = 3 oz dates
2 c wine	15 threads saffron
4 T fresh parsley	½ t cinnamon
1 ½ T fresh hyssop	½ t ginger
⅛ t cloves	2 t more wine
¼ t cubebs	½ t salt

Cut chicken into separate joints, add broth and wine and set to boil. Chop herbs and grind cubebs in a mortar; add herbs, dates, cloves, cubebs, and mace and cook about 35 minutes uncovered. Mix cinnamon and ginger with remaining wine, add them and salt to chicken, cover and let simmer another 30 minutes. Should be served with bread (or rice, although that is less appropriate for 15th-century England) to sop up the sauce.

Notes: One could also interpret "smyting to gobbetys" as taking the meat off the bones and cutting up; my gobbets are the size of the thigh or half the breast. I assume the parsley and hyssop are intended to be fresh since they are being washed. Fresh hyssop tastes somewhat like parsley but rather more bitter and spicier; I would suggest, if you can't get it, substituting more fresh parsley rather than dried hyssop, which is pretty tasteless.

Cold Sage Chicken
Goodman p. 277

Take your chicken and quarter it and set to cook in salt and water, then set it to get cold. Then bray ginger, cinnamon powder, grain of Paradise, and cloves and bray them well without straining; then bray bread dipped in chicken broth, parsley (the most), sage, and a little saffron in the leaf and color it green and run it through a strainer (and some there be that run therewith yolk of egg) and moisten with good vinegar, and when it is moistened set it on your chicken and with and on the top of the aforesaid chicken set hard boiled eggs cut into quarters and pour your sauce over it all.

½ chicken, quartered	4 T parsley
¼ t ginger	3 leaves sage
½ t cinnamon	10 threads saffron
¼ t grains of paradise	2 egg yolks
less than ⅛ t cloves	1 T vinegar
3 slices of bread	4 hard boiled eggs

Douce Ame
Form of Cury p. 35

Take good cowmilk and do it in a pot. Take psel., sage, Hissop, savory, and other good herbs. Hew them and do them in the milk and seethe them. Take capons half y-roasted and smite them on pieces and do thereto pine and honey clarified. Salt it and color it with saffron and serve it forth.

2 ¼ c milk	2 lb chicken
¼ c fresh parsley	1 T pine nuts
1 t dried sage	½ T honey
1 t hyssop	¼ t salt
1 t dried savory	a pinch saffron
other herbs to taste	

Bake chicken about 40 minutes at 350°. Simmer in milk about 45 minutes.

Conyng, Hen, or Mallard
Two Fifteenth Century p. 80

Take conyng, hen or mallard, and roast him almost enough; or else chop him, and fry him in fresh grease; and fry onions minced, and cast altogether into a pot, and cast thereto fresh broth and half wine; cast thereto cloves, maces, powder of pepper, canel; then stepe fair bread with the same broth and draw it through a strainer with vinegre. And when it hath well boiled, cast the liquor thereto, and powder ginger, and vinegre, and season it up, and then thou shall serve it forth.

4 ½ lb duckling, or 3 lbs chicken or 3 lb rabbit	¼ t mace
	¼ t pepper
	1 t cinnamon
lard for frying	6 slices bread
½ lb onions	2 T red wine vinegar
2 c chicken broth	¼ t ginger
1 c wine	[½ t salt]
⅛ t cloves	1 T vinegar

Roast the duck, chicken or rabbit for about an hour and a quarter. Bone the meat, or break it into small pieces. Chop onions and fry them in 2 t of the drippings for about five minutes, until they turn yellow. Add dismembered chicken (or …), broth, wine, cloves, mace, pepper and cinnamon to the pot, bring to a simmer, and cook twenty minutes.

Meanwhile, tear up the bread, spoon about 1 c of the liquid from the pot over the bread, and let it soak for 3-4 minutes. Add 2 T vinegar, force through a strainer or mash very thoroughly, and add to the pot along with ginger and another T of vinegar. Bring back to a boil, stirring, and serve.

Chicones in Mose
Curye on Inglysch p. 86
(*Utilis Coquinario* no. 17)

To make chicones in mose. Tak blaunched almoundes & grynde hem smale & tempere hem with clene watere, & do hem in a pot & put þerto floure of rys & sugre & salt & safroun, & boyle hem togedere. & ley þe yelkes of harde sothe eyren in disches, & tak rosted chikenes & tak þe lemes & þe wynges & þe braun, & cut þat oþer del on lengthe, & ley it in þe disches with yolkes and take the sauce and hilde hit into the disches & do aboue clowes & serue it forth.

4 lb chicken	1 T sugar
8 eggs	½ t salt
1 c blanched almonds	8 threads saffron
1 c water	8 whole cloves
1 T rice flour	

Roast the chicken for about an hour and 35 minutes, preheating oven to 450° and turning down to 350° when the chicken is put in. While it is baking, put eggs in cold water and bring to a boil; after 15 minutes remove them, separate the yolks and set aside. Grind the almonds fine. Shortly before the chicken is done, combine almonds with water, bring to a boil, stir in the rice flour, sugar, salt and saffron and cook until thickened.

Cut legs and wings off the chicken, remove white meat and cut into strips. Arrange on a platter with the egg yolks on the chicken and pour the sauce over. Put on a few whole cloves for ornament and serve forth.

Garbage
Two Fifteenth Century p. 72

Take faire Garbage, chikenes hedes, ffete, lyvers, And gysers, and wassh hem clene; caste hem into a faire potte, And caste fressh broth of Beef, powder of Peper, Canell, Clowes, Maces, Parcely and Sauge myced small; then take brede, stepe hit in þe same brothe, Drawe hit thorgh a streynour, cast thereto, And lete boyle ynowe; caste there-to pouder ginger, vergeous, salt, And a litull Safferon, And serve hit forthe.

1 lb chicken livers	½ c fresh parsley, packed
1 lb gizzards	1 t fresh sage
2 ½ c beef broth	3 ½ oz bread
⅛ t pepper	¼ t ginger
½ t cinnamon	3 T verjuice
⅛ t cloves	½ t salt
¼ t mace	10 threads saffron

Cut up gizzards to remove the thin bits of gristle connecting the lumps of meat. Wash and chop parsley and sage. Put broth, meat, herbs, pepper, cinnamon, mace and cloves into a pot and bring to a boil. Simmer uncovered 1 hour 10 minutes. About 15 minutes before it is done simmering, remove about ¾ cup of the broth and tear up the bread into it; let soak briefly and mash thoroughly with a mortar and pestle. Put back into pot, bring back to a boil and cook, stirring, about 5 minutes, add remaining ingredients and cook a couple of minutes, stirring, and serve. Note that the original has chickens' heads and feet, which we have left out because they are not easy to get hold of.

Almond Fricatellae
Platina p. 150 (book 9)

Pass almonds that have been well cleaned and ground through a strainer with milk and rosewater. And to these add the breast of a chicken, boiled and ground separately, and blend in well some meal, two or three egg whites, and sugar. When this has been prepared, as you wish, fry them either in oil or liquamen.

2 oz almonds	½ c meal
⅜ c milk	½ t salt
1 ½ t rosewater	1 T sugar
1 lb chicken breasts	oil or lard
5 egg whites	

Blanch and grind almonds. Mix with rosewater and some milk. Boil chicken breasts about 10 minutes. Cut up chicken breasts and run them through a blender or food processor, using egg whites and remaining milk if necessary to make them sufficiently liquid to blend. Combine egg whites, almonds, and remaining ingredients. Make into patties or spoon into oil and flatten with a pancake turner. Fry about 1 minute a side in ½" oil until brown. They are good served with salt sprinkled over them.

For the meal, I use whole wheat (the kind you get in a health food store that looks like hard brown rice) ground in an electric coffee grinder (a sort of miniature food processor, also useful for grinding almonds and spices). You can use flour instead, but it does not come out the same.

Meat Dishes

Boiled Meats Ordinary
The English Huswife p. 47

You shall take a racke of mutton cut into peeces, or a leg of mutton cut in peeces: for this meat and these joints, are the best, Although any other joint, or any fresh beefe will likewise make good pottage: and having washt your meat well, put it into a cleane pot with faire water, and set it on the fire: then take violet leaves, endive, succory [chiccory?], strawberie leaves, spinage, langdebeefe, marygold flowers, Scallions, and a little persly, and chop them very small together, then take halfe so much oatmeale well beaten as there is herbes, and mix it with the herbes, and chop all very wel together: then when the pot is ready to boile, skumme it very wel and then put in your herbes: And so let it boil with a quicke fire, stirring the meat oft in the pot, till the meat be boild enough, and that the hearbes and water mixt together without any separation, which will be after the consumption of more then a third part: then season them with salt, and serve them up with the meat either with sippets or without.

1 lb mutton or lamb	3 scallions
2 ½ c water	1 t salt
2 T parsley	7 oz oats ≅ 1 ⅜ c
14 oz mixed greens ≅ 5 c	
(Greens: endive lettuce, Belgian endive, spinach, …)	

Cut lamb into bite-sized pieces. Put in a pot with water, bring to a simmer. Chop greens, including parsley and scallions, and mix with oatmeal (steel-cut oats, since rolled oats are long out of period). Add the oatmeal and greens to the pot, along with salt. Simmer 45 minutes to 1 hour—perhaps a little longer if you are using mutton.

Variants: If you want the pottage green but without visible herbs, beat the oatmeal and herbs in a stone mortar with a wooden pestle. Strain it, using some warm water from the pot. If you want it without herbs, use lots of onions and more oatmeal than before.

Pottage with Whole Herbs
English Huswife, book 2, p. 48

Take mutton, veal or kid, break the bones but do not cut up the flesh, wash, put in a pot with water. When ready to boil and well skimmed, add a handful or two of small oatmeal. Take whole lettuce, the best inner leaves, whole spinach, whole endive, whole chiccory, whole leaves of colaflorry or the inward parts of white cabbage, with two or three onions. Put all into the pot until done. Season with salt and as much verjuice as will only turn the taste of the pottage; serve up covering meat with whole herbs and addorning the dish with sippets.

1 lb veal	5 flowerettes cauliflower
1 ½ c oatmeal	2 small onions
3 ½ oz lettuce	½ T salt
1 c spinach	2 T verjuice
1 small endive	6 slices of toast
2 oz chicory	

Note: "Oatmeal" should be steelcut/Irish oatmeal, not moden rolled oats.

Cook veal whole about ½ hour in enough water to cover. Add vegetables as soon as the water comes to a boil and is skimmed.

Stwed Mutton
Two Fifteenth Century p. 72

Take faire Mutton that hath ben roste, or elles Capons, or suche oþer flessh, and mynce it faire; put hit into a possenet, or elles bitwen ii siluer disshes; caste thereto faire parcely, And oynons small mynced; then caste there-to wyn, and a litull vynegre or vergeous, pouder of peper, Canel, salt and saffron, and lete it stue on þe faire coles, And þen serue hit forthe; if he have no wyne ne vynegre, take Ale, Mustard, and A quantite of vergeous, and do þis in þe stede of vyne or vinegre.

Wine Version
1 ½ lb boned lamb	1 t pepper
¼ c parsley	½ t cinnamon
1 ¼ lb onions	1 t salt
¾ c wine	3 threads saffron
2 T vinegar	½ c water

Beer Version
Substitute 1 c dark beer and ½ t ground mustard for the wine. Substitute 4 T of verjuice for the vinegar if you have it.

Roast the lamb (before boning) at 350° for about 1 hour, then chop it into bite sized pieces. Chop onions fine. Combine all ingredients (and the juices from roasting the lamb) in a covered stew pot; use enough water so that there is just enough liquid to boil the meat in. Simmer it about ½ hour and serve it forth. It is good over rice.

Beef y-Stewed
Two Fifteenth Century p. 6

Take faire beef of the ribs of the forequarters, and smite in fair pieces, and wash the beef into a fair pot; then take the water that the beef was sodden in, and strain it through a strainer and seethe the same water and beef in a pot, and let them boil together; then take canel, cloves, maces, grains of paradise, cubebs and onions y-minced, parsley and sage, and cast thereto, and let them boil together; and then take a loaf of bread, and stepe it with broth and vinegar, and then draw it through a strainer, and let it be still; and when it is near enough, cast the liquor thereto, but not too much, and then let boil once, and cast saffron thereto a quantity; then take salt and vinegar, and cast thereto, and look that it be poynant enough, and serve forth.

1 medium onion = 6 oz	⅛ t cloves
¼ c parsley	½ t cinnamon
⅛ t grains of paradise	2 slices bread = 3 oz
⅛ t cubebs	12 threads saffron
1 t fresh sage	1 T vinegar
1 lb beef	1 t salt
¼ t mace	1 t more vinegar

Chop onions and herbs, grind grains of paradise and cubebs. Put beef in a pot, add 1 ½ c water, bring to a boil, add parsley, sage, onion, and spices. Simmer about 45 minutes covered. Tear up bread, put to soak in 1 T vinegar and 5/8 c broth from the meat. After 45 minutes put bread through a strainer (or a food processor); add that, saffron, salt and 1 t vinegar to the meat. Adjust salt and vinegar to your taste, bring back to a boil and serve.

Bruet of Savoy
Du Fait de Cuisine no. 3

And again, another potage, that is a bruet of Savoy: to give understanding to him who will be charged with making this bruet, to take his poultry and the meat according to the quantity which he is told that he should make, and make ready his poultry and set to cook cleanly; and meat according to the quantity of potage which he is told to make, and put to boil with the poultry; and then take a good piece of lean bacon in a good place [a good cut?] and clean it well and properly, and then put it to cook with the aforesaid poultry and meat; and then take sage, parsley, hyssop, and marjoram, and let them be very well washed and cleaned, and make them into a bunch without chopping and all together, and then put them to boil with the said potage and with the meat; and according to the quantity of the said broth take a large quantity of parsley well cleaned and washed, and brayed well and thoroughly in a mortar; and, being well brayed, check that your meat is neither too much or too little cooked and salted; and then according to the quantity of broth have white ginger, grains of paradise, and a little pepper; and put bread without the crust to soak with the said broth so that there is enough to thicken it; and being properly soaked, let it be pounded and brayed with the said parsley and spices, and let it be drawn and strained with the said broth; and put in wine and verjuice according as it is necessary. And all of the things aforesaid should be put in to the point where there is neither too little nor too much. And then, this done, put it to boil in a large, fair, and clean pot. And if it happens that the potage is too green, put in a little saffron, and this will make the green bright. And when it is to be arranged for serving, put your meat on the serving dishes and the broth on top.

2 lbs chicken pieces	¾ c more parsley
1 ¼ lb veal	1 t ground ginger
3 stalks marjoram	1 t grains of paradise
2 stalks parsley	¼ t pepper
1 stalk fresh sage	1 ½ t verjuice
1 stalk hyssop	2 T wine
4 slices bacon	[⅛ t salt]
4 slices white bread	[8 threads saffron]

Tie sage, parsley, and marjoram with string and put them in a pot; cut up leg quarters, slice veal, add them along with enough water to cover. Cut off about half the fat from the bacon (or start with lean bacon if you can find it); cut the remainder in small pieces. Simmer for about ½ hour. Drain off broth, put bread in broth; grind up the rest of the spices and the additional ¾ c parsley. Soak the bread in about 1 c broth then add parsley and spices, put through the strainer. Add wine and verjuice, boil about 10 minutes, serve with the sauce over the meat.

Cormarye
Curye on Inglysch p. 109
(*Forme of Cury* no. 54)

Take colyaundre, caraway smale grounden, powdour of peper and garlec ygrounde, in rede wyne; medle alle þise togyder and salt it. Take loynes of pork rawe and fle of the skyn, and pryk it wel with a knyf, and lay it in the sawse. Roost it whan þou wilt, & kepe þat fallith þerfro in the rostyng and seeþ it in a possynet with faire broth, and serue it forth wiþ þe roost anoon.

1 t caraway	1 ½ c red wine
3 cloves garlic	½ t salt
1 t ground coriander	1 ½-3 lb pork roast
½ t pepper	½ c chicken broth

Grind caraway in a mortar, then grind garlic with it (or use a spice grinder and a garlic press). Combine with coriander, pepper, wine and salt to make a marinade. Stick pork with a knife lots of times. Put pork in marinade and let it marinate over night, turning it once or twice. Heat oven to 450°, put in pork, turn down to 350°, roast until it is done (170° on a meat thermometer), basting with the marinade every ten or fifteen minutes. It should take about an hour and a half to two hours, depending on the size and shape of the roast; for larger roasts the rule is about half an hour/pound (if you use more than a three pound roast, you probably want to scale up the amount of marinade). Collect the drippings from the broth, combine with half their volume of chicken broth, simmer for at least 15 minutes and serve over the pork.

Meat Casserole (Cazuela De Carne)
De Nola no. 124

You must take meat and cut it into pieces the size of a walnut, and gently fry it with the fat of good bacon; and when it is well gently fried, cast in good broth, and cook it in a casserole; and cast in all fine spices, and saffron, and a little orange juice or verjuice, and cook it very well until the meat begins to fall apart and only a little broth remains; and then take three or four eggs beaten with orange juice or verjuice, and cast it into the casserole; and when you wish to eat, give it four or five stirs with a large spoon, and then it will thicken; and when it is thick, remove it from the fire; and prepare dishes, and cast cinnamon upon each one. However, there are those who do not wish to cast in eggs or spice, but only cinnamon and cloves, and cook them with the meat, as said above, and cast vinegar on it so that it may have flavor; and there are others who put all the meat whole and in one piece, full of cinnamon, and whole cloves, and ground spices in the broth, and this must be turned little by little, so that it does not cook more at one end than the other. And so nothing is necessary but cloves and cinnamon, and those moderately.

[Another recipe from this book says: "all manner of fine spices, which are: good ginger, and good cinnamon, and saffron, and grains of paradise, and nutmeg, and mace..."]

1 ½ lb lamb	¼ t cinnamon at end
1 slice of bacon	*fine spices:*
1 ½ c chicken broth	⅛ t ginger
15 threads saffron	¼ t grains of paradise
2 T verjuice	⅛ t mace
2 eggs	½ t cinnamon
1 T more verjuice	⅛ t nutmeg

Cut the meat into bite sized pieces. Fry the bacon to render out the fat; fry the meat in the bacon fat (more like simmering because of liquid from the lamb) for about ten minutes. Add broth, fine spices, saffron, and 2 T verjuice, cook for an hour and a quarter until only a little liquid remains. Beat 2 eggs into the additional 1 T verjuice, add to casserole, cook another couple of minutes. Serve with a little more cinnamon sprinkled over.

Cow's Meat
Anthimus p. 11

Cow's meat however, steamed and cooked in a casserole should be eaten, in a gravy. First, it should be put to soak in one water, and then it should cook in a reasonable quantity of fresh water, without adding any water as it cooks, and when the meat is cooked, put in a vessel about a half mouthful of vinegar, and put in the heads of leeks and a little pennyroyal, parsley root, or fennel, and let it cook for an hour; then add honey to half the quantity of the vinegar, or sweeter according to taste. Then let it cook on a slow fire, shaking the pot frequently with the hands, and the sauce will well season the meat. Then grind: pepper fifty grains; costum and spikenard, a half solidus each; cloves, one tremissis. All these grind well in an earthen mortar, add a little wine, and when well ground, put into a vessel and stir well, so that before it is taken from the fire it may warm up a little and put its strength into the gravy. Moreover, where there is honey, or must, or caroenum, put in one of these as it says above, and do not let it cook in a copper kettle, but in an earthen vessel; it makes flavor the better.

1 ¾ lb beef	2 t honey
3 c water	2 T wine
3 leeks	½ t pepper
4 t vinegar	½ t cloves
1 t fennel seed	1 t spikenard
(*or* pennyroyal or parsley root)	

Cut beef into 1" pieces. Bring beef and water to a boil, turn down heat to low and cook covered 45 minutes. Wash and slice leeks, using only the half starting at the white end. Grind fennel seed and add vinegar, honey, leeks and fennel to stew. Cook uncovered on moderate heat one hour. Grind pepper, cloves, and spikenard (we don't know what "costum" is) together, add wine and grind some more. Put this with stew and cook ten minutes and serve.

As spikenard is related to lavender, we have used lavender when we could not get spikenard.

Fylettes en Galentyne
Two Fifteenth Century p. 8 (Good)

Take fair pork, the fore quarter, and take off the skin; and put the pork on a fair spit, and roast it half enough; then take it off and smite it in fair pieces, and cast it on a fair pot; then take onions and shred them and peel them, and not too small, and fry in a pan of fair grease; then cast them in the pot to the pork; then take good broth of mutton or of beef, and cast thereto, and cast thereto powder pepper, canel, cloves, and mace, and let them boil well together; then take fair bread, and vinegar, and steep the bread with the same broth, and strain it on blood, with ale, or else with saunders, and salt, and let them boil enough, and serve it forth.

2 lb pork roast	¼ t cloves
2 big onions	¼ t mace
2 T lard	¼ loaf of bread = 4-5 oz
4 c beef broth	¼ c vinegar
¼ t pepper	small pinch of saunders
1 t cinnamon	½ t salt

Put the pork in a 450° oven, turn down to 325°, and roast until about half done—140° on the meat thermometer. Cut it in slices, put it in a pot. Cut up the onions, not too fine, fry in lard until they are limp. Put them in the pot, along with the broth and spices. Bring to a boil and simmer for about half an hour. Meanwhile, soak your bread in vinegar and enough of the broth from the pot to get it thoroughly soggy, add saunders and salt and force it through a strainer (or use a food processor to reduce to mush). Add it and the salt, boil another ten or fifteen minutes.

Alternatives: add ½ c of ale (good), or else use ½ c of blood instead of the saunders, reducing the beef broth by ½ c to compensate.

Brawn en Peuerade
Two Fifteenth Century p. 11

Take Wyne an powder Canel, and draw it þorw a straynour, an sette it on þe fyre, and lette it boyle, an caste þer-to Clowes, Maces, an powder Pepyr; þan take smale Oynonys al hole, an par-boyle hem in hot watere, an caste þer-to, and let hem boyle to-gederys; þan take Brawn, an lesshe it, but nowt to þinne. An if it sowsyd be, lete it stepe a whyle in hot water tyl it be tendere, þan caste it to þe Sirip; þen take Sawnderys, an Vynegre, an caste þer-to, an lete it boyle alle to-gederys tyl it be y-now; þen take Gyngere, an caste þer-to, an so serue forth; but late it be nowt to þikke ne to þinne, but as potage shulde be.

1 lb small onions (~10)	¾ t pepper
4 c wine	2 ¼ lb pork
½ t cinnamon	½ t saunders
½ t cloves	¼ c vinegar
½ t mace	½ t ginger

Simmer onions in wine with spices (cinnamon, cloves, mace, pepper) for about 15 minutes, then slice meat and add it. Add saunders and vinegar. Cook together at moderate heat about one hour, then add ginger and remove from heat.

Autre Vele en Bokenade
Two Fifteenth Century p. 13

Take Vele, an Make it clene, and hakke it to gobettys, an sethe it; an take fat brothe, an temper up þine Almaundys þat þou hast y-grounde, an lye it with Flowre of Rys, and do þer-to gode powder of Gyngere, & Galyngale, Canel, Maces, Quybybis, and Oynonys y-mynsyd, & Roysonys of coraunce, & coloure yt wyth Safroun, and put þer-to þin Vele, & serue f.

1 lb stew veal	1 ½ t cinnamon
2 ½ c water	½ t mace
4 oz almonds	½ t cubebs
1 ½ c broth from veal	2 oz onion
2 T rice flour	5 T currants
½ t ginger	8 threads saffron
¼ t galingale	[½ t salt]

Cook veal in water about 20 minutes; grind almonds, mix with the rest of the ingredients in a small pot (including the broth from the veal). Simmer about 20 minutes (veal is also still cooking). Combine sauce and veal.

Mete of Cypree
Curye on Inglysch p. 55
(*Diuersa Cibaria* no. 56)

Vor mete of Cypree. Vurst nim of alemauns, & hwyte of heom one pertie, ah hwyte summe hole & þe oþur do to grinden. Soþþen nim þe hole alemauns & corf heom to quartes; soþþen nim fat broþ & swete of porc oþur of vþur vlehs; tempre þin alemauns & soþþen drauh out þi milke & so þe do hit in an veyre crouhe. Soþþen nim þe braun of chapouns oþur of hennen oþur of porc, & ef noed is let hakken, & soþþen do in a morter þat hit beo wel igronden, & soþþen nym hit & do hit to þe milke. Soþþen nim blod of cycchen oþur of oþur beste, & soþþen grind hit & do hit to þe vlesche. Soþþen do þe crouhe to þe vure & seoþ hit wel; & soþþen nym gode poudre of spices: gynger, kanel, maces, quibibes, and so zeoþ hit wiþ þilke metee. Soþþen nim wyn & sucre & make me an stronge soupe. Do hit in þilke to zeoþen. Soþþen nym flour of ris & do a quantite þat hit beo wel þikke. Soþþen nim þin alemauns icoruen & frie heom wel in grece; soþþen nim gynger & par yt wel & heuw hit. Soþþen nym þin alemauns yfried & þi gynger to þe dressur, & so do hit to þilke mete, & soþþen nym saffron & colore wel þi mete: & gef þat to gode men vor god mete & riche.

Version with modernized English: For meat of Cyprus. First take of almonds, & blanche of them one part, the white should be whole & the other do to grind. Then take the whole almonds & carve them to quarters; then take fat broth & suet of pork or of other flesh; temper thine almonds & then draw out thy milk & then do it in a fair crock. Then take the meat of capons or of hens or of pork, & if need is let it be hacked, & then do in a mortar that it be well ground, & then take it & do it to the milk. Then take blood of chicken or of other beast, & then grind it & do it to the flesh. Then do the crock to the fire & seethe it well; & then take good powder of spices: ginger, canel, maces, cubebs, and so seethe it with that meat. Then take wine & sugar & make me a strong soup. Do it in that to seethe. Then take flour of rice & do a quantity that it be well thick. Then take thine almonds carved & fry them well in grease; then take ginger & pare it well & hew it. Then take thine almonds yfried & thy ginger to the dresser, & so do it to this meat, & then take saffron & color well thy meat: & give that to good men for good meat & rich.

⅓ c almonds	⅛ t mace
1 c chicken broth	4 t wine
¾ lb pork (or chicken)	4 t sugar
[blood]	2 T rice flour
¼ t cubebs	2 T slivered almonds
⅛ t ginger	2 t lard
¼ t cinnamon	½ T fresh ginger

Grind whole almonds in food processor. Add ½ c of the broth, run the food processor, strain out liquid, put back residue; add another ¼ c broth, repeat; add another ¼ c, repeat. Grind meat and add to liquid; add blood if you can get it. Put on the heat; grind cubebs and add spices. Cook about 10 minutes, stirring frequently; add wine and sugar. Cook another couple of minutes, add rice flour; cook a minute and remove from heat. While meat is cooking, fry the slivered almonds in grease, cut ginger into very little pieces. When meat is done, sprinkle almonds and ginger over and serve.

See p. 21 for a fish (Lenten) version of this dish.

Froys
Curye on Inglysch p. 65
(*Diuersa Servicia* no. 18)

For to make a froys. Nym veel and seþ yt wel & hak it smal, & grynd bred, peper & safroun and do þereto & frye yt, & presse yt wel vpon a bord, & dresse yt forþe.

1 lb veal	⅜ t pepper
2 slices bread	[½ t salt]
10 threads saffron	2 ½ T lard for frying

Put veal in pot, cover with water, bring to a boil and cook 15 minutes. Cut it to ¼" pieces, including fat. Grind bread in food processor, crush saffron into about 1 T of the broth, and mix meat, bread, pepper and salt. Melt lard; fry mixture 4-5 minutes over moderately high flame until pieces are getting browned. Press out excess lard on cutting board with a spatula and transfer to serving dish.

Froyse out of Lentyn
Two Fifteenth Century p. 45

Take Eyroun & draw þe yolkes & þe whyte þorw a straynoure; þan take fayre Bef or vele, & sethe it tyl it be y-now; þan hew cold oþer hote, & melle to-gederys þe eggys, þe Bef, or vele, & caste þer-to Safroun, & Salt, & pouder of Pepir, & melle it to-gederys; þan take a fayre Fryingpanne, & sette it ouer þe fyre, & caste þer-on fayre freysshe grece, & make it hot, & caste þe stuf þer-on, & stere it wel in þe panne tyl it come to-gederys wel; cast on þe panne a dysshe & presse it to-gederys, & turne it onys, & þanne serue it forth.

1 ¼ lb beef steak	⅜ t pepper
15 threads saffron	¾ t salt
8 eggs	2 oz bacon fat

Cut meat into 2 inch chunks, boil in water 20 minutes. Cut into pea sized pieces. Grind 15 threads of saffron in 2 T warm water. Pass eggs through a strainer or simply beat them. Render out bacon fat, mix everything together, then cook the mixture in a frying pan, stirring frequently until set up, about five minutes. Press it all together and flip it, then invert onto a plate and serve.

Egredouncye
Two Fifteenth Century p. 31

Take Porke or Bef, wheþer þe likey, & leche it þinne þwerte; þen broyle it broun a litel, & þen mynce it lyke Venyson; choppe it in sewe, þen caste it in a potte & do þer-to Freyssh brothe; take Erbis, Onynonys, Percely & Sawge, & oþer gode erbis, þen lye it vppe with brede; take Pepir & Safroun, pouder Canel, Vynegre, or Eysel Wyne, Broþe an Salt, & let yet boyle to-gederys, tylle þey ben y-now, & þan serue it forth rennyng.

½ lb pork or beef	¼ c bread crumbs
1 small onion = 2 oz	⅛ t pepper
1 oz fresh parsley	6 threads saffron
5 leaves fresh sage	¼ t cinnamon
[½ t rosemary]	2 T wine vinegar
[¼ t oregano]	⅓ c more beef broth
1 ½ c beef broth	½ t salt

Chop meat and then brown in a frying pan with chopped onions; put with herbs and 1½ c broth and bring to a boil, adding bread crumbs as it comes to a boil; add remaining ingredients and simmer for about five minutes, then remove from heat. Good over rice.

Fricassee of Whatever Meat You Wish
Platina p. 91 (book 6)

You make a fricassee from fowl or whatever meat you choose in this way: in a pot with lard, close to the fire, put meat or birds well cleaned and washed, whether cut up finely or in slices. Stir this often with a spoon so that it does not stick to the side of the pot; when it is nearly cooked, take out most of the lard and put in two egg yolks beaten with verjuice and pour in juice and spices mixed into the pot. To this dish add some saffron so that it is more colorful. Likewise, it will not detract from the enjoyment of it to sprinkle finely chopped parsley over the dish. Then serve it immediately to your guests.

1 lb boneless chicken	⅛ t cloves
2 egg yolks	¼ t cinnamon
2 T verjuice	[¼ t salt]
3 threads saffron	1 T parsley
3 T chicken broth	¼-⅓ c lard
¼ t pepper	

Cut up meat. Beat egg yolks with verjuice. In another small dish, crush saffron into a little of the broth, then add the rest of the broth and spices. Chop parsley. Heat lard. Fry meat about 8 minutes, stirring often, then add egg yolk mixture and broth mixture. Cook another two minutes. Remove from heat and sprinkle parsley on top.

Bourbelier of Wild Pig
Menagier p. M-23 (Good)

First you must put it in boiling water, and take it out quickly and stick it with cloves; put it on to roast, and baste with a sauce made of spices, that is ginger, cinnamon, clove, grain, long pepper and nutmegs, mixed with verjuice, wine, and vinegar, and without boiling use it to baste; and when it is roasted, it should be boiled up together. And this sauce is called boar's tail, and you will find it later (and there it is thickened with bread: and here, not).

3 lb pork roast	½ t long pepper
60 whole cloves	⅛ t nutmeg
¼ t ginger	½ c verjuice
⅛ t cinnamon	1 c wine
⅛ t cloves	½ c vinegar
¼ t grains of paradise	

Preheat oven to 450°. Stud roast with whole cloves, baste with a mixture of the remaining ingredients, then put into oven. Immediately after putting it in, turn oven down to 350°. Roast meat 1 hour 45 minutes (for this size roast), basting every 15 minutes.

Gourdes in potage
Curye on Inglysch p. 99
(*Forme of Cury* no. 10)

Take yong gowrdes; pare hem and kerue hem on pecys. Cast hem in gode broth, and do þerto a gode pertye of oynouns mynced. Take pork soden; grynde it and alye it þerwith and wiþ ʒolkes of ayren. Do þerto safroun and salt, and messe it forth with powdour douce.

1 lb pork	¾ t salt
3 ¼ lb opo gourd	3 egg yolks
½ lb onions	1 ½ T poudre douce (p. 4)
40 threads saffron	

Cut pork into large chunks (2" or so), put it in a pot with 1 c of water, boil for about 15 minutes. Peel and slice and quarter gourd (see p. 4). Put gourds and onions in pot with pork broth. Bring to a boil, simmer 30 minutes (until gourds are soft).

Grind up the pork in a food processor or mash it in a mortar. Stir the pork, saffron, salt and egg yolks into the simmering liquid. Simmer another ten minutes. Combine spices to make your poudre douce, serve with pottage with poudre douce sprinkled over it.

Mortrewys of Flesh
Two Fifteenth Century p. 14

Take porke, and seþe it wyl; þanne take it vppe and pulle a-way þe swerde [skin], an pyke owt þe bonys, and hakke it and grynd it smal; þenne take þe sylf brothe, & temper it with ale; þen take fayre gratyd brede, & do þer-to, and seþe it, an coloure it with saffroun, & lye it with ʒolks of eyroun, and make it euen salt, & caste powder gyngere, a-bouyn on þe dysshe.

1 lb+ pork roast	3 egg yolks
1 c ale (or beer)	1 t salt
⅔ c bread crumbs	1 t ginger
3 threads of saffron	

Simmer a small pork roast for 45 minutes. Take it out. Separate the meat from the bones and fat. Chop it up small–if you have a large mortar mush it in that. Mix 2 c of the broth from the pork with ale and bread crumbs. Boil it, add saffron, mix in egg yolks to thicken. Add salt. Pour over the meat. Sprinkle powdered ginger over all and serve.

Picadinho de Carne de Vaca: Beef Hash
Portuguese p. P-2

Wash tender beef and chop fine. Next add cloves, saffron, pepper, ginger, minced green herbs, onion juice, vinegar and salt. Saute it all in oil and let cook until water dries up. Serve on slices of bread.

2 lb beef	¼ c parsley
¼ t cloves	4 t onion juice
20 threads saffron	2 T wine vinegar
1 t pepper	¾ t salt
1 t ginger	2 T oil
4 t cilantro	6 slices bread
2 t mint	

Chop meat to a little coarser than hamburger, using a food processor; mix everything but oil and bread. The herbs chosen are those mentioned commonly in other recipes in this cookbook. Heat oil over moderately high heat in a large frying pan and add beef mixture; cook about 20 minutes, stirring constantly until water comes out of the meat, then occasionally until water dries up. We considered it done when it still looked moist but there was no longer standing liquid. Serve over bread or toast; also good on rice.

Brawune Fryez
Two Fifteenth Century p. 43

Take Brawune, and kytte it þinne; þan take þe yolkes of Eyroun, and sum of þe whyte þer-with; þan take mengyd Flowre, an draw þe Eyroun þorw a straynoure; þen take a gode quantyte of Sugre, Saferoun, and Salt, and caste þer-to, and take a fayre panne with Fressche gres, and set ouer þe fyre; and whan þe grece is hote, take þe Brawn, an putte in bature, and turne it wyl þer-yn, an þan putte it on þe panne with þe grece, and late frye to-gederys a lytil whyle; þan take it vppe in-to a fayre dyssche, and caste Sugre þer-on and þan serue forth.

10 oz pork	2 threads saffron
2 egg yolks	¼ t salt
2 eggs	oil or lard to fry
½ c flour	~ 2 t sugar on top
1 T sugar	

Slice meat thin (¼" or less). Beat eggs and egg yolks and combine with flour, sugar, saffron and salt to make a batter, crushing the saffron into ½ t water before mixing it in. Melt lard and heat over moderate heat. Dip strips of meat into the batter on both sides and fry until brown, about half a minute to a minute on each side (it is hard to give exact time since that depends on the heat of the lard). Sprinkle sugar on top and serve.

Alows de Beef or de Motoun
Two Fifteenth Century p. 40

Take fayre Bef of þe quyschons, and motoun of þe bottes, and kytte in þe maner of Stekys; þan take raw Percely, and Oynonys smal y-scredde, and yolkys of Eyroun soþe hard, and Marow or swette, and hew alle þes to-geder smal; þan caste þer-on poudere of Gyngere and Saffroun, and tolle hem to-gederys with þin hond, and lay hem on þe Stekys al a-brode, and caste Salt þer-to; þen rolle to-gederys, and putte hem on a round spete, and roste hem til þey ben y-now; þan lay hem in a dysshe, and pore þer-on Vynegre and a lityl verious, and pouder Pepir þer-on y-now, and Gyngere, and Canelle, and a fewe yolkys of hard Eyroun y-kremyd þer-on; and serue forth.

⅓ c parsley	½ lb lamb or beef
¼ c onion	¼ t more ginger
3 hard-boiled egg yolks	¼ c vinegar
1 T lamb fat or marrow	pinch pepper
¼ t ginger	[salt to taste]
4 threads saffron	¼ t cinnamon

Mix chopped parsley, finely chopped onions, 2 egg yolks, and fat or marrow; chop it all together and add ginger and saffron. Slice the meat ¼" thick; slices should be about 6" by 2". Spread with parsley, etc. mixture, roll up on skewers or toothpicks, broil about 10-12 minutes until brown. Mix sauce with the remaining ingredients and pour over. Makes 6-8 rolls 2" long and 1" to 1 ½" in diameter.

The Flesh of Veal
Platina p. 94 (book 6)

From the haunch of veal take the lean meat and slice it into long thin slices; stroke them with the back of the knife so that they do not break; right away sprinkle them with salt and ground fennel, then on the meat spread marjoram and parsley, with finely diced lard, and sprinkle aromatic herbs over the slices and immediately roll them up and put them on a spit near the fire, taking care that they do not dry out too much. When they are cooked serve them immediately to your guests.

3 T parsley
2 t fresh marjoram
2 T fresh basil
1 t salt
1 t fennel seed, ground
¾ lb lean veal
1 T lard
¼ t dry thyme

Chop parsley, marjoram and basil coarsely. Sprinkle salt and fennel onto the meat slices, dot with lard, sprinkle on remaining herbs. Roll meat up in the direction that the fibers run, since otherwise it will tear, and secure it with toothpicks or skewers. Bake 40 minutes at 350°.

Corat
Curye on Inglysch p. 100
(*Forme of Cury* no. 14)

Take the noumbles of calf, swyne, or of shepe; perboile hem and kerue hem to dyce. Cast hem in gode broth and do þerto erbes, grene chybolles smale yhewe; seeþ it tendre, and lye with yolkes of eyren. Do þerto verious, safroun, powdour douce and salt, and serue it forth.

1 lb calf heart
2 ½ c beef broth
4 oz spinach
6 oz scallions
4 oz turnip greens
8 egg yolks
¼ c verjuice
12 threads saffron
1 T poudre douce (p. 4)
1 t salt

Parboil heart in 4 c water: bring water to boil, add heart, bring back to boil, total time about 4 minutes. Drain. Cut heart in ½"-1" cubes. Put with broth and chopped washed greens, simmer about 20 minutes. Stir in beaten egg yolks, turn off heat. Add verjuice, saffron (crushed into a little water), poudre douce, salt, and serve it forth.

Numbles means innards. We suspect the title of the recipe is derived from the French word for "heart" and therefore use heart, but it is also good made with kidney.

Chopped Liver
Du Fait de Cuisine no. 61

For the chopped liver: he who has the charge of the chopped liver should take kids' livers—and if there are not enough of those of kids use those of veal—and clean and wash them very well, then put them to cook well and properly; and, being cooked, let him take them out onto fair and clean boards and, being drained, chop them very fine and, being well chopped, let him arrange that he has fair lard well and properly melted in fair and clean pans, then put in to fry the said chopped liver and sauté it well and properly. And then arrange that he has a great deal of eggs and break them into fair dishes and beat them all together; and put in spices, that is white ginger, grains of paradise, saffron, and salt in good proportion, then put all of this gently into the said pans with the said liver which is being fried while continually stirring and mixing with a good spoon in the pans until it is well cooked and dried out and beginning to brown. And then when this comes to the sideboard arrange the aforesaid heads [reference to preceding recipe in the original] *on fair serving dishes, and on each dish next to the heads put and arrange the aforesaid chopped liver.*

½ lb calf liver
3 eggs
¼ t ginger
¼ t grains of paradise
8 threads saffron, ground
¼ t salt
2 T lard

Simmer liver for about 5 minutes, drain, then chop very fine. Beat the eggs, add spices. Melt the lard, add liver and eggs, stir constantly until cooked.

Meat, Cheese and Egg Pies

Tart on Ember Day
Ancient Cookery p. 448 (Good)

Parboil onions, and sage, and parsley and hew them small, then take good fat cheese, and bray it, and do thereto eggs, and temper it up therewith, and do thereto butter and sugar, and raisyngs of corince, and powder of ginger, and of canel, medel all this well together, and do it in a coffin, and bake it uncovered, and serue it forth.

1 lb onions
7 oz cheese
⅓ c parsley
2 T chopped fresh sage
 (or 1 ½ t dried)
4 eggs
3 T melted butter
1 T sugar
4 T currants
¼ t ginger
1 t cinnamon
9 " pie crust

Chop the onions and boil 10 minutes, drain. Grate cheese. Mix everything and put in pie crust. We have used several kinds of cheese, all of which work in this recipe.

Spinach Tart
Goodman p. 278 – "A Tart" (Good)

To make a tart, take four handfuls of beet leaves, two handfuls of parsley, a handful of chervil, a sprig of fennel and two handfuls of spinach, and pick them over and wash them in cold water, then cut them up very small; then bray with two sorts of cheese, to wit a hard and a medium, and then add eggs thereto, yolks and whites, and bray them in the cheese; then put the herbs into the mortar and bray all together and also put therein some fine powder. Or instead of this have ready brayed in the mortar two heads of ginger and onto this bray your cheese, eggs and herbs and then cast old cheese scraped or grated onto the herbs and take it to the oven and then have your tart made and eat it hot.

⅓ lb spinach *and/or* beet greens	6 oz Parmesan
½ cup fresh parsley	6 oz mozzarella
2 T dried *or* ¼ c fresh chervil	5 eggs
1 or 2 leaves fresh fennel, *or* 1 t fennel seed, ground	½ t ginger
	[½ t salt]
	9" pie crust

Chop greens, chop or grate cheese and mix filling in a bowl. Make pie crust and bake at 400° for about 10 minutes. Put filling in crust and bake about 40 minutes at 350°. We usually substitute spinach for beet leaves, dried chervil for fresh, and fennel seed for fresh fennel leaves because of availability.

Malaches of Pork
Curye on Inglysch p. 134
(*Form of Cury* no. 162)

Hewe pork al to pecys and medle it with ayren & chese igrated. Do þerto powdour fort, safroun & pynes with salt. Make a crust in a trap; bake it wel þerinne, and serue it forth.

13 oz boneless pork	¾ t powder fort (p.4)
½ lb parmesan	¼ c pine nuts
3 eggs	½ t salt
8 threads saffron	

Cut up the pork raw into ½"-¼" cubes. Grate cheese and mix with eggs in a bowl. Crush saffron into a teaspoon or so of water. Combine everything. Make a 9" pie crust, prebake about 10 minutes at 350°. Put filling in crust and bake at 350° for 45-50 minutes.

We have also used mozzarella and cheddar for the cheese, but parmesan is better.

Mushroom Pastries
Menagier p. M-25

Mushrooms of one night are the best, and are small and red inside, closed above; and they should be peeled, then wash in hot water and parboil; if you wish to put them in pastry add oil, cheese, and powdered spices.

Fine Powder of Spices (Menagier p. M-40): Take an ounce and a drachm of white ginger, a quarter-ounce of hand-picked cinnamon, half a quarter-ounce each of grains and cloves, and a quarter-ounce of rock sugar, and grind to powder.

1 lb mushrooms	¼ t cinnamon
9 oz parmesan	⅛ t grains of paradise
1 T olive oil	⅛ t cloves
1 t ginger	¼ t sugar

Slice mushrooms and parboil (put into boiling water and cook two minutes); drain. Grate or chop cheese. Grind grains of paradise and mix up spices. Mix mushrooms, ⅔ of cheese, spices and oil. Put mixture into crust, put remaining cheese over. Makes scant 9" pie. Bake about 20-25 minutes at 350°.

To Make a Chicken Tart
Due Libri di Cucina B: no. 42

If you want to make a pie of chickens, one can do it in four ways. Take them and dismember them and fry them in lard and get boiled shoulder meat beaten very well and good cheese with it and good finest spices and eggs that you need, and put the chickens and these things together, and make the pie, and annoint it of the top with yolks of egg with saffron, and to all these things one must give salt.

3 c flour	⅛ t cloves
1 c water	⅛ t pepper
¼ t salt	¼ t cinnamon
2 ½ oz parmesan	⅛ t galingale
¾ lb pork shoulder	¼ t ginger
1 lb chicken	2 egg yolks
3 T lard	10 threads saffron
4 eggs	¼ t salt
⅛ t nutmeg	

Knead together flour, water and salt, roll out to about a 10" circle, use it to line a 9" greased pie pan. With a fork prick the shell on the bottom and along the bottom edge so as to minimize lifting from steam underneath. Bake 25 minutes at 350°.

Cut pork into several chunks, boil in 2 c water for about half an hour. Drain it.

Dismember the chicken to the smallest coherent pieces, fry in the lard at medium high for 5-10 minutes until brown. Put into the pie crust.

Grate the cheese, mash the pork in a large mortar then combine it with eggs, spices, cheese and salt. Use this to fill in the pie crust under and between the pieces of chicken—the endoring will look better on chicken than on the mashed pork mixture. Grind the saffron in a small mortar, add egg yolks, stir together so the saffron colors the egg yolks, use the mixture to paint the top of the tart.

Bake ½ hour at 350°. Serve.

It works better with boneless chicken quarters, since then you can cut the pie without running into chicken bones, but pretty clearly that isn't how the original was done. It may have used a bigger pie and smaller chickens, which would reduce the problem. Or the pie might have been eaten out of the crust rather than cut in wedges in the modern fashion.

Chawettys
Two Fifteenth Century p. 48

Take buttys of Vele, and mynce hem smal, or Porke, and put on a potte; take Wyne, and caste per-to pouder of Gyngere, Pepir, and Safroun, and Salt, and a lytel verpous, and do hem in a cofyn with yolks of Eyroun, and kutte Datys and Roysonys of Coraunce, Clowys, Maces, and pen ceuere pin cofyn, and lat it bake tyl it be y-now.

1 ½ lb pork or veal	5 threads saffron
double 9" pie crust	¾ t salt
⅜ c dates	1 t verjuice
⅜ c currants	¾ c red wine
½ t mace	¼ t cloves
¾ t ginger	9 egg yolks
¾ t pepper	

Cut the meat up fine (½" cubes or so). Simmer it in a cup and a half of water for about 20 minutes. Make pie crust, fill with meat, chopped dates and currants. Mix spices, wine, verjuice and egg yolks and pour over. Put on a top crust. Bake in a 350° oven for 50 minutes, then 400° for 20 minutes or until the crust looks done.

For Tarts owte of Lente
Pepys 1047 p. 27

Take nesche chese and pare hit and grynd hit yn a morter and breke egges and do therto and then put yn butter and creme and mess all well to gethur put not to moche buttr ther yn if the chese be fatte make a coffyn of dowe and close ht above with dowe and collor hit above with the yolkes of eggs and bake hit well and sue hit furth.

7 ½ oz soft cheese	1 c cream
3 eggs	double 9" pie crust
1 T butter	1 egg yolk

Mix ingredients (we used havarti for the cheese), put in a pie shell, cover, bake 45 minutes at 375°; allow to cool before serving.

Nourroys Pies (or Lorez Pies?)
Taillevant

Take meat well cooked and hashed fine, pine nuts, currants and cottage cheese chopped fine, and a little sugar and a little salt.

To make little Lorez pies, like great pies or those above, and fry them, and don't let them be too large, and whoever wishes to make "lettuces" or "little ears," must make rounds of pastry, the one larger than the other, and fry in deep fat until they are as hard as if cooked on the hearth; and if you wish, gild them with gold leaf or silver leaf or saffron.

3 c chopped cooked pork	2 T sugar
2 T pine nuts	½ t salt
1 ½ c currants	double 9" pastry
4 oz farmer's cheese	

Make as a 2 crust pie, bake 45 minutes at 350°, 10 minutes at 400°. Or make small ones and fry them (we haven't tried that).

Malaches Whyte
Curye on Inglysch p. 133
(Form of Cury no. 160)

Take ayren and wryng hem thurgh a cloth. Take powdour fort, brede igrated, & saffron, & cast þerto a gode quantite of buttur with a litull salt. Medle all yfere. Make a foyle in a trap & bake it wel þerinne, and serue it forth.

8 threads saffron	5 eggs
1 c bread crumbs	⅜ c whole wheat flour
¼ t salt	¾ c white flour
1 ½ t powder fort (p. 4)	another ¼ t salt
½ c butter	¼ c water

Grind the saffron with a few of the bread crumbs in a mortar. Mix that with the rest of the bread crumbs, ¼ t salt, powder fort and melted butter. In another bowl, force eggs through cheese cloth, then add them to the bread crumb mix. Make a pie crust by mixing flours and ¼ t salt, stirring in ¼ c water and kneading smooth. Roll it out and put it in a 9" pie shell, put in the filling, bake about 30 minutes at 350°.

(Forcing the eggs through the cheese cloth produces something like very slightly beaten eggs; the white and the yolk are not as well mixed as if you applied an egg beater for thirty seconds.)

Crustade
Two Fifteenth Century p. 50

Take veal, and smite in little pieces into a pot, and wash it fair; then take fair water, and let it boil together with parsley, sage, savory, and hyssop small enough and hew; and when it is on boiling, take powder pepper, canel, cloves, maces, saffron, and let them boil together, and a good deal of wine therewith. When the flesh is y-boiled, take it from the broth all clean, and let the broth cool; and when it is cold, take eyroun, the white and the yolks, and cast through a strainer, and put them into the broth, so many that the broth be stiff enough; then make fair coffins, and couch 3 pieces or 4 of the flesh in a coffin; then take dates, and cut them, and cast thereto; then take powder ginger, and a little verjuice, and put into the broth and salt; and than put the broth on the coffins, bake a little with the flesh ere thou put thyne liquor thereon, and let all bake together till it be enough; then take it out, and serve them forth.

2 lb veal	a pinch of saffron
1 T parsley	½ c wine
½ t sage	4 eggs
½ t savory	2 9" pie crusts
½ t hyssop	1 lb of dates
½ t pepper	½ t ginger
1 T cinnamon	1 T verjuice
½ t cloves	~ ½ t salt
½ t mace	

Boil veal and herbs and spices for 1 to 1 ½ hours. Boil spices with wine. Let the veal broth cool; separate it from the meat. Add beaten eggs to about 1 c of the broth to stiffen it. Make two pie crusts. Put in meat. Cut up dates and put them in. Add ginger and verjuice to broth, also salt. Bake until it hardens. Add wine with spices and eggs. Bake about 30 minutes at 325°.

Another Crust with Tame Creatures
Platina pp. 90-91 (book 6)

If you want to put pigeons and any other birds in a crust, first let them boil; when they are almost cooked, take them out of the pot. Then cut them into nice pieces and fry them in a pan with a goodly amount of lard. Next put them in a deep dish or an earthen pot that has been well greased, and where a crust has been rolled out on the bottom. To this dish you may add plums and cherries or sour fruit without going wrong. Then take verjuice and eight eggs, more or less depending on the number of guests, if there are a few, with a little juice, beaten with a spoon; to this add parsley, marjoram, and finely cut mint, which can be blended after being cut up, and put all this near the fire, but far from the flame. It must be a slow heat so that this does not boil over. All the while, it should be stirred with a spoon until it sticks to the spoon because of its thickness. Finally pour this sauce into the pastry crust and put it near the fire and when it seems to have cooked enough, serve it to your guests.

3 chicken leg quarters	½ t marjoram
3 T lard	2 t mint
⅓ lb plums	5 eggs
or sour cherries	2 T verjuice
one 9" pie crust	¼ c chicken broth
4 T parsley	½ t salt

Boil chicken 20 minutes. Cut the meat off the bones and fry in lard for 5 minutes. Cut the plums up finely and put in the crust with the meat. Wash and chop herbs, and mix eggs, verjuice, broth, herbs and salt, and cook this at a low heat for about 10 minutes (until thick) and add to crust. (Platina comments elsewhere that he doesn't always bother to mention salt, so we have added it here.) When it is all assembled, bake at 400° for 15 minutes, then at 350° for 25 minutes.

Pork Doucetty
Two Fifteenth Century p. 55 (Good)

Take pork, and hack it small, and eyroun y-mellyd together, and a little milk, and melle him together with honey and pepper, and bake him in a coffin, and serve forth.

½ to ⅔ lb of pork chops	2 t honey
6 eggs	pinch of pepper
3 T milk	1 9" pie crust

Cook pork in the oven or boil it about 20 minutes. Make a pie crust, prick it, and put it in a 400° degree oven for about 10 minutes. Mix remaining ingredients. Cut pork into small pieces and add to mixture. Put it in the pie crust and bake at 350° for about 40 minutes.

Koken van Honer
Grewe 13th century

One should make a pastry shell of dough, and cut up into it a chicken, and add bacon [speck], cut as peas, pepper and cumin and egg yolks well beaten with saffron, and take the shell and bake it in an oven. It is called "koken van honer."

1 ½ lb chicken	⅛ t pepper
(or ¾ lb boneless)	¼ t cumin
9" pie shell	6 egg yolks
3 pieces of bacon	4 threads saffron

Bone and cut up chicken, put in pie shell; add bacon cut small; sprinkle on spices. Beat egg yolks with saffron and pour over. Bake 45 minutes at 350°.

Flampoyntes Bake
Two Fifteenth Century p. 53

Take fayre Buttes of Porke, and sepe hem in fayre Watere, and clene pyke a-way þe bonys and þe Synewes, and hew hem and grynd hem in a mortere, and temper with þe Whyte of Eyroun, and Sugre, and pouder of Pepir, and Gyngere, and Salt; þan take neyssche Cruddis [soft curds], grynd hem, and draw þorw a straynoure; and caste þer-to Aneys, Salt, pouder Gyngere, Sugre; and þan take þe Stuffe of þe Porke, and putte it on euelong cofyn of fayre past; and take a feþer, and endore þe Stuffe in þe cofyn with þe cruddys; and whan it is bake, take Pynes, and clowys, and plante þe cofyn a-boue, a rew of on, and rew of a-nother; and þan serue forth.

2 lbs pork chops	½ t anise seed
7 egg whites	⅛ t salt
4 t sugar	¼ t ginger
¼ t pepper	1 ½ t sugar
¾-1 t ginger	1 9" pie crust
⅜ t salt	1 T whole cloves
1 c cottage cheese	2 T pine nuts

Bring one quart water to a boil, add meat, boil 15 minutes covered. Drain and let meat cool. Cut the meat up, removing bones and fat. Chop fine and grind in food processor. Add egg whites, sugar, pepper, ginger, salt, mix well. Blend cheese in food processor and put into separate bowl; grind anise seed in mortar and add anise, salt, ginger and sugar to cheese. Put meat in unbaked pie crust, spread cheese mixture above it. Decorate with cloves and pine nuts. Bake at 350° 50 minutes to 1 hour. 1 t of ginger in the meat was liked by some people and considered too much by others; adjust to your taste.

Crustade Gentyle
Two Fifteenth Century p. 55

Take a Cofyn y-bake; þan grynd Porke or Vele smal with harde yolkys of Eyroun; þan lye it with Almaunde Milke, & make hem stondyng; take Marow of bonys, & ley on þe cofynee, & fylle hem fulle with þin comade, & serue f[orth].

1 c white flour	1 lb ground pork
½ c whole wheat flour	⅙ c almonds
⅜ c water	⅚ c water
3 eggs	~2 ½ lb marrow bones
½ t salt	

Knead flours and water to a smooth dough, roll out, and use to line 9" pie pan. Bake at 350° for 20 minutes. Hard boil eggs and add egg yolks and salt to the ground pork. Make about ⅔ c almond milk (see p. 7), add to pork mixture, and stir to a uniform consistency. Force the marrow out of the marrow bones— you should end up with about 4 oz of marrow—lay it in chunks about the pie crust, and fill up with the pork mixture. Bake at 350° for 1 hour.

Herbelade
Two Fifteenth Century p. 54

Take Buttes of Porke, and smyte hem in pecys, and sette it ouer the fyre; and sethe hem in fayre Watere; and whan it is y-sothe y-now, ley it on a fayre bord, and pyke owt alle the bonys, and hew it smal, and put it in a fayre bolle; than take ysope, Sawge, Percely a gode quantite, and hew it smal, and putte it in a fayre vessele; than take a lytel of the brothe, that the porke was sothin in, and draw thorw a straynoure, and caste to the Erbys, and gif it a boyle; thenne take owt the Erbys with a Skymoure fro the brothe, and caste hem to the porke in the bolle; than mynce Datys smal, and caste hem ther-to, and Roysonys of Coraunce, and pynes, and drawe thorw a straynoure yolkes of Eyroun ther-to, and Sugre, and pouder Gyngere, and Salt, and coloure it a lytel with Safroune; and toyle yt with thin hond al thes to-gederys; than make fayre round cofyns, and harde hem a lytel in the ovyn; than take hem owt, and with a dysshe in thin hond, fylle hem fulle of the Stuffe; than sette hem ther-in a-gen; and lat hem bake y-now, and serue forth.

3 pork chops	⅓ c pine nuts
3 c fresh parsley	5 egg yolks
1 t dried leaf sage	1 T sugar
2 T hyssop	½ t powdered ginger
½ c chopped dates	½ t salt
½ c currants	9" pastry shell

Boil pork chops until cooked (about 20 minutes), take out, remove the bones and cut up the meat. Chop parsley, boil herbs in the pork broth. Mix pork, cooked herbs, and remaining ingredients in bowl. Make pie crust and bake 10 minutes to harden. Put filling in the pie crust. Bake 30 minutes at 375°.

To Make Short Paest for Tarte
A Proper Newe Book p. 37

Take fyne floure and a curscy of fayre water and a dysche of swete butter and a lyttel saffron, and the yolkes of two egges and make it thynne and as tender as ye maye.

1 c flour	6 threads saffron
5 t water	2 egg yolks
5-6 T very soft butter	

Cut butter into flour, then crush saffron into 1 t of water; mix that and the rest of the water with the egg yolks and stir it into the flour-butter mixture.

To Make a Tarte of Beans
A Proper Newe Book of Cookery p. 37

Take beanes and boyle them tender in fayre water, then take theym oute and breake them in a morter and strayne them with the yolckes of foure egges, curde made of mylke, then ceason it up with suger and halfe a dysche of butter and a lytle synamon and bake it.

½ lb (1 ¼ c) dry fava beans	4 T sugar
4 egg yolks	6 T butter
½ c curds (cottage cheese)	4 t cinnamon

crust: (from short paest for tarte, p. 45)
1 c flour   6 threads saffron
5 t water   2 egg yolks
5-6 T very soft butter

Put beans in 2 ½ c of water, bring to boil and let sit, covered, 70 minutes. Add another cup of water, boil about 50 minutes, until soft. Drain beans and mush in food processor. Cool bean paste so it won't cook the yolks. Mix in yolks; add cottage cheese (do not drain); add sugar, butter (soft or in small bits) and cinnamon, then mush it all together to a thick liquid.

Make crust according to the previous recipe. Roll smooth and place in 9" pie plate. Crimp edge. Pour into raw crust and bake at 350° for about 50 minutes (top cracks). Cool before eating.

This would probably be good with fresh fava beans, but we have not tried it that way.

Desserts, Appetizers, Etc.

Prince-Bisket
Hugh Platt p. 14

Take one pound of very fine flower, and one pound of fine sugar, and eight eggs, and two spoonfuls of Rose water, and one ounce of Carroway seeds, and beat it all to batter one whole houre: for the more you beat it, the better your bread is: then bake it in coffins, of white plate, being basted with a little butter before you put in your batter, and so keep it.

4 c flour (1 lb)	2 t rose water
2 c sugar (1 lb)	4 t caraway seeds
5 eggs	

Beat all ingredients together one whole hour (or do a fourth of a recipe at a time in a food processor, processing it for several minutes or until the blades stall); there is a visible change in texture at that point. Spoon out onto a greased cookie sheet as 3" biscuits and bake about 20 minutes at 325°. You end up with very hard biscuits which keep forever.

Excellent Small Cakes
Digby p. 221

Take three pound of very fine flower well dried by the fire, and put to it a pound and a half of loaf sugar sifted in a very fine sieve and dried; 3 pounds of currants well washed, and dried in a cloth and set by the fire; when your flour is well mixed with the sugar and currants, you must put in it a pound and a half of unmelted butter, ten spoonfuls of cream, with the yolks of three newlaid eggs beat with it, one nutmeg; and if you please, three spoonfuls of sack. When you have wrought your paste well, you must put it in a cloth, and set it in a dish before the fire, till it be through warm. Then make them up in little cakes, and prick them full of holes; you must bake them in a quick oven unclosed. Afterwards ice them over with sugar. The cakes should be about the bigness of a hand breadth and thin; of the size of the sugar cakes sold at Barnet.

Scaled down version:

3 c flour	2 ½ T cream
¾ c sugar	1 egg yolk
2 ½ c currants	¼ t nutmeg
⅜ lb butter	2 t sack

(This assumes that "spoonful" = T)

Mix flour, sugar, and currants, then cut butter into the mixture as one would for piecrust. Add cream, egg yolk, nutmeg, and sack (we used sherry). Knead together, warm it. Bake cakes about 20 minutes at 350°.

Icing: about ⅓ c sugar and enough water so you can spread it.

To Make an Excellent Cake
Digby p. 219 (Good)

To a peck of fine flour take six pounds of fresh butter, which must be tenderly melted, ten pounds of currants, of cloves and mace, ½ an ounce of each, an ounce of cinnamon, ½ an ounce of nutmegs, four ounces of sugar, one pint of sack mixed with a quart at least of thick barm of ale (as soon as it is settled to have the thick fall to the bottom, which will be when it is about two days old), half a pint of rosewater; ½ a quarter of an ounce of saffron. Then make your paste, strewing the spices, finely beaten, upon the flour: then put the melted butter (but even just melted) to it; then the barm, and other liquours: and put it into the oven well heated presently. For the better baking of it, put it in a hoop, and let it stand in the oven one hour and a half. You ice the cake with the whites of two eggs, a small quantity of rosewater, and some sugar.

Scaled down to one sixteenth of the original

2 c flour	¼ c yeast residue from beer
¼ t cloves	(or 1 t yeast in 3 T water)
¼ t mace	8 threads saffron
½ t cinnamon	1 T rosewater
¼ t nutmeg	2 T sack (or sherry)
½ T sugar	2 c currants
⅜ lb butter	

icing:
⅛ egg white (about 2 t)
¼ t rosewater   2 T sugar

Mix flour, spices, and sugar. Melt butter, mix up yeast mixture, and crush the saffron in the rosewater to extract the color. When the butter is melted, stir it into the flour mixture, then add sack, yeast mixture, and rosewater-saffron mixture. Stir this until smooth, then stir in currants. Bake at 350° in a greased 10" round pan or a 7"x11" rectangular pan for 40 minutes. Remove from pan and spread with a thin layer of icing. We usually cut it up into bar cookies.

Pastry Which They Call Canisiones
Platina p. 144 (book 8)

When you have rolled out your pastry made of meal with sugar and rosewater and formed it like a crust, put into it the same mixture as the one I said in the section on marzapan [Take almonds that have soaked in fresh water for a day and night and when you have cleaned them as carefully as can be, grind them up, sprinkling them with fresh water so that they do not make oil. And if you want the best, add as much finest sugar as almonds. When all this has been well ground and dissolved in rosewater...]; this time, it should be formed like rolls and cooked in the oven as I said before, with a gentle flame.

pastry:	*filling*:
2 c flour	¾ c almonds, soaked
¼ c sugar	½ c sugar
2 t rosewater	1 t rosewater
~10 T water	2 t water

Mix pastry ingredients and knead to a dry but not stiff dough. Divide in half, roll each half out to about 12" across. Coarsely grind the filling together. Spread thinly onto pastry, leaving ½" margin around the edges, and roll up like a jelly roll; seal seams tightly to avoid leakage. Bake 40 minutes at 350°. Slice when warm; crumbles when cool.

This makes two rolls about 12 inches long. Best when fresh; they dry out by the next day. Note the similarity between this recipe and the Islamic pastry khushkananaj, p. 116.

To Make Iumbolls
Hugh Platt p. 12

Take ½ a pound of almonds being beaten to paste with a short cake being grated, and two eggs, two ounces of caraway seeds, being beaten, and the juice of a lemon: and being brought into paste, roll it into round strings: then cast it into knots, and so bake it in an oven and when they are baked, ice them with rose water and sugar, and the white of an egg being beaten together, then take a feather and gild them, then put them again into the oven, and let them stand in a little while, and they will be iced clean over with a white ice: and so box them up and you may keep them all the year.

¼ lb almonds	1 egg
1 oz shortbread	1 t rose water
1 oz caraway seeds	½ c sugar
½ lemon, juiced	½ egg white

Grind almond fine in food processor, crush shortbread cookies with mortar and pestle, grind caraway seeds briefly in spice grinder and mix these three ingredients. Beat lemon juice and egg together and add to dry ingredients. Mix and roll into ¼" diameter strings and lay on greased cookie sheet in loops. Bake at 375° for 25 minutes. Mix up icing and put onto cookies; put back in hot oven with heat turned off for 5 minutes

Quinces in Pastry
Du Fait de Cuisine no. 70

Again, quinces in pastry: and to give understanding to him who should prepare them let him arrange that he has his fair and good quinces and then let him clean them well and properly and then make a narrow hole on top and remove the seeds and what they are wrapped in, and let him take care that he does not break through on the bottom or anywhere else; and, this being done, put them to boil in a fair and clean cauldron or pot in fair water and, being thus cooked, take them out onto fair and clean boards to drain and put them upside down without cutting them up. And then let him go to the pastry-cooks and order from them the little crusts of the said pastries to put into each of the said little crusts three quinces or four or more. And when the said little crusts are made fill the holes in the said quinces with very good sugar, then arrange them in the said little crusts and cover and put to cook in the oven; and, being cooked enough, let them be served.

3 quinces	⅝ c sugar	[⅛ t ginger]
pie crust:		
1 ¼ c flour	3 ½ T water	6 ½ T butter

Core the quinces without cutting through to the bottom. Simmer them in water about 15 minutes. Make pie crust, divide in half, roll out bottom crust and put in 7" pie pan. Set quinces upright on top of the bottom crust, fill with sugar, put top crust over them. Bake at 450° for 15 minutes, then at 350° for 35 minutes.

Note: there is a similar recipe in Two Fifteenth Century Cookery Books p. 51. The differences are that the quinces are peeled, they may be replaced by warden pears, there is a little powdered ginger in with the sugar, and the sugar may be replaced by honey with pepper and ginger.

Tartys in Applis
Curye on Inglysch p. 78
(*Diuersa Servicia* no. 82)

For to make tartys in applis, tak gode applys & gode spycis & figys & reysons & perys, & wan þey arn wel ybrayed colour wyþ safroun wel & do yt in a cofyn, & do yt forth to bake wel.

2 c flour	½ cup raisins
~⅔ c water	⅔ t cinnamon
1 large apple	½ t nutmeg
1 large pear	¼ t ginger
1 c figs	5 threads saffron

Knead water into the flour until you have a dough that can be rolled out; use it to line a 9" pie pan. Peel, core and chop the apples and pears; chop the figs. Put all of the fruit and spices into a food processor and process to a homogeneous but not liquid texture. Pour the mixture into the pie crust and bake at 350° for 45 minutes.

A Tarte of Strawberries
A Proper Newe Book p. 39

Take and strain them with the yolks of four eggs, and a little white bread grated, then season it up with sugar and sweet butter and so bake it.

2 c strawberries	⅓ c sugar
4 egg yolks	4 T butter, melted
½ c bread crumbs	8" pie shell

Force strawberries through a strainer or run through a blender, then mix with everything else. Bake crust for 10 minutes, then put filling into the crust and bake at 375° for 20 minutes. You may make the crust using the recipe for Short Paest (page 45), which is from the same source.

A Tart with Plums, Which can be Dried or Fresh
Sabina Welserin no. 70

Let them cook beforehand in wine and strain them and take eggs, cinnamon and sugar. Bake the dough for the tart. That is made like so: take two eggs and beat them. Afterwards stir flour therein until it becomes a thick dough. Pour it on the table and work it well, until it is ready. After that take somewhat more than half the dough and roll it into a flat cake as wide as you would have your tart. Afterwards pour the plums on it and roll out after that the other crust and cut it up, however you would like it, and put it on top over the tart and press it together well and let it bake. So one makes the dough for a tart.

¾ lb prunes	1 T sugar
1 ½ c red wine	1 t cinnamon
4 eggs	1 ¼ c flour

Simmer the prunes in the wine for about 40 minutes until they are quite soft. Remove the pits, force them through a strainer. Add two eggs, sugar, cinnamon.

Beat two more eggs well with a fork, then beat and gradually stir in about 1 ¼ c flour. Knead the dough smooth; you may need to add a few drops of water at the end. Divide in two slightly unequal portions. Roll out the larger to fit a 9" pie pan. Roll the smaller not quite as large, cut into strips. Pour the prune goo onto the larger crust, cover with a lattice made from the strips. Bake at 325° for about 40 minutes.

An Apple Tart
Sabina Welserin no. 74

Peel the apples and take the cores cleanly out and chop them small, put two or three egg yolks with them and let butter melt in a pan and pour it on the apples and put cinnamon, sugar and ginger thereon and let it bake. Roast them first in butter before you chop them.

2 lb apples	¼ t ginger
5 T butter	1 t cinnamon
3 egg yolks	2 eggs
¼ c sugar	1 ¼ c flour

Peel, quarter and core apples; unless they are small, cut each quarter in half lengthwise. Melt 1 T butter in large frying pan and fry apple pieces 10 minutes at medium to medium high, stirring frequently. Make crust as in the previous recipe. Chop apples (about ½" by ¼" pieces.) Put apples in a bowl and mix with egg yolks. Melt the remaining 4 T of butter and stir it in along with sugar and spices. Take ⅔ of the dough, roll it and stretch it out until it is large enough to line a 9" pie pan. Put filling in, then roll and stretch out the rest of the dough and cut for some kind of ornamental top crust—I made a lattice crust. Bake at 325° for 40-50 minutes, at which point the crust should be browning.

A Flaune of Almayne
Ancient Cookery p. 452 (Good)

First take raisins of Courance, or else other fresh raisins, and good ripe pears, or else good apples, and pick out the cores of them, and pare them, and grind them, and the raisins in a mortar, and do then to them a little sweet cream of milk, and strain them through a clean strainer, and take ten eggs, or as many more as will suffice, and beat them well together, both the white and the yolk, and draw it through a strainer, and grate fair white bread, and do thereto a good quantity, and more sweet cream, and do thereto, and all this together; and take saffron, and powder of ginger, and canel, and do thereto, and a little salt, and a quantity of fair, sweet butter, and make a fair coffin or two, or as many as needs, and bake them a little in an oven, and do this batter in them, and bake them as you would bake flaunes, or crustades, and when they are baked enough, sprinkle with canel and white sugar. This is a good manner of Crustade.

⅔ c raisins	¼ t ginger
3 pears or apples	½ t cinnamon
½ c whipping cream	½ t salt
3 eggs, beaten	5 T butter
4 T breadcrumbs	9" pie crust
pinch of saffron	1 T sugar + 1 t cinnamon

A blender works well as a substitute for a mortar to mash the apples and raisins; mix the liquids in with the apples and raisins before blending. Bake at 375° for about an hour. Sprinkle on cinnamon sugar.

Torta of Herbs in the Month of May
Platina p. 136 (book 8) (Good)

Cut up and grind the same amount of cheese as I said in the first and second tortae ["a pound and a half of best fresh cheese"]. When you have ground this up, add juice from bleta, a little marjoram, a little more sage, a bit of mint, and a good bit of parsley; when all this has been ground in a mortar, add the beaten whites of 15 or 16 eggs and half a pound of liquamen or fresh butter, and mix. There are those who put in some leaves of parsley and marjoram that have been cut up but not ground, and half a pound [surely a typo for half an ounce, as in the previous recipes in this cookbook] of white ginger and eight ounces of sugar. When all of these have been mixed together, put this in a pot or deep dish that has been well greased on the coals at a distance from the flame so that it does not absorb the smoke; and stir it continually and let it boil until it thickens. When it is nearly done transfer it into another pot with the crust and cover it with your lid until it is all cooked with a gentle flame. When it is done and put on a plate, sprinkle it with best sugar and rose water.

[*Notes*: earlier torta recipes refer to a pastry crust rolled thin and both top and bottom crusts. "Blette–Name given in some parts of France to white beet or chard." *Larousse Gastronomique.*]

¾ lb Monterey Jack	double 9" pie crust
⅜ c spinach or chard	[¼ c parsley]
¼ t marjoram	[2 t marjoram]
½ t sage	[¼ oz ginger]
1 t fresh mint	[½ c sugar]
½ c fresh parsley	1 T sugar
5 egg whites	¼ t rosewater
¼ lb butter	

Grate cheese. Spinach or chard (measured unchopped) is chopped and ground in a mortar with a T of water to provide spinach juice. Mix the juice with the marjoram, sage, mint, and ½ c parsley—all fresh if available, and remove the stems from the parsley—and grind in mortar or food processor; mix with grated cheese. Beat egg whites lightly, melt butter and add; put in pie crust and cover with top crust. Adding additional chopped but not ground parsley and marjoram is an option; sugar and ginger, for a dessert pie, are another option (ginger seems to mean fresh ginger root, which should be finely chopped). Bake at 400° for 10 minutes, then at 350° for about another 40 minutes, then sprinkle with mixed sugar and rosewater.

Torta from Gourds
Platina p. 136 (book 8)

Grind up gourds that have been well cleaned as you are accustomed to do with cheese. Then let them boil a little, either in rich juice or in milk. When they are half-cooked and have been passed through a strainer into a bowl, add as much cheese as I said before [a pound and a half]. Take half a pound of belly or fat udder boiled and cut up or, instead of this, if you wish, take the same amount of either butter or liquamen, add half a pound of sugar, a little ginger, some cinnamon, six eggs, two ladles of milk, a little saffron, and blend thoroughly. Put this preparation in a greased pan or in a pastry shell and cook it over a slow fire. There are those who add strips of leaves, which they call lagana, instead of the upper crust. When it is cooked and set on a plate, sprinkle it with sugar and rosewater.

½ lb gourd (see p. 4)	⅛ t ground ginger
½ c milk	½ t cinnamon
8 oz cheddar cheese	6 threads saffron
2 oz butter	double 9" pastry shell
¼ c sugar	2 T sugar
1 egg	1 T rosewater
½ c milk	

Grind gourd finely with a grater and boil in ½ c milk for six minutes on low heat while being stirred; drain in strainer and throw away liquid, then force cooked gourd through strainer. Grate or cut up cheese; mix with gourd, butter, sugar, egg, another ½ c milk, ginger, cinnamon, and saffron. Put in pie shell and cover with top crust. Bake in 350° oven for 65 minutes; at this point it is bubbly and needs to set for a while. Sprinkle top with sugar and rosewater. Makes one 9 inch pie.

Torta from Red Chickpeas
Platina p. 142 (book 8)

Grind up red chickpeas that have been well cooked with their own juice and with a little rosewater. When they have been ground, pass them through a strainer into a bowl. Add a pound of almonds so ground up that it is not a chore to pass them through the strainer, two ounces of raisins, three or four figs ground up at the same time. And besides this, add an ounce of pine kernels coarsely ground, and as much sugar and rosewater as you need, and just so much cinnamon and ginger; and blend. Put the mixture into a well-greased pan with the pastry crust on the bottom. There are those who add starch or pike eggs, so that this torta is more firm; when it is cooked, put it almost above the fire to make it more colored. It should be thin and sprinkled with sugar and rosewater.

1 lb almonds	⅜ c water
1 oz pine nuts	1 t cinnamon
15 oz can chickpeas	½ t ginger
2 oz raisins	pastry for 2 9" pie crusts
4 figs	[starch or pike eggs]
½ c sugar	2 t more sugar
⅛ c rosewater	1 t more rosewater

Grind almonds finely, but not to dust. Chop pine nuts coarsely. Grind chickpeas in a food processor with the liquid from the can, then grind raisins and figs. Stir these and the sugar, rosewater, extra water, cinnamon, and ginger together. The pie crust can be rolled out and put on a 10"x15" cookie sheet or it can be made into two 9" pie shells. The filling is spread on top; it will be thicker if made as two pies. Mix extra sugar and rosewater together and sprinkle on top. Bake 30 to 40 minutes for the cookie-sheet version, or 50-60 minutes for the pie version, in a 375° oven until golden brown.

To Make a Custarde
Proper Newe Booke p. 23

A Custarde the coffyn must be fyrste hardened in the oven, and then take a quart of creame and fyve or syxe yolkes of egges, and beate them well together, and put them into the creame, and put in Suger and small Raysyns and Dates sliced, and put into the coffyn butter or els marrowe, but on the fyshe daies put in butter.

1 pie crust	¼ c sugar
¼ c dates	⅓ c raisins
3 egg yolks	3 t butter (or marrow)
2 c cream	

Make pie crust and pre-bake for 10-15 minutes at 400°. Chop dates. Beat the egg yolks, add cream, sugar, raisins and dates and pour into pie crust. Dot pie with butter. Bake at 350° for 1 hour 15 minutes.

To Make Cheesecakes
Digby p. 214

Take 12 quarts of milk warm from the cow, turn it with a good spoonfull of runnet. Break it well, and put it in a large strainer, in which rowl it up and down, that all the whey may run out into a little tub; when all that will is run out, wring out more. Then break the curds well; then wring it again, and more whey will come. Thus break and wring till no more come. Then work the curds exceedingly with your hand in a tray, till they become a short uniform paste. Then put to it the yolks of 8 new laid eggs, and two whites, and a pound of butter. Work all this long together. In the long working (at the several times) consisteth the making them good. Then season them to your taste with sugar finely beaten; and put in some cloves and mace in subtle powder. Then lay them thick in coffins of fine paste and bake them.

Judging by the cottage cheese recipe in *Joy of Cooking*, 12 quarts of milk would yield about 4.5 lbs of cottage cheese. It sounds as though either creamed cottage cheese or fresh cheese corresponds to what Digby is making. The following quantities are for half of Digby's quantity, with an adjustment for egg sizes.

2 lbs creamed cottage cheese	½ c sugar
1 egg yolk	¼ t cloves
2 large eggs	¼ t mace
½ lb of butter	2 9" pie crusts

Cook at 350° for 70 minutes. Let cool 1 hour before serving.

Custard Tart
Platina p. 147 (book 8)

Make a little crust as I said in the section on rolls. Put in two egg yolks that have been well beaten, milk, cinnamon and sugar, and stir it near the hearth until it thickens.

½ t cinnamon	4 egg yolks
½ c sugar	9" pie crust
2 c milk	

Mix cinnamon and sugar together, mix in milk, add yolks and beat well, pour into pre-baked tart shell. Bake at 375° 50-60 minutes. To make little tarts, make half again the amount of crust and make into about 15 little tart shells by pressing the dough down into muffin tins. Bake about 10-15 minutes in 400° oven, then pour in filling and bake about 40 minutes at 375°.

Darioles
Ancient Cookery p. 37

Take cream of almonds, or of cow milk, and eggs, and beat them well together; and make small coffins, and do it therein; and do thereto sugar and good powders, or else take good fat cheese and eggs, and make them of divers colors, green, red, or yellow, and bake them and serve them forth.

pastry for 2 9" pie crusts	colorings:
1 ⅓ c milk and cream	6 threads saffron
⅓ c sugar	2 T parsley
2 eggs	3/16 t saunders
⅙ t salt	

Make pastry into tart shells in muffin tins and bake about 10 minutes. Make filling, divide in three and color one part with saffron, extracting the color with 1 t of water, one with saunders, and one with parsley juice—parsley mashed and strained with 2 t water. Pour into tart shells and bake. The recipe makes 15 tarts.

Tart de Bry
Forme of Cury p. 74

Take a crust inch deep in a trap. Take yolks of ayren raw and cheese ruayn and medle it and the yolks together and do thereto powder ginger, sugar, saffron, and salt. Do it in a trap, bake it and serve it forth.

Note: according to the Oxford English Dictionary, ruen cheese is a kind of soft cheese.

1 lb 3 oz Brie cheese	3 T sugar
6 egg yolks	⅜ t ginger
8 threads saffron	1/16 t salt
1 t water	9" pie crust

Mash cheese and egg yolks together. Crush saffron into water to draw out the color, then mix that and the sugar, ginger and salt with the cheese. Put in crust and bake 50 minutes at 350°. Cool before eating.

White Torta
Platina p. 135 (book 8)

Prepare a pound and a half of best fresh cheese, chopped especially fine. Add twelve or fifteen egg whites, half a pound of sugar, half an ounce of white ginger, half a pound of pork liquamen and as much fresh butter. Blend in as much milk as you need. When you have blended this, put it into a pastry crust rolled thin and put it all in a pan and set it to bake on the hearth with a gentle flame. Then, to give it color, put coals on the lid. When it is cooked and taken from the pan, sprinkle ground sugar over it, with rosewater.

1 lb fresh ricotta	⅓ oz fresh ginger
8 egg whites	½ c milk
¼ lb butter	10" pastry shell
¼ lb lard	~2 t sugar
⅔ c sugar	1 t rosewater

Beat egg whites to soft peaks. Soften butter and lard together at room temperature. Fold together cheese and egg whites, then add sugar, minced ginger, lard and butter. Mix until fairly uniform. Add milk, fill shell. Bake at 325° for 40 minutes. When oil separates, it is done. Put under broiler to brown top lightly. Sprinkle sugar and rosewater, spread on with spoon bottom. Cool until set.

This is a little less butter and lard than Platina suggests, but we found it too fatty using his quantities. Our interpretation of "add egg whites" is pretty free—it would be worth trying to follow the recipe more literally.

Flathonys
Two Fifteenth Century p. 73 (Good)

Take mylke, and yolkes of egges, and ale, and drawe hem thorgh a straynour, with white sugur or blak; And melt faire butter, and put thereto salt, and make faire coffyns, and put hem into a Nowne til thei be a litull hard; then take a pile, and a dissh fastned there-on, and fill the coffyns therewith of the seid stuffe and late hem bake a while. And then take hem oute, and serue hem forthe, and caste Sugur ynogh on hem.

9" pie shell	¼ c sugar
½ c milk	4 T butter
4 egg yolks	1 t salt
⅓ c ale	

Bake a pie shell. Beat together milk, egg yolks, ale, sugar. Melt butter, add salt, beat into the liquid, trying to keep the butter from separating out (the hard part). Pour into the pie shell, bake at 350° about 20-30 minutes. Sprinkle on sugar (about 1 T) after the flathon is reasonably solid.

Creme Boylede
Two Fifteenth Century p. 8

Take creme or mylke, and brede of paynemayn, or elles of tendre brede, and breke it on the creme, or elles in the mylke, an set it on the fyre tyl it be warme hot; and thorw a straynour throwe it, and put it into a fayre potte, an sette it on the fyre, an stere euermore: an whan it is almost y-boylyd, take fayre yolkes of eyron, an draw hem thorw a straynowr and caste hem ther-to, and let hem stonde ouer the fyre tyl it boyle almost, an till it be skylfully thikke; than caste a ladel-ful, or more or lasse, of boter ther-to, an a good quantite of whyte sugre, and a litel salt, an than dresse it on a dysshe in maner of mortrewys.

5-10 slices white bread	6 T melted butter
1 quart light cream	½ c sugar
8 lightly beaten egg yolks	1 t salt

Tear up bread and soak it in the cream. Heat until hot to the touch but not boiling. Pass through a coarse sieve or mash thoroughly. Heat again, stirring constantly. When almost boiling, stir in egg yolks. Keep heating, stirring, not boiling, until it thickens. Stir in butter, sugar, salt. Serve in bowls.

Milkemete
Two Fifteenth Century p. 106

Take faire mylke and floure, and draue hem þorgh a streynour, and sette hem ouer the fire, and lete hem boyle awhile; And then take hem vppe, and lete hem kele awhile/ And þen take rawe yolkes of eyren and drawe hem thorgh a streynour, and caste thereto a litull salt, And set it ouer the fire til hit be som-what thik, And lete hit nogt fully boyle, and stere it right well euermore. And put it in a dissh al abrode, And serue it forth fore a gode potage in one maner; And then take Sugur a good quantite, And caste there-to, and serue it forth.

3 c milk	¼ t salt
¾ c flour	4 T sugar
4 egg yolks	

Mix milk and flour thoroughly, trying to remove lumps, and force through a strainer; dissolve the lumps that didn't go through in some of the milk and repeat. Bring it to a low simmer on medium to medium low heat (about 10 minutes) and simmer about 5 minutes, stirring constantly with a whisk. Remove from heat, let cool ½ hour to 125°. Beat egg yolks with salt, add to pot and stir in thoroughly with a whisk. Heat about ten minutes, bringing it to near a boil. Add sugar and serve.

Papyns
Two Fifteenth Century p. 9

Take fayre Mylke and Flowre, an drawe it þorw a straynoure, an set it ouer þe fyre, an let it boyle a-whyle; þan take it owt an let it kele; þan take yolkys of eyroun y-draw þorwe a straynour, an caste ther-to; þan take sugre a gode quantyte, and caste þer-to, an a lytil salt, an sette it on þe fyre tyl it be sum-what þikke, but let it nowt boyle fullyche, an stere it wyl, an putte it on a dysshe alle a-brode, and serue forth rennyng.

2 c milk	¾ c sugar
4 T flour	⅛ t salt
4 egg yolks	

Beat together the milk and flour; keep it over a very low flame about 5 minutes until it will coat a clean spoon. Add egg yolks, sugar and salt and put over a medium flame, stirring constantly for about ½ hour (until it thickens).

Principal Dish (Manjar Principal)
De Nola no. 13

For a half dozen dishes, take a half azumbre of strained milk and six egg yolks and four ounces of grated aged cheese, and just as much of grated hard bread; and thoroughly mix the cheese and the grated bread with the egg yolks and beat it very well, and thin it with a little milk; and then take a half pound of sugar and remove two ounces of that sugar to grind with the cinnamon to cast on the dishes; and the other portion that remains will be six ounces that you will cast into the milk; and set it to heat on your coals away from the fire; and when it is hot, remove it from the fire, and cast the abovementioned beaten eggs into it, stirring it constantly in one direction until it is good and thick; and sample it for taste; and if it is good, set it aside to rest while the meal is prepared, and dish it out with your sugar and cinnamon on top.

(*azumbre:* approximately two liters.)

4 oz parmesan cheese	4 c milk
4 oz bread crumbs	1 c sugar
6 egg yolks	2 t cinnamon

Grate cheese into bowl, stir in bread crumbs and egg yolks. Stir in ½ c milk, set aside.

Put 3 ½ c milk and ¾ c sugar in sauce pan and cook at just below boiling, stirring frequently for about 15 minutes. Remove from the heat, stir in the egg mixture stirring in one direction only. If it doesn't thicken, put back on a low heat, stirring constantly until it does. Remove from heat, let cool.

Serve with cinnamon sugar (¼ c sugar, 2 t cinnamon).

Slow Or Smooth Dish
(Manjar Lento o Suave)
De Nola no. 14

For half a dozen dishes, take a half azumbre of strained milk, and half a dozen egg yolks, and beat them well, and thin them with a little milk; and set the other milk to heat alone by itself on a fire of coals away from the fire; and when it is hot, remove it from the fire, and cast the beaten egg yolks into it, and three or four ounces of sugar, and return it to the coals; and if you wish to give it color, cast in a little saffron, and then return it to the coals, stirring it constantly in one direction until it is thick so that it seems good to you; and then sample it for taste; and if it is good, set it aside from the fire to rest, and grind sugar and cinnamon to cast upon the dishes.

[*Azumbre:* approximately 2 liters.]

4 c milk	[6 threads saffron]
6 egg yolks	1 T sugar
⅜ c sugar	1 t cinnamon

Beat egg yolks with 2 T of the milk. Heat the rest of the milk for about 10 minutes over medium heat then remove from heat. Stir egg yolk mixture and sugar into the milk, crush saffron (optional) into a little of the milk mixture and add. Put back on medium heat and cook about 45 minutes, stirring, until thick. Remove from heat and let cool. Sprinkle on additional sugar and cinnamon and serve.

Pipefarces
Goodman p. 286

Take the yolks of eggs and flour and salt and a little wine and beat them well together and cheese cut into strips and then roll the strips of cheese in the paste and fry them in an iron pan with fat therein. One does likewise with beef marrow.

8 egg yolks	~1 ½ T wine
2 T flour	½ pound cheese
½ t salt	oil to fry

Use enough wine to make a thick paste. Works better with hard cheese such as cheddar.

A Fritur þat Hatte Emeles
Curye on Inglysch p. 53
(*Diuersa Ciberia* no. 46)

Nym sucre, salt, & alemauns & bred, & grind am togedre; & soþþen do of ayren. & soþþen nim grece oþur botere oþur oyle, and soþþen nim a dihs, & smeore heom; & soþþen nym bliue [quickly, according to the editor of Curye on Inglysch], & cose wiþ sucre drue: & þis beoþ þin cyueles in leynten ase in oþur time.

1 c bread crumbs	4 eggs
½ c sugar	butter or oil
⅛ t salt	more sugar
1 c almonds	

Grind bread, sugar, salt and almonds together. Mix eggs and add to dry mixture. Put ½ inch of oil in skillet. Deep fry, turn fritter over, remove, drain on paper towel. Put on plate and sprinkle with sugar. Makes 36 1" diameter fritters.

Frytour of Erbes
Curye on Inglysch p. 132
(*Form of Cury* no. 156)

Take gode erbys; grynde hem and medle hem with flour and water, & a lytel yest, and salt, and frye hem in oyle. And ete hem with clere hony.

¼ t yeast	1 T oregano
2 ¼ c water	2 ½ t sage
⅛ t salt	1 ½ t thyme
3 c flour	oil to fry in
6 T parsley	honey

Dissolve yeast in ½ c water, add salt to flour; when yeast is foamy, add yeast and the rest of the flour to the water. Let sit while herbs are chopped and ground; note that quantities of herbs are after chopping. Divide batter in 4, add one kind of herb to each; or add four times as much of any one of the herbs to the whole batter. Fry in ¼" deep oil by half tablespoonfuls. Makes about 3 dozen 2.5" fritters. Serve with honey.

Lente Frytoures
Two Fifteenth Century p. 96 (Good)

Take good flour, ale yeast, saffron and salt, and beat all together as thick as other manner fritters of flesh; and then take apples, and pare them, and cut them in manner of fritters, and wet them in the batter up and down, and fry them in oil, and cast them in a dish, and cast sugar thereon enough, and serve them forth hot.

5 apples	6 threads saffron
2 ⅓ c flour	2 t salt
1 ½ c water	oil for frying
2 T yeast	sugar sprinkled over

Pare apples and slice into sixteenths. Beat together everything else, dip apple pieces in the batter and fry them in a deep skillet with about ¾" of oil.

Note: The ale yeast would presumably be berme, skimmed from fermenting ale, and would provide the necessary liquid for the batter. I use water plus dried yeast instead; you can also replace the water with ale.

Losenges Fryes
Two Fifteenth Century p. 97

Take flour, water, saffron, sugar and salt, and make fine paste thereof, and fair thin cakes; and cut them like losenges and fry them in fine oil, and serve them forth hot in a dish in lenten time.

a pinch of saffron	½ t salt
½ c water	oil for frying
½ c sugar	2 ¼ c flour

Crush saffron in water to extract color and flavor, put in a bowl and mix in sugar and salt, add flour and mix lightly until moistened. Heat about 1 inch of oil in a frying pan. Roll out dough to about ¼ inch thick or a little thinner. Cut in small diamonds, fry a few at a time since they cook very quickly.

Frictella from Apples
Platina p. 150 (book 9)

Morsels of apple that have been cleaned and cored, you fry in liquamen or a little oil, and spread them on a board so that they dry. Then roll them in a preparation such as we described earlier and fry again. Preparation described earlier: to grated cheese, aged as well as fresh, add a little meal, some egg whites, some milk, a bit more sugar, and grind all this together in the same mortar.

3 green cooking apples	2 egg whites
oil to fry in	5 T milk
¼ cup grated cheddar cheese	1 T sugar
1 cup flour (or meal—p. 31)	

Frytour Blaunched
Curye on Inglysch p. 132
(Form of Cury no. 153)

Take almaundes blaunched, and grynde hem al to doust withouten eny lycour. Do perto poudour of gyngeuer, sugur, and salt; do pise in a thynne foile. Close it perinne fast, and frye it in oile; clarifie hony with wyne, & bake it perwith.

½ lb blanched almonds	~ ¾ c water
½ t ginger	oil
1 T sugar	⅔ c honey
¼ t salt	¼ c Rhine wine
3 c flour	

Grind almonds thoroughly: ½ lb = 1 ½ c whole = 2 c ground. Stir together with ginger, sugar and salt. Mix flour with enough water to make a slightly sticky dough. Roll out dough very thin and cut into 2 ¼" squares. Place a teaspoon of ground almond mix on each dough square. Fold corners to center and seal. Fry in ½"-1" of oil in a frying pan until brown, drain on paper towels, then place in baking pan. Heat honey and wine together; pour over fritters and bake at 350° for 10 minutes. Makes about 100.

Puffy Fricatellae
Platina p. 153 (book 9)

Flour with salt, water and sugar and spread it into a dough that is not too hard, but thin. Then cut them into shape with something for that purpose or with the opening of a ladle. And when you fry them, they puff up, but nothing is inside them.

1 c flour
2 T sugar
¼ t salt
⅜-½ c water
oil (for frying)

Mix flour with sugar, salt, and water. Knead smooth. Roll out dough to ~⅛" thickness and cut into circles 1"-2" in diameter—a small wine cup or similar object can be used to cut them. Put frying pan to heat on medium high with about ½" of oil; put in pieces of dough until they puff up and turn brown, and then flip over, frying about 2 minute on a side. Drain and serve.

Fritter of Milk
Form of Cury p. 68

Take of curds and press out the whey. Do thereto sugar, white of eyroun. Fry them. Do thereto and lay on sugur and mess forth.

1 c dry curd cottage cheese
3 T sugar
4 egg whites
more sugar

Mix together cottage cheese, sugar and egg whites. Drop by tablespoonfuls into hot oil, fry about 1 minute on each side (light to dark brown). Drain on paper towels, sprinkle with the additional sugar, serve. Should make about 40 fritters.

Rice Fricatellae
Platina p. 151 (book 9)

Spread rice that has been well cooked on a flat surface to rid it of excess moisture; mash it if you wish. Add a sufficient quantity of ground almonds and moisten with rosewater and the juice from the cooked-down rice. Next, into these things, blend flour and sugar. When they have been mixed, fry them in oil, as you wish.

½ c rice
¾ c unblanched almonds
1 t rosewater
½ c flour
¼ c sugar
⅜ c olive oil

Simmer rice in 2 c water about 30 minutes. Drain, keeping the water that comes out. Put the lid back on, let it steam another five or ten minutes. Spread it out, mash with a fork. Grind almonds medium fine (not to flour but to very small crunchies). Mix with rosewater and ¼ c of the leftover rice juice. Add flour and sugar. Mix it all together to a uniform consistency. Form into patties 2"-3" across, ½" thick. Fry over medium high heat, starting with ¼ c oil and adding more as necessary. After frying one side, turn it over and press down on it with the pancake turner, thus making it a little thinner. Makes about 25 fricatellae.

Longe Frutours
Two Fifteenth Century p. 73

Take Mylke And make faire croddes there-of in maner of chese al tendur, and take oute þe way clene; then put hit in a faire boll, And take yolkes of egges, and white, and menge floure, and caste thereto a good quantite, and drawe hit þorgh a streynoure into a faire vessell; then put hit in a faire pan, and fry hit a litull in faire grece, but lete not boyle; then take it oute, and ley on a faire borde, and kutte it in faire smale peces as thou list, And putte hem ayen into the panne til thei be browne; And then caste Sugur on hem, and serue hem forth.

1 cup cottage cheese
2 eggs
1 c flour
6-8 T butter or oil
2 T sugar

Mix cottage cheese, egg, and flour in a bowl. Heat butter or oil in a large skillet over medium-high heat, put half the mixture in the skillet, pat to about ¼" thick. Cook about two minutes until it will hold together, flip, cook another two minutes, remove from pan to a cutting board. Slice into pieces, return to pan and fry until browned—about three minutes a side. Remove from pan, sprinkle with sugar, serve.

Golden Morsels
Platina p. 148 (book 8)

Toast white bread crumbs, soak them in rosewater with beaten eggs and ground sugar. Take them out, fry them in a pan with butter or liquamen [chicken or pork fat], spread out so they do not touch each other. When fried, put in dishes and sprinkle with sugar, rosewater, and saffron.

The version of this recipe in Martino's cookbook, on which Platina apparently based his recipes, starts out: *Have some slices of white bread pared that does not have crust and make the slices be four [or square], a little toasted so much that every part be colored from the fire. ...*

10 eggs
5 T sugar
2 t rosewater (or more)
1 lb white bread
16 threads saffron
1 t more rosewater
1 c more sugar
⅛ lb butter or lard

Beat eggs. Beat in sugar and rosewater. Cut crust off the bread, slice thin, put into egg mixture and let soak. Crush saffron into remaining rosewater, mix with remaining sugar and set aside. Melt butter or lard in frying pan; when hot enough (test with small piece of bread stuff) put chunks of bread stuff into lard and fry until just browned on both sides. Drain briefly on paper towels, put into dish and sprinkle with sugar and rosewater mixture.

Mincebek [or, funnel cakes]
Anglo-Norman no. 4 p. 863
(Elizabeth's translation, guided by the Hieatt and Jones translation)

And another dish, which has the name mincebek. Take amydon [wheat starch] and grind it in a mortar, and if you do not have this, take fine white flour; and take almond milk or tepid water, and put in it a little yeast or a little sourdough; and then temper it; and take a bowl and make a hole in the middle, and pour the mincebek through the hole into oil or into grease; and then take sugar and make a syrup to boil; and dip[?] the mincebek in it, and put some on top [or, put salt on it]; and then serve them.

¼ c sourdough
2 c water for dough
1 c white flour
1 c whole wheat flour
oil for frying
½ c water for syrup
2 c sugar

Mix sourdough and water, stir into the mixed flour, stirring until pretty smooth. Let rise about 4 hours. Heat oil in frying pan. For syrup, bring water to a boil, add sugar and cover. When the sugar is dissolved and the syrup again clear, it is ready. Pour some of the batter into a funnel and dribble around into oil at a medium heat, then fry until brown, turning at least once. Each mincebek comes out of the oil onto a paper towel to drain briefly, then is dipped (tongs are useful) into the syrup, then onto the plate to serve.

Cryspes
Two Fifteenth Century p. 44 (Good)

Take white of eyroun, milk, and flour, and a little berme, and beat it together, and draw it through a strainer, so that it be running, and not too stiff, and cast suger thereto, and salt; then take a chafer full of fresh grease boiling, and put thine hand in the batter, and let thine batter run down by thy fingers into the chafer; and when it is run together on the chafer, and is enough, take and nym a skimmer, and take it up, and let all the grease run out, and put it on a fair dish, and cast thereon sugar enough, and serve forth.

4 egg whites
⅔ c milk
1 c flour
1 T dried yeast
3 T sugar
½ t salt

Take egg white, milk, and flour and a little yeast and beat it together, being careful not to let the flour make lumps. Add sugar and salt. Pour into a pan of hot oil, so that they puff up and brown, turn them, drain them, sprinkle on sugar and serve them.

To make it more like a funnel cake than a pancake, which seems to fit the description better, I use a slotted spoon; the batter runs through the slots into the hot grease. Of course, you could always let thine batter run down by thine fingers instead–but make sure no one is watching.

Ryschewys Closed and Fried
Two Fifteenth Century p. 45

Take figs, and grind them small in a mortar with a little oil, and grind with them cloves and maces; and then take it up into a vessel, and cast thereto pines, saunders and raisons of corinth and minced dates, powdered pepper, canel, salt, saffron; then take fine paste of flour and water, sugar, saffron and salt, and make fair cakes thereof; then roll thine stuff in thine hand and couch it in the cakes and cut it, and fold them in ryshews, and fry them up in oil; and serve forth hot.

25 figs	1 t cinnamon
2 t oil	¼ t salt
1 t cloves	4 threads saffron
1 t maces	*pastry*:
¼ c pine nuts	2 c flour
¼ t saunders	½ c water
⅓ c currants	1 T sugar
5 ½ oz dates	⅛ t salt
⅛ t pepper	1 thread saffron

Cuskynoles
Curye on Inglysch p. 52
(*Diuersa Cibaria* no. 45)

Make a past tempred wiþ ayren, & soþþen nim peoren & applen, figes & reysins, alemaundes & dates; bet am togedere & do god poudre of gode speces wiþinnen. & in leynten make þi past wiþ milke of alemaundes. & rolle þi past on a bord, & soþþen hew hit on moni perties, & vche an pertie beo of þe leynþe of a paume & an half & of þreo vyngres of brede. & smeor þy past al of one dole, & soþþen do þi fassure wiþinnen. Vchan kake is portiooun. & soþþen veld togedere oþe zeolue manere, ase þeos fugurre is imad: & soþþe boille in veir water, & soþþen rost on an greudil; & soþþen adresse.

Modernized English: Make a paste tempered with eggs, & so then take pears & apples, figs & raisins, almonds & dates; beat them together & do good powder of good spices within. & in Lent make thy paste with milk of almonds. & roll thy paste on a board, & so then hew it in many parts, & each part be of the length of a palm & a half & of three fingers of breadth. & smear thy paste all on one half, & so then do thy filling within. Each cake is a portion. & so then fold together of the same manner, as this figure is made: [see below] & so then boil in fair water, & so then roast on a griddle; & so then dress.

•	•	•	•	•
•	•	•	•	•
•	•	•	•	•

¾ c water	3 oz unblanched almonds
4 ½ c flour	3 oz pitted dates
3 beaten eggs	1 ½ t cinnamon
5 oz apple	½ t ginger
5 oz pear	⅔ t cloves
3 oz figs	1 ½ t nutmeg
4 oz raisins	

Stir cold water into the flour, then stir in egg, stir and knead until smooth. Wash and core the apple and pear. Put them, along with the remaining ingredients, into a food processor and process to a uniform mush. Roll out dough as six 12"x15" sheets. Cut each sheet into 10 6"x3" pieces. Either:

Version 1: Spread 1 T of filling on all of one piece, put another piece over it (sandwich—dough, filling, dough). Using the back of a reasonably thick knife, press the edges and the lines, to give the 3x5 pattern shown.

Version 2: An earlier version of this recipe (*Two Anglo-Norman Culinary Collections*) shows the figure as a 3x3 grid. That fits the text more closely. You cut pieces about 3"x6", spread 1 ½ to 2 t of filling on half of one piece, fold them to 3"x3" with the filling inside, then press a tic-tac-toe pattern with the back of your knife, giving a 3x3 grid of miniature ravioli.

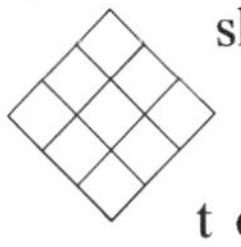

Either version should about use up the filling, but I don't promise it will come out exactly even. If there is extra filling, make more dough.

Boil about 4 minutes, then broil at medium distance about 4 minutes a side, watching to be sure they do not burn.

Lenten version of the dough
1 ¾ c almond milk to 4 c. flour. After being worked together, knead the paste four or five minutes until it is springy and elastic and smooth.

Good Membrillate Which Is A Pottage Of Quinces
Buen Membrillate Que Es Potaje De Membrillos
De Nola no. 106

You must take as many quinces as you wish to make dishes, and quarter them, and remove the core and the pips from them, and pare off the skin; and when they are well-peeled, wash them with tepid water; then remove them from that water and set them to cook in cold water; and when they begin to get mushy, then they are cooked; and remove them from the kettle and grind them well in a mortar; and blend them with a little of that same water of theirs, and strain them through a woolen cloth; and then take three pounds of unpeeled almonds, but only wash them in cold water, or tepid which would be better, and grind them well in a mortar; and when they are well-ground, strain them through a woolen cloth, having been blended with tepid water (and if it is a meat day, blend it with meat broth); and cast the milk in with the quinces; and then cast into the pot all manner of fine spices, which are: good ginger, and good cinnamon, and saffron, and grains of paradise, and nutmeg, and mace, and if it is a meat day, you will cast in two egg yolks for each dish; and if it is a fish day, it is not needful; and when it is quite thick, prepare dishes, and [cast] upon them sugar and cinnamon.

5 quinces	3 egg yolks
¼ c almonds	1 T sugar
1 c lamb broth	½ t cinnamon
1 t spice mixture*	

Peel, quarter, core quinces, wash, put to cook in cold water, bring to a boil, simmer, total cooking time about 20 minutes. Mash, adding 1 T of the water they cooked in, and force through cheese cloth.

Grind almonds, use with ⅔ c lamb broth to make ½ c almond milk (p. 7). Combine with the quince mush. Add 1 t of the spice mixture (see below) and egg yolks. Stir together, cook for about 5 minutes. Sprinkle sugar and cinnamon over at the end.

Spice mixture: 1 part ginger, 3 parts cinnamon, 1 part grains of paradise (measured before grinding), ½ part nutmeg, ½ part mace.

Strawberye
Two Fifteenth Century p. 29

Take Strawberys, and waysshe hem in tyme of yere in gode red wyne; þan strayne þorwe a clope, and do hem in a potte with gode Almaunde mylke, a-lay it with Amyndoun oþer with þe flowre of Rys, and make it chargeaunt and lat it boyle, and do þer-in Roysonys of coraunce, Safroun, Pepir, Sugre grete plente, pouder Gyngere, Canel, Galyngale; poynte it with Vynegre, and a lytyl whyte grece put þer-to; coloure it with Alkenade, and droppe it a-bowte, plante it with graynys of Pomegarnad, and þan serue it forth.

1 pint strawberries	¼ c sugar
¼ c red wine	¼ t ginger
1 ¾ c almond milk: (p. 7)	¼ t cinnamon
½ c almonds	⅛ t galingale
1 ½ c water	¼ t vinegar
4 T wheat starch	¾ t lard
¾ c currants	[alkanet]
8 threads saffron	pomegranate
⅛ t pepper	seeds

Wash strawberries in water, then mix with wine and force through wire strainer using a pestle. Mix with almond milk and wheat starch, then boil about 10 minutes, until thick enough to stick to the spoon. Add currants, then remaining ingredients as it cooks. Make sure the spices are ready when you start boiling it. We used not very sweet strawberries; one might use less sugar or more vinegar if they were sweeter.

Gaylede
Two Fifteenth Century p. 22

Take almond milk and flour of rice, and do thereto sugar or honey, and powdered ginger and galingale; then take figs and carve them a-two or raisins whole or hard wastel diced and color it with saunders, and seethe it and dress it in.

almond milk (p. 7):	2 t ginger
1 c ground almonds	1 t galingale
1 c water	1 c halved figs
1 c rice flour	1 ½ c raisins
6 T honey	a pinch of saunders

Chare de Wardone
Two Fifteenth Century p. 88

Take peer Wardons, and seth hem in wine or water; And then take hem vppe, and grinde hem in a morter, and drawe hem thorgh a streynoure with the licour; And put hem in a potte with Sugur, or elles with clarefiede hony and canell ynowe, And lete hem boile; And then take hit from the fire, And lete kele, and caste there-to rawe yolkes of eyren, til hit be thik, and caste thereto powder of ginger ynowe; And serue hit forth in maner of Ryse. And if hit be in lenton tyme, leve the yolkes of eyren, And lete the remnaunt boyle so longe, til it be so thikk as though hit were y-tempered with yolkes of eyren, in maner as A man setheþ charge de quyns; And then serue hit forth in maner of Rys.

1 ½ lb pears	1 ½ T honey
¾ c white wine	¼ t ginger
½ t cinnamon	4 egg yolks

Peel and core pears and chop into ½" pieces. We used Bartletts; we don't know what wardons are like. Simmer in the wine for 35 minutes. Remove from liquid, grind with a mortar and pestle, force through a strainer. Return to pan, add cinnamon and honey, bring to boil, simmer for a bit and remove from heat. Let cool somewhat and then stir in ginger and egg yolks. Serve.

A Good Filling
Daz Buoch von Guoter Spise p. B-4 (#12)

This is how you want to make a food. Trim fine pears and divide in four. And lay them in a pot and cover the pot and coat it with dough, so that the vapor can (not?) get out. Then cover the pot with a broad cover and lay there about glowing coals and let it slowly bake. So take then the pears out [of the fire?] and add clean honey therein, as much as the pear is, and boil it together so that it becomes thick and give it out. So you can make also from apples and from quinces but one should add pepper enough thereto.

4 large apples	⅙ cup water
⅛ teaspoon pepper	~2 ½ c honey
½ cup flour	

Peel and core the apples (or pears or quinces), cut in quarters, put them in a baking dish, sprinkle with pepper. Knead together flour and water to make the dough, make it into a strip, put it on the edge of the dish and jam the lid down onto it to seal the lid on the baking dish. Bake at 350° for 45 minutes. Remove from heat, mix with honey (which should be the same volume as the apples) in a clean pot. Simmer it for ½ hour until it begins to thicken a little.

It is not clear how this was meant to be eaten; it is very good as a spread, sweet and strong.

Taylours
Two Fifteenth Century p. 94

Take almondes, and grynde hem raw in a morter, and temper hit with wyne and a litul water; And drawe hit þorgh a streynour into a good stiff mylke into a potte; and caste thereto reysons of coraunce, and grete reysons, myced Dates, Clowes, Maces, Pouder of Peper, Canel, saffron a good quantite, and salt; and sette hem ouere the fire, And lete all boyle togidre awhile; And alay hit up with floure of Ryse, or elles grated brede, and caste there-on pouder ginger in þe dissh.

⅓ c almonds	pinch black pepper
¾ c chardonnay	¼ t cinnamon
¾ c water	4 threads saffron
⅓ c each of currants, raisins, and dates	pinch salt
	⅓ c bread crumbs (*or* rice flour)
~1/16 t cloves	⅛ t powdered ginger
~1/16 t mace	

Make up almond milk with wine and water (see p. 7). In a medium pot put dried fruit, all spices but ginger, and the almond milk. Bring to a boil over moderate high heat and cook 5 minutes, add bread crumbs, remove from heat and stir. Sprinkle ginger on top. This has a very thick pudding consistency.

To make Marmelade of Quinces or Damsons
Platt no. 31 p. 19

When you have boyled your Quinces or Damsons sufficiently, straine them; then dry the pulp in a pan on the fire; and when you see that there is no water in it, but that it beginneth to be stiffe, then mix two pound of sugar with three pound of pulpe; this marmelade will bee white marmelade; and if you desire to haue it looke with an high colour: put your sugar and your pulp together so soone as your pulp is drawne, and let them both boile together, and so it will look of the colour of ordinary marmeade, like vnto a stewed warden; but if you dry your pulp first, it will look white, and take lesse sugar: you shall know when it is thick enough, by putting a little into a sawcer, letting it coole before you box it.

2 ½ lbs quinces
2 ⅙ c sugar

Peel, core and slice the quinces. Put in pot with water to cover, bring to a boil and simmer covered for 40 minutes. Drain off the water and force the quinces through a strainer. Combine quince pulp with sugar and heat on high about 2 minutes until it starts to simmer. Turn down to medium low and cook for 1 ½ hours stirring almost continually. Towards the end the mixture will visibly hang together more; test by putting a bit of it on a cold plate to see if it gets stiff. Put in a container and let cool; it will end up solid enough to be cut in chunks. Refrigerate if you do not intend to eat it in the next few days. This is a fairly basic quince paste recipe and tastes rather bland. *(This is the "high color" version, not the "white marmelade" version.)*

Tostee
Curye on Inglysch p. 119
(*Form of Cury* no. 96)

Take wyne and hony and found it togyder and skym it clene, and seeþ it long. Do þerto powdour of gynger, peper and salt. Tost brede and lay the sewe þerto; kerue pecys of gynger and flour it þerwith, and messe it forth.

½ c wine
½ c honey
¼ t ground ginger
⅛ t pepper
⅛ t salt
8 slices toast
⅓ oz candied ginger

Mix wine and honey, simmer over moderate heat 20-25 minutes; remove from heat and mix in powdered ginger, pepper, and salt. Make toast, spread honey mixture on it and put slivers of ginger on top.

Gingerbrede
Curye on Inglysch p. 154
(*Goud Kokery* no. 18) (Good)

To make gingerbrede. Take goode honey & clarifie it on þe fere, & take fayre paynemayn or wastel brede & grate it, & caste it into þe boylenge hony, & stere it well togyder faste with a sklyse þat it bren not to þe vessell. & þanne take it doun and put þerin ginger, longe pepper & saundres, & tempere it vp with þin handes; & than put hem to a flatt boyste & strawe þeron suger, & pick þerin clowes rounde aboute by þe egge and in þe mydes, yf it plece you, &c.

1 c honey
1 ½ c breadcrumbs
1 t ginger
¼ t long pepper
¼ t saunders
1 T sugar
30-40 whole cloves
[or 5 t sugar, pinch powdered cloves]

Bring honey to a boil, simmer two or three minutes, stir in breadcrumbs with a spatula until uniformly mixed. Remove from heat, stir in ginger, pepper, and saunders. (If you can't get long pepper, substitute ordinary black pepper.) When it is cool enough to handle, knead it to get spices thoroughly mixed. Put it in a box, cookie tin, or the like, squish it flat and thin, sprinkle with sugar and stick cloves ornamentally over the surface. Leave it to let the clove flavor sink in; do not eat the cloves.

An alternative way of doing it is to roll into small balls, roll in sugar mixed with a pinch of cloves; we like to flatten them a little to avoid confusion with hais (p. 117). This is suitable if you are making them today and eating them tomorrow.

Payn Ragoun
Curye on Inglysch p. 113
(*Forme of Cury* no. 68)

Take hony and sugur cipre and clarifie it togydre, and boile it with esy fyre, and kepe it wel fro brennyng. And whan it hath yboiled a while, take vp a drope þerof wiþ þy fyngur and do it in a litel water, and loke if it hong togydre; and take it fro the fyre and do þerto pynes the triddendele & powdour gyngeuer, and stere it togydre til it bigynne to thik, and cast it on a wete table; lesh it and serue it forth with fryed mete, on flessh dayes or on fysshe dayes.

1 c honey	1 c pine nuts
1 c sugar	2-3 t ginger

Mix honey and sugar, cook over low heat, stirring frequently, until temperature reaches 270°, stirring constantly once it is over 250°; about ½ hour. Test by dropping small amount of syrup into water to see if it holds shape. Remove from heat, add pine nuts and ginger. Spread onto wet marble slab. Let cool until it can be cut into pieces, then serve. Result is very stretchy, almost like taffy.

Pynade
Curye on Inglysch p. 79
(*Diuersa Servicia* no. 91)

For to make a pynade, tak hony and rotys of radich & grynd yt smal in a morter, & do to þat hony a quantite of broun sugur. Tak powder of peper & safroun & almandys, & do al togedere. Boyl hem long & held yt on a wet bord & let yt kele, & messe yt & do yt forth.

4 radishes = 2 ½ oz	½ c brown sugar
½ c honey	½ t pepper
1 c slivered almonds	10 threads saffron

Cut radish up small, put it in the spice grinder or a mortar with ¼ c honey and grind small. Slightly crush the almonds. Mix all ingredients in a small pot. Simmer, stirring, until candy thermometer reaches between 250° and 270°. Dump out in spoonfuls onto a greased marble slab or a wet cutting board—the latter works if you have gotten up to 270° but sticks at 250°. Let it cool.

I got it to 270° without serious scorching by stirring continuously near the end. When it cools fully, the 250° is firm but chewable, the 270° between chewable and crunchy.

On Pine Kernels
Platina p. 42 (book 3)

They are often eaten with raisins and are thought to arouse hidden passions; and they have the same virtue when candied in sugar. Noble and rich persons often have this as a first or last course. Sugar is melted, and pine kernels, covered with it, are put into a pan and moulded in the shape of a roll. To make the confection even more magnificent and delightful, it is often covered with thin gold leaf.

½ c = 2 ¾ oz pine nuts	½ c sugar

Heat the sugar in a frying pan about 10 min, until it carmelizes to a light brown, stirring as necessary. Stir in the pine nuts. Shape roughly into long, thin shapes with a spoon and/or spatula. When it is cool enough to touch but still soft, roll them between your wet hands to get cylinders. This is a guess at what he means by "the shape of a roll" and could easily be wrong—you could try to find a pan that would provide the shape instead.

The Recipe for Sesame Candy
Mappae Clavicula p.71

The recipe for sesame candy. Put white pure honey near a moderate fire in a tinned pan and stir it unceasingly with a spatula. Place it alternately near the fire and away from the fire, and while it is being stirred more extensively, repeatedly put it near and away from the fire, stirring it without interruption until it becomes thick and viscous. When it is sufficiently thickened, pour it out on a slab of marble and let it cool for a little. Afterwards, hang it on an iron bolt and pull it out very thinly and fold it back, doing this frequently until it turns white as it should. Then twist and shape it on the marble, gather it up and serve it properly.

1 c honey	⅜ c sesame seeds

Cook the honey, using a candy thermometer, removing it from the heat whenever it starts boiling too hard. About an hour gets it to 250°, about 20 minutes more to 270°. At either of those temperatures it works, but ends up soft rather than crisp. At about 280° it becomes crisp—the problem is to keep it from scorching.

When you reach the desired temperature, pour it out on a buttered marble slab (or equivalent). Sprinkle on toasted sesame seeds if you like them (note that the original has sesame seeds only in the title!). Let it cool about 5 minutes, until you can handle it with your bare hands and it is no longer liquid. Then pull it with your hands like taffy (i.e. pull, fold, pull, fold, etc.). You will find that as you pull it it turns to a silky pale gold color.

Drinks

Hippocras
Goodman p. 299

To make powdered hippocras, take a quarter of very fine cinnamon selected by tasting it, and half a quarter of fine flour of cinnamon, an ounce of selected string ginger, fine and white, and an ounce of grain of Paradise, a sixth of nutmegs and galingale together, and bray them all together. And when you would make your hippocras, take a good half ounce of this powder and two quarters of sugar and mix them with a quart of wine, by Paris measure. And note that the powder and the sugar mixed together is the Duke's powder.

4 oz stick cinnamon   1 oz ginger
2 oz cinnamon   1 oz grains of paradise
"A sixth" (probably of a pound: 2 ⅔ oz)
   of nutmegs and galingale together

Grind them all together. To make hippocras add ½ ounce of the powder and ½ lb (1 cup) of sugar to 2 quarts of boiling wine (the quart used to measure wine in Paris c. 1393 was about 2 modern U.S. quarts, the pound and ounce about the same as ours). Strain through a sleeve of Hippocrates (a tube of cloth, closed at one end).

Weak Honey Drink (More commonly called Small Mead)
Digby p. 107

Take nine pints of warm fountain water, and dissolve in it one pint of pure White-honey, by laving it therein, till it be dissolved. Then boil it gently, skimming it all the while, till all the scum be perfectly scummed off; and after that boil it a little longer, peradventure a quarter of an hour. In all it will require two or three hours boiling, so that at last one third part may be consumed. About a quarter of an hour before you cease boiling, and take it from the fire, put to it a little spoonful of cleansed and sliced Ginger; and almost half as much of the thin yellow rind of Orange, when you are even ready to take it from the fire, so as the Orange boil only one walm in it. Then pour it into a well-glased strong deep great Gally-pot, and let it stand so, till it be almost cold, that it be scarce Luke-warm. Then put to it a little silver-spoonful of pure Ale-yest, and work it together with a Ladle to make it ferment: as soon as it beginneth to do so, cover it close with a fit cover, and put a thick dubbled woollen cloth about it. Cast all things so that this may be done when you are going to bed. Next morning when you rise, you will find the barm gathered all together in the middle; scum it clean off with a silver-spoon and a feather, and bottle up the Liquor, stopping it very close. It will be ready to drink in two or three days; but it will keep well a month or two. It will be from the first very quick and pleasant.

9 pints water   1 pint honey = 1 ½ lb
1 T fresh ginger   ½ T fresh orange peel
½ t yeast

Dissolve the honey in the water in a large pot and bring to a boil. Let it boil down to ⅔ the original volume (6 ⅔ pints), skimming periodically. This will take about 2 ½ to 3 hours; by the end it should be clear. About 15 minutes before it is done, add the ginger, sliced and peeled. Peel an orange to get only the yellow part, not the white; a potato peeler works well for this. At the end of the boiling, add the orange peel, let it boil a minute or so, and remove from the heat. Let the mead cool to lukewarm, then add the yeast. The original recipe appears to use a top fermenting ale yeast, but dried bread yeast works. Cover and let sit 24-36 hours. Bottle it, using sturdy bottles; the fermentation builds up considerable pressure. Refrigerate after three or four days. Beware of exploding bottles. The mead will be drinkable in a week, but better if you leave it longer.

This recipe is modified from the original by lengthening the time of fermentation before bottling. This change is intended to reduce the incidence of broken bottles. 2 liter plastic soda bottles are unaesthetic, but they are safer than glass.

Caudell
Two Fifteenth Century p. 96

Take faire tryed yolkes of eyren, and cast in a potte; and take good ale, or elles good wyn, a quantite, and sette it ouer þe fire. And whan hit is at boyling, take it fro the fire, and caste þere-to saffron, salt, Sugur; and ceson hit vppe, and serue hit forth hote.

7 egg yolks	2 pinches salt
2 c ale or wine	1 T sugar
6 threads saffron	

Put egg yolks and ale in a pot and heat to boiling, stirring constantly; remove from heat, add seasonings, and serve.

Sauces

Savoury Tosted or Melted Cheese
Digby p. 228

Cut pieces of quick, fat, rich, well tasted cheese, (as the best of Brye, Cheshire, &c. or sharp thick Cream-Cheese) into a dish of thick beaten melted Butter, that hath served for Sparages or the like, or pease, or other boiled Sallet, or ragout of meat, or gravy of Mutton: and, if you will, Chop some of the Asparages among it, or slices of Gambon of Bacon, or fresh-collops, or Onions, or Sibboulets [green onions], or Anchovis, and set all this to melt upon a Chafing-dish of Coals, and stir all well together, to Incorporate them; and when all is of an equal consistence, strew some gross White-Pepper on it, and eat it with tosts or crusts of White-bread. You may scorch it at the top with a hot Fire-Shovel.

½ lb butter	⅛ lb Brie
½ lb cream cheese	¼ t white pepper

Melt the butter. Cut up the cheese and stir it into the butter over low heat. You will probably want to use a whisk to blend the two together and keep the sauce from separating (which it is very much inclined to do). When you have a uniform, creamy sauce you are done. You may serve it over asparagus or other vegetables, or over toast; if you want to brown the top, put it under the broiling unit in your stove for a minute or so. Experiment with some of the variations suggested in the original.

Jance
Du Fait du Cuisine no. 46

Now it remains to be known with what sauce one should eat the pilgrim capons: the pilgrim capons should be eaten with the jance, and to advise the sauce-maker who should make it take good almonds and blanch and clean them very well and bray them very well; and take the inside of white bread according to the quantity which he needs, and let him have the best white wine which he can get in which he should put his bread to soak, and with verjuice; and when his almonds are well brayed put in a little garlic to bray with them; and take white ginger and grains of paradise according to the quantity of sauce which he needs, and strain all this together and draw it up with the said white wine and a little verjuice and salt also, and put it to boil in a fair and clean pot.

2 c white bread	3 cloves garlic
1 c white wine	½ t ginger
2 t verjuice	½ t grains of paradise
or 1 t vinegar	2 c white wine
6 oz almonds	½ t salt

Crumble bread, soak with 1 c wine and verjuice; blanch and grind almonds (or start with blanched almonds), then grind garlic with them. Add ground spices, mix with bread, force through a strainer, put into a pot with additional wine and salt, bring to a boil and cook over low heat about ten minutes. Makes about 3 cups.

Note: the "pilgrim capons" mentioned are roasted capons with lampreys, with which this sauce was intended to be served.

Cameline Sauce
Goodman p. 286

Note that at Tourney to make cameline they bray ginger, cinnamon and saffron and half a nutmeg moistened with wine, then take it out of the mortar; then have white bread crumbs, not toasted but moistened in cold water and brayed in the mortar, moisten them with wine and strain them, then boil all together and put in brown sugar last of all; and that is winter cameline. And in summer they do the same but it is not boiled.

	Sweet	Spicy	Sweet & spicy
ginger	1 t	1 t	1 t
cinnamon	1 t	1 t	1 t
saffron	10 threads	10 thrds	10 thrds
nutmeg	1 whole	½ whole	½ whole
wine	2 T	½ c	½ c
bread crumbs	3 T	2 T	2 T
brown sugar	2 T	1 t	1 T
cold water	2 c	1 c	1 c

We tried several versions of the winter cameline sauce and liked all of them. Grind smoothly until well ground, add bread crumbs, grind smooth, add water and wine, bring it to a boil, simmer until thickened and add the brown sugar.

Mirrauste de Manzanas — Mirrauste of Apples
De Nola no. 243

You must take the sweetest apples and peel off their skin, and quarter them. And remove the core and the pips, and then set a pot to boil with as much water as you know will be necessary. And when the water boils, cast in the apples and then take well toasted almonds and grind them well in a mortar. Dissolve them with the broth from the apples, and strain them through a woollen cloth with crustless bread soaked in said apple broth. And strain everything quite thick, and after straining it cast in a good deal of ground cinnamon and sugar. And then send it to the fire to cook and when the sauce boils remove it from the fire. And cast in the apples which remain, well drained of the broth, but see that the apples should not be scalded, so that you can prepare dishes of them, and when they are made cast sugar and cinnamon on top.

(This is a Lenten version of Mirrauste, a sauce served with roast birds.)

1 ½ lb apples	3 slices white bread
2 ½ c water	¾ t cinnamon
½ c roasted almonds	2 T+2 t sugar

Peel apples, quarter, core. Bring water to a boil, add apples, bring back to a boil and cook about 10 minutes until soft to a fork but not starting to fall apart. Grind almonds fine in food processor, remove crusts from bread. When apples are cooked, remove them from broth and put aside. Soak bread in ¾ c apple broth; regrind almonds with another ½ c apple broth, mix with bread. Force it through metal strainer. Mix ½ t cinnamon with 2 T sugar and add them. Heat to a boil, stirring to keep it from sticking. Remove from heat, add apples, mix remaining cinnamon and sugar and sprinkle over, serve.

A Garlic Sauce with Walnuts or Almonds
Platina p. 133 (book 8)

To almonds or walnuts that have been coarsely ground add as much cleaned garlic as you like and likewise, as need be, grind them up well, sprinkling them all the while so they do not make oil. When they are ground up put in white breadcrumbs softened in juice of meat or fish, and grind again. And if it seems too stiff it can be softened easily in the same juice. [See next recipe.]

A More Colored Garlic Sauce
Platina p. 133 (book 8)

Prepare this in the same way as above. But do not moisten it in water or juice, but in must of dark grapes, squeezed by hand and cooked down for half an hour. The same can be done with juice of cherries.

⅛ c walnuts	1 ½ c grape juice
½ T garlic	4-6 t vinegar
¼ c bread crumbs	¼ c water

Boil down the grape juice for must.

Another Pottage Of Coriander Called The Third
Otro Potaje De Culantro Llamado Tercio
De Nola no. 30

You must take green coriander, and cut it finely, and grind it in a mortar together with dry coriander, and then take toasted almonds and toasted hazelnuts, and grind them separately in a mortar; and when they are well-ground, mix them with the almonds, and resume grinding everything together; and when it is well-ground, strain it through a woolen cloth, and set it to cook in the pot; and cast in all fine spices with saffron, and vinegar, and sugar; and set it to cook with little fire just until it is a little thickened; and remove it from the fire, and prepare dishes, and upon them cast sugar and cinnamon.

½ c hazelnuts	4 threads saffron
4 oz cilantro	1 T sugar
½ c roasted almonds	2 T white wine vinegar
½ t ground coriander	2 T more sugar
½ c water	2 t cinnamon
½ t de Nola fine spices (p. 34)	

Toast hazelnuts, dry-frying them in a frying pan 5 minutes or so, and peel off skins. Wash cilantro and remove the stems. Grind almonds and hazlenuts separately in a food processor or a mortar.

Chop cilantro finely and add ground coriander. Put in nuts. Process in a food processor to a thick paste. Add ½ c of water and rub through a wire mesh strainer.

Add spices, sugar and vinegar, and cook on low about 10 minutes until it thickens enough to hold its shape when scooped up. Mix remaining sugar and cinnamon and sprinkle on top when you serve it.

(We don't know if this would be served by itself or possibly as a sauce; it might work well as a side dish with red meat. Or it might have been intended as a Lenten dish.)

Mustard
Menagier p. M-36

If you wish to provide for keeping mustard a long time do it at wine-harvest in sweet must. And some say that the must should be boiled. Item, if you want to make mustard hastily in a village, grind some mustard-seed in a mortar and soak in vinegar, and strain; and if you want to make it ready the sooner, put it in a pot in front of the fire. Item, and if you wish to make it properly and at leisure, put the mustard-seed to soak overnight in good vinegar, then have it ground fine in a mill, and then little by little moisten it with good vinegar: and if you have some spices left over from making jelly, broth, hippocras or sauces, they may be ground up with it, and then leave it until it is ready.

4 t mustard seed	¼ t hippocras spices (p. 64)
½ c vinegar	

Soak the mustard seed overnight in 5 T of the vinegar, then grind with the rest.

Blank Desure
Curye on Inglysch p. 76
(*Diuersa Servicia* no. 78)

For to make blank desure, tak þe yolkes of egges sodyn & temper it wiþ mylk of a kow. & do þerto comyn & safroun & flowre of ris or wastel bred myed, & grynd in a morter & temper it vp wyþ þe milk; & mak it boyle & do þerto wit of egges coruyn smal. & tak fat chese & kerf þerto wan þe licour is boylyd, & serue it forth.

6 eggs	¼ c breadcrumbs
¼ t ground cumin	*or* 1 T rice flour
12 threads saffron	¾ c milk
½ lb fat cheese (Swiss or …)	

Boil eggs until hard, about 12 minutes. Run cold water over them to cool, then peel and take egg yolks out. Mash yolks in a mortar with some of the milk until smooth. Add cumin and saffron threads and grind some more, being careful to crush the saffron in. Add breadcrumbs and the rest of the milk. Chop egg whites small and grate cheese or cut it into little bits. Put egg yolk mixture into a pot and heat at medium, stirring constantly until it just starts to boil; add egg whites and cheese and heat, stirring, until cheese melts, about 7 minutes total from starting to heat egg yolks.

Lemon Dish (Limonada)
De Nola no. 17

Take blanched almonds and peel them, and grind them in a mortar, and blend them with good hen's broth; and then take new raisins, and clean them well of the seeds, and grind them by themselves and strain them through a woolen cloth; and after they are strained, mix them with the almonds, and put everything in the pot where it must cook; and put sugar and a little ginger in that same way, and set it to cook, constantly stirring it with a stick of wood. And when it is cooked, put a little lemon juice, and then stir it a little with the wooden stirrer so that the lemon juice is well-mixed within it. And then dish it out and cast fine sugar on the dishes.

½ lb blanched almonds	3 T+ sugar
10 ½ oz chicken broth	¾ t ginger
¼ c raisins	4 T lemon juice

Blanch the almonds, grind them to a coarse meal and put them in a pan with chicken broth. Grind the raisins and pass through fine metal strainer, ending up with ~10 t pulp and juice combined. Mix that in. Add sugar and ginger. Cook about 10 minutes on a low heat, stirring constantly. Add lemon juice. Cook briefly, turn off, serve with sugar sprinkled on.

This could be used as a sauce over meat. If the raisins are dry, put them in boiling water for a while to plump them out before grinding. Could try using grapes, on the theory that new raisins mean raisins too new to have been dried.

Pasta, Rice, etc.

Losyns
Curye on Inglysch p. 108
(*Forme of Cury* no. 50)

Take good broth and do in an erthen pot. Take flour of payndemayn and make þerof past with water, and make þerof thynne foyles as paper with a roller; drye it harde and seeþ it in broth. Take chese ruayn grated and lay it in disshes with poudre douce, and lay þeron loseyns isode as hoole as þou myght, and above powdour and chese; and so twyse or thryse, & serue it forth.

½ to ¾ c water	1 T poudre douce (p. 4)
2 c flour	5 c beef broth
1 lb mozzarella	

Stir the water into the flour; knead 5-10 minutes until smooth. Divide in four portions, roll each out to about 12" diameter. Cut in lozenges (diamonds), leave to dry. This produces 9 ½ oz dried pasta, which will keep at least three weeks.

Grate cheese and mix up poudre douce. Bring broth to a boil, put in pasta, cook 10-12 minutes and drain. Put ⅓ of the cheese in a dish, sprinkle about ⅓ of the poudre douce over it, and layer ⅓ of the hot pasta on top; repeat this twice, reserving a little poudre douce to sprinkle on top. Let sit a couple of minutes to melt cheese and serve.

To Make Gnochi
Due Libri di Cucina B: no. 69

He who wants to make nochi, take flour and bread crumbs, and put in a little water, and take the eggs and break them with it, and get a wet slice and put it to boil, and when they are cooked, draw them forth and throw on them enough cheese.

½ c whole wheat flour	[¼ t salt]
½ c bread crumbs	2 eggs
3 T water	½ oz parmesan

Combine everything except the cheese, roll out, cut into pieces about 1"x1"x1", boil for ½ hour. Sprinkle on grated cheese and serve it.

Potaje de Fideos (Pottage of Noodles)
De Nola no. 59

Clean the fideos of the dirt which they have and when they are well cleaned put them on the fire in a very clean pot with good fatty broth of chicken or mutton which is well salted and when the broth begins to boil, cast the fideos in the pot with a piece of sugar, and when they are more than half cooked, cast into the pot with the chicken or mutton broth, milk of goats or sheep, or in place of those, almond milk, for that can never be lacking, and cook it all well together, and when the fideos are cooked remove the pot from the fire and let it rest a bit and prepare dishes, casting sugar and cinnamon upon them; but as I have said in the chapter on rice, there are many who say concerning pottages of this kind which are cooked with meat broth that one should cast in neither sugar nor milk, but this is according to each one's appetite, and in truth, with fideos or rice cooked with meat broth, it is better to cast grated cheese on the dishes, which is very good.

Translator's notes: My modern Spanish dictionary translate "fideos" as "vermicelli"; I do not know what medieval fideos were like. I suspect the phrase "clean the fideos of the dirt which they have" is a scribal error. An almost identical phrase is at the beginning of the previous recipe, which is for baked rice. There it makes sense; even today, packages of rice have instructions to check it for small pebbles and other impurities. I cannot see why pasta would need cleaning.

2 ½ c chicken broth	1 c goat's milk
8 oz spaghetti	(*or* sheep or almond)
½ t sugar	1 T sugar + 1 t cinnamon
	or ½ c Parmesan

Bring broth to a boil and cook spaghetti in boiling broth 8 minutes (or just over half the maximum cooking time given on the package), then add sugar and goat's milk and cook another 6 minutes. Let sit off the heat about 15 minutes, during which time most of the liquid gets absorbed. Mix in either the cinnamon sugar or the (grated) cheese. For larger quantities, reduce the proportionate amount of broth: for three times this amount, for example, use two and a half times the amount of broth.

To Make Ravioli
Sabina Welserin no. 31

Take spinach and blanch it as if you were making cooked spinach, and chop it small. Take approximately one handful, when it is chopped, cheese or meat from a chicken or capon that was boiled or roasted. Then take twice as much cheese as herb, or of chicken an equal amount, and beat two or three eggs into it and make a good dough, put salt and pepper into it and make a dough with good flour, as if you would make a tart, and when you have made little flat cakes of dough then put a small ball of filling on the edge of the flat cake and form it into a dumpling. And press it together well along the edges and place it in broth and let it cook about as long as for a soft-boiled egg. The meat should be finely chopped and the cheese finely grated.

Cheese version

¼ lb spinach	2 c flour
¼ lb cheese	½-¾ c water
⅛ t pepper	½ t salt (for dough)
1 egg	

Chicken version

¼ lb spinach	½ egg
3 oz chicken	1 c flour
⅛ t salt	¼-⅜ c water
⅛ t pepper	¼ t salt (for dough)

Put spinach into boiling water for 1-2 minutes, take out, cool, drain, squeeze dry. Boil chicken (if you are doing the chicken version) about 15 minutes. Chop cheese (or chicken) fine. Chop spinach fine. Combine with salt (chicken version), pepper, egg.

Knead flour and water into a smooth dough. Make about 1 ¼" ball of dough, roll out to aprox 4" circle on floured board, put 1 t filling in the middle, pinch the edges together around the filling like a pirogi. Bring the chicken stock plus spinach water to a boil, boil the ravioli in it for 3-4 minutes.

Macrows
Forme of Cury p. 46

Take and make a thin foil of dowh, and kerve it on peces, and cast hem on boiling water and seeth it wele. Take chese and grate it and butter cast bynethen and above as losyns (p. 68). and serve forth.

2 c flour	3 c grated cheese
~⅔ c cold water	4 T butter

Knead flour and cold water into a smooth, elastic dough. Roll it out thin and cut into broad strips (1"-2" wide). Boil it about 5-10 minutes (until tender). Put it in a dish, layered with grated cheese—we used Swiss and Parmesan—and butter. You may want to heat it briefly in an oven (although the recipe does not say to do so).

To Make Pot Torteli
Due Libri di Cucina B: no. 53

If you want to make torteli of meat of fresh mixed pork, boil it so that it is cooked, and beat it with a knife so that it is very good, and take the pot and boil it and grind it in a mortar and put in up to six eggs that are boiled and mix with the meat and put in good spices and put in some good dry, grated cheese, and you want to make this pie in a pie-shell [skin—another possible translation for the word] of lasagna and one should not boil it in meat broth and it should be given for dish with a long meat pottage of pepper, and it is good.

1 lb pork shoulder	1 t cinnamon
4 hard boiled eggs.	2 ½ oz parmesan
1 ½ t pepper	5 c flour
2 t ginger	~2 c water.
¼ t cloves	

Boil the pork shoulder, cut into several pieces, for about half an hour. Cut it up and beat it, using the back of a knife (or a mortar and pestle). Combine with eggs, spices, and grated cheese to make the filling for the tortelli.

Knead together flour and water, roll it out and cut it into about 60 pieces, each about 2"x3". Place a small amount of the filling in each, fold the pasta around it, and boil in water for about ten minutes.

To Make Lesagne
Due Libri di Cucina B:no. 67

He who wants to make lesanga, take good white flour and boil it in capon broth. If it is not so much, put in some other water, and put in some salt to boil with it, and dump it in a broad, flat bowl, and put in enough cheese, and throw over it the cuttings of the fat of the capon.

2 ½ c flour	1 ½ c parmesan cheese
1 c water	½ c rendered chicken fat

chicken broth sufficient to boil the pasta

Knead together flour and water, roll it out as two approximate circles about 10" in diameter, cut each into about five pieces. Boil the pieces in chicken broth for about ten minutes. Spread on each piece about 2 ½ T grated parmesan cheese and 1T rendered chicken fat and serve it.

Tartlettes
Curye on Inglysch p. 109
(*Form of Cury* no. 51)

Take pork ysode and grynde it small with safroun; medle it with ayren, and raisouns of coraunce, and powdour fort and salt, and make a foile of dowhgh and close the fars þerinne. Cast þe tartletes in a panne with faire water boillyng and salt; take of the clene flessh with oute ayren & boile it in gode broth. Cast þer powdour douce and salt, and messe the tartletes in disshes & helde the sewe þeronne.

½ lb pork	3 c flour
15 threads saffron	1 ⅛ c water
3 eggs	¼ lb more pork
½ c currants	2 c chicken broth
1 t powder fort (see p. 4)	1 t poudre douce
1 t salt (¼ + ½ +¼)	(see p. 4)

Cut two thirds of the pork into slices ½" thick, boil about 10 minutes in 6 c water, take out and cut the slices into about 1"x2" pieces.

Grind saffron in mortar. Combine pork and saffron in food processor (or mortar) and grind. Then add eggs, currants, powder fort and ¼ t salt and combine. Knead flour with about 1 ⅛ c water, and roll it out in 3 11"x14" pieces. Make into ravioli about 2"x2", stuffed with the pork mixture. Put 3 quarts water, ½ t salt in a pot, bring to a boil. Put in tartlettes, boil about 15 minutes and remove from water. Meanwhile grind the rest of the pork fine and cook in broth with another ¼ t salt and poudre douce about 15 minutes. Pour this over the tartelettes (including the broth) and serve.

Cressee
Anglo-Norman p. 874

Take best white flour and eggs, and make pasta dough; and in the pasta dough put fine choice ginger and sugar. Take half of the pastry, [which is or should be] colored with saffron, and half [which is or should be] white, and roll it out on a table to the thickness of your finger; then cut into strips the size of a piece of lath; stretch it out on a table as illustrated; then boil in water; then take a slotted spoon and remove the cressees from the water; then arrange them on, and cover them with, grated cheese, add butter or oil, and serve.

2 eggs	~35 threads saffron
1 ⅓ c flour	3 ½ oz parmesan cheese
¾-1 t ginger	1 T butter or oil
2 T sugar	

Knead the eggs and the flour together, along with the ginger and sugar until smooth; a tiny amount of water may help. Divide the dough in half. Grind the saffron in a mortar, then add ½ t water to extract the color; add the resulting liquid to half the dough and knead it in.

Roll out each half to about ⅜" thick. Cut in ¾" strips. Interlace the strips, with the yellow going one way, the plain the other. Use a drop of water at each point where the strips cross to stick them together, then roll the whole thing slightly with a rolling pin at the end. The result is a criss-cross fabric of strips of dough.

Cook in boiling water for about ten minutes. Spread half the cheese on a plate, take the cressee out of the water, drain it, put it on the plate on top of the cheese, put the rest of the cheese on top of the cressee, add olive oil or butter, serve.

Using about 12 threads of saffron tastes fine, but gives too pale a color from an aesthetic point of view. Using four times that much saffron makes it look good, but has too strong a saffron taste unless you really like saffron.

Ryse of Fische Daye
Curye on Inglysch p. 127
(*Forme of Cury* no. 129)

Blaunche almaundes & grynde hem, & drawe hem vp wyt watur. Weshce þi ryse clene, & do þerto sugur roche and salt: let hyt be stondyng. Frye almaundes browne, & floriche hyt þerwyt, or wyt sugur.

7 oz almonds	1 t salt
~4 ½ c of water	3 oz slivered almonds
2 c rice	1 T sugar on top
2 T sugar	

Make 4 c of almond milk (see p. 7). Add rice to almond milk, also sugar and salt, bring to a boil and simmer covered 20 minutes; let stand 25 minutes. Lightly grease frying pan with oil and put in almonds, cook while stirring for 5 minutes at low to moderate heat. Sprinkle almonds and extra sugar on rice and serve.

Frumente
Curye on Inglysch p. 98
(*Forme of Cury* no. 1)

To make frumente. Tak clene whete & braye yt wel in a morter tyl þe holes gon of; seþe it til it breste in water. Nym it vp & lat it cole. Tak good broþ & swete mylk of kyn or of almand & tempere it þerwith. Nym yelkys of eyren rawe & saffroun & cast þerto; salt it; lat it nought boyle after þe eyren been cast þerinne. Messe it forth with venesoun or with fat motoun fresch.

2 c water
1 c cracked wheat
4 threads saffron
⅓ c chicken broth
⅓ c milk
 (or almond milk p. 7)
2 egg yolks
½ t salt

Bring water to a boil. Add wheat and bring back to a boil, cook about 10 min, then remove lid and cool, with occasional stirring to hasten the cooling and break up the pasty lumps. Crush saffron into a little of the broth; add saffron, broth and milk to the wheat and heat. When heated through, stir in egg yolks and salt. Frumenty was traditionally served with venison; this recipe also suggests serving with mutton.

Miscellaneous

Stuffed eggs
Platina book 9

Cook fresh eggs for a long time so that they are hard, then take the egg from the shell and split it through the middle, so as not to lose any of the white. After you have taken out the yolk, grind up part of it with good cheese, aged as well as fresh, and raisins; save the other part to color the dish. Likewise add a little finely chopped parsley, marjoram and mint. There are those who also put in two or more egg whites, along with some spices. With this mixture fill the whites of the eggs and when they are stuffed, fry them over a gentle flame, in oil. When they are fried, make a sauce from the rest of the yolks and raisins ground together, and when you have moistened them in verjuice and must, add ginger, clove, and cinnamon and pour over the eggs and let them boil a little together.

8 eggs
1 oz Romano
1 oz fresh mozzerella
⅜ c raisins
1 ½ T parsley
1 T marjoram
1 T mint
~1 T oil
[1 egg white]
[additional spices]
2 T verjuice
2 T grape juice
⅛ t ginger
⅛ t clove
¼ t cinnamon

Hard boil eggs, cool, cut in half as for deviled eggs. Set aside 3 yolks. Grate the hard cheese, slice thin the soft cheese, chop herbs fine. Put the remaining 5 yolks in a bowl with both cheeses and mix. Grind ⅛ c raisins in a mortar. Add egg and cheese mix to the mortar, grind all together. Add herbs to the mixture and stir in. Fill eggs and put back together with a toothpick. There may be some leftover filling.

Grind remaining ¼ c raisins, mash into them the egg yolks set aside at the beginning, stir in grape juice, verjuice, and spices to make the sauce. Heat oil in a frying pan and have ready a small pot. Fry the eggs in the oil, four at a time, rolling them around to get them fried on all sides, for about a minute, then put into the pot. When all are fried, pour the sauce over them and heat that pot for about a minute, stirring them around to heat through, serve.

There is an Islamic version of stuffed eggs on p. 125.

How One Makes Almond Butter
Grewe: *XIIIth c.* p.35, recipe 3

One should take almond kernels and add water to make milk thereof and place it in a pot and heat it up over the embers and add saffron well crushed, and salt and vinegar to taste, and heat it until it thickens. When it has become sufficiently thick, place it in a cloth sewn together as a bag and hang it on a wall until the liquid has drained off, and then take it out, and make butter of it.

½ c almonds
2 c water
6 threads saffron
¼ t salt
2 t vinegar

Make 1 ½ c almond milk. Bring to a slow boil. Add saffron, salt and vinegar. Simmer about 15 minutes (it ends up about as thick as heavy cream). Pour it into a linen cloth (over a bowl) and leave it to drain for an hour. The result has about the texture of butter. Yields 3-4 T. Use more saffron if you like saffron and want it yellower.

To Make Quince Marmalade (Condoignac)
Le Menagier M-50

Take quinces and peel them, then cut in quarters and take out the eye and the seeds, then cook them in good red wine and then strain through a strainer: then take honey and boil it for a long time and skim it, then put your quinces in it and stir thoroughly, and keep boiling until the honey is reduced by half; then throw in powdered hippocras, and stir till cold, then divide into portions and keep it.

2 lb quince	1c honey
2 c red wine	½ t Duke's Powder (p. 64)

Peel, core and quarter your quinces. Put them in a pot with the wine, and simmer until the quinces are very soft—about an hour. Strain off the liquid and force the quinces through a strainer or a potato ricer or something similar. Add the honey, simmer gently, stirring if necessary to keep it from burning (if sufficiently gentle it mostly isn't) until the mixture is substantially thicker, which may take about an hour and a half. Add Duke's powder. Let it cool, stirring occasionally, and put it in a jar.

Sawgeat
Curye on Inglysch p. 135
(*Forme of Cury* no. 169)

Take sawge; grynde it and temper it vp with ayren. Take a sauseges & kerf hym to gobetes, and cast it in a possynet, and do þerwiþ grece & frye it. Whan it is fryed ynowgh, cast þerto sawge with ayren; make it not to harde. Cast þerto powdour douce & messe it forth. If it be in ymbre day, take sauge, buttur, & ayren, and lat stonde wel by þe sauge, & serue forth.

1 ½ T sage	⅜ lb mild breakfast sausage
4 large eggs	1 t poudre douce (see p. 4)
2 T oil	

Mix ground sage into eggs. Heat oil on high, fry sausage on high 5 minutes until browned. Turn heat to low, give it a minute or two to cool, add eggs, fry scrambling for 2 minutes. Remove excess grease; sprinkle poudre douce on top.

Arbolettys
Two Fifteenth Century p. 20

Take milk, butter and cheese and boil in fere; then take eyroun and caste thereto; then take parsley and sage and hack it small, and take powdered ginger and galingale, and cast it thereto, and then serve it forth.

¼ lb cheddar cheese	¼ c parsley
½ c milk	2 T sage
⅛ lb butter	1 t ginger
5 eggs	1 t galingale

Cut up cheese, heat milk, melt butter and cheese in it, stir together, then add beaten eggs. Chop parsley and sage fine, add along with the spices, cook until the mixture thickens, serve.

To Make Pescoddes
A Proper Newe Book of Cookery p. 33

Take marybones and pull the mary hole out of them, and cutte it in two partes, then season it with suger, synamon, ginger and a little salte and make youre paeste as fyne as ye canne, and as shorte and thyn as ye canne, then frye theym in swete suette and caste upon them a lyttle synamon and ginger and so serve them at the table.

pie crust (for 9" pie)	pinch salt
2 oz marrow	2 T lard for frying
2 t sugar	cinnamon (to cast on)
¼ t cinnamon	ginger (to cast on)
¼ t ginger	

Mix up pie crust. Mix marrow (from marrow bones), sugar, cinnamon, ginger, salt to a uniform paste. Roll pie crust very thin, cut into circles about water glass size (2 ¾"). Spread thin layer of marrow mixture across each round, fold it in half, seal the edges. Brown it in hot lard. Sprinkle with cinnamon and ginger and serve it forth.

White Pudding
Icelandic p. 216

One shall take sweet milk and well crushed wheat bread and beaten egg and well ground saffron and let it all boil until it grows thick. Then pour it upon a dish and throw in butter. This is called white pudding.

4 slices bread (4 oz)	6 threads saffron
2 eggs	3 T butter
1 c milk	

Turn bread into crumbs. Beat eggs, mix with milk and beat. Grind saffron and add, then add crumbs. Heat for about 5 minutes, put in dish and add butter.

Lord's Salt
Icelandic p. 215

One shall take cloves and mace, cardamom, pepper, cinnamon, ginger an equal weight of each except cinnamon, of which there shall be just as much as of all the others, and as much baked bread as all that has been said above. And he shall cut it all together and grind it in strong vinegar; and put it in a cask. That is their salt and it is good for half a year.

How to Make Use of the Salt Spoken of Above
Icelandic p. 215

When a man wants to use of this salt, he shall boil it in a pan over coals without flame. Then he shall take venison of hart or roe and carefully garnish with fat and roast it. And cut it up well burned; and when the salt is cold than the meat shall be cut up therein with a little salt. Then it can lie for three weeks. So a man may long keep geese, ducks, and other game if he cuts them thin. This is the best salt the gentry have.

1 t cloves	1 ½ t ginger
1 ⅛ t mace	1 t salt
½ T cardamom	8 t breadcrumbs
1 ³⁄₁₆ t pepper	2 c strong vinegar
5 t cinnamon	

Grind cardamom and mix all spices together. (This quantity is 2 g of all spices except the cinnamon, of which there is 10 g; it adds up to 3 ½ T total.) To use, add 1 t of salt to the spice mixture, the breadcrumbs and the vinegar, simmer it briefly, cool it, then mix it in with your meat and close up the container. This quantity will preserve a 2 c container of cooked, sliced meat or fowl (1 to 1 ½ lb).

We tried this recipe in order to have a way of storing meat without refrigeration for long events, such as Pennsic. In our experience, meat preserved this way keeps several weeks without refrigeration; we have done so repeatedly without health problems, but see warning below. The meat tastes strongly of the vinegar and spices when you rinse off the preserving mixture; we generally use the meat in recipes that call for vinegar and then leave out the vinegar.

Ordinary vinegar is 5%, which is just barely strong enough, so we normally mix it with stronger vinegar ("75 grain" or 7.5%) from a gourmet food store.

!Warning!

Preserving foods can be dangerous; if you experiment with this recipe, be careful. According to our researches, either using vinegar of at least 5% acidity or boiling for 15 minutes before eating will protect you from botulism; we strongly advise doing both. We take no responsibility for the result of trying this recipe; before doing so, you may want to read up on methods and hazards of preserving food.

Islamic Dishes: Middle East and al-Andalus

Bread

Making Bread of Abu Hamza
al-Warraq p. 123

Use as much as needed of fine samidh flour (high in starch and bran free). This bread is dry.

The dough is made similar to that of barazidhaj, except that this bread is a little thinner and smaller, it is pricked a lot with feathers [before baking], and neither buraq (bakers' borax) nor any sweetening ingredients are used in making it. However, you need to knead into it (olive oil from unripe olives), the amount of which depends on how much oily you want it to be. Moreover, after you stick them to the inside wall of the tannur and they are fully baked, take them out and stack them at the top of the oven. Keep them there until they are completely dry. Store them in wicker baskets and use them as needed.

Barazidhaj: Take 1 makkūk [7½ pounds] good quality, pure flour, and mix with it 2 uqiyas yeast, and 20 dirhams salt and (bakers' borax). Mix them into dough [by adding water] and knead vigorously. Cover it and let it ferment.

Divide dough into small portions, the weight of each should be 1 Levantine uqiya (1 ½ ounces), brush each portion with 2 dirhams (olive oil from unripe olives), and flatten it on a wooden board to medium thinness. Prick the breads with feathers, but not much, and cover them with a dry piece of cloth.

(One fifth of the recipe)
3 ⅓ c semolina	1 ½ c water
1 T sourdough	1 ½ t salt
3 T olive oil	additional 4 T olive oil

Knead all ingredients except the additional oil together, let rise overnight, divide into 1 oz portions (about 40 of them), flour the portions. Press flat to a thickness of ⅛ to ¼", prick all over with a feather (I used a wooden skewer). Brush with olive oil—about 4 T for the whole batch. Bake at 350° for 15-20 minutes—longer the thicker they are. Take out. Turn off the oven, open the door to let it cool a little, then put the loaves back in on the oven rack, dry for half an hour at about 150-200°.

A Recipe for Ka'k Made for Abu 'Ata Sahl bin Salim al-Katib
al-Warraq pp. 123-4

Take 1 kerylaja (2 ½ pounds) or 1 makkūk (7 ½ pounds) fine samith flour. Make it into dough using 100 dirham ground sesame seeds that have not been extracted of their oil (i.e. tahini), 1 uqiyya almond oil, and 2 dirhams salt. For each makkūk add 2 uqiyyas white sugar and 3 dirhams saffron. Knead the mixture with 10 dirhams yeast [and some water].

When dough is fully fermented, rub it with a little fat and rose water beaten together. Roll it out on a board into a square and cut it out into small squares. Bake them in the tannur by sticking them [into the inner wall]. When done, take them out and leave them at the top of the tannur for a short while to dry out, God willing.

(One fifth of the recipe)
3 ⅓ c semolina	.3 g saffron= (150 threads)
2 ounces tahini	t sourdough
1 t+ almond oil	1 ½ c water
⅕ t salt	T olive oil
scant T sugar	T rose water

Combine all ingredients except oil and rose water and knead it smooth. Leave overnight to rise. Knead in oil (or animal fat) and rose water. Roll out about ¼" thick, cut into squares 1.5"-2" on a side, put on a baking stone in a 400 degree oven, bake about 20-30 minutes until they begin to get brown. They taste very strongly of saffron, which some like and some do not.

Loaf Kneaded with Butter
Andalusian p. A-23

Take three ratls of white flour and knead it with a ratl of butter and when the mixing is complete, leave it to rise and make bread from it; send it to the oven in a dish and when it has cooked, turn it on the other side in another dish and return it to the oven. When it is thoroughly cooked, take it out of the oven, then cover it a while and present it.

½ lb butter	1 c water
5 c flour	¾ lb =~1 ¼ c sourdough
1 t salt	

Note: we assume that "make bread from it" requires water and leavening.

Soften butter and mix into flour; add salt. Mix lukewarm water with sourdough starter and stir into flour mixture; knead until smooth. Transfer to a greased ceramic or pyrex baking dish, cover with a damp cloth, let rise 3-4 hours. Heat oven to 350°. Bake bread about 55 minutes, remove from dish, invert and bake another 20 minutes. Remove from oven, cover with cloth for 10 minutes, then serve.

Recipe for Folded Bread from Ifriqiyya
Andalusian p. A-57

Take coarsely ground good semolina and divide it into three parts. Leave one third aside and knead the other two well and it is made from it. Roll out thin bread and grease it. Sprinkle some of the remaining semolina on top and fold over it and roll it up. Then roll it out a second time and grease it, sprinkle some semolina on top and fold it over like muwarraqa [p. 121]. Do this several times until you use up the remaining third of the semolina. Then put it in the oven and leave it until it sets. Remove it when tender but not excessively so. If you want, cook the flatbreads at home in the tajine. Then crumble it and with the crumbs make a tharid like fatir, either with milk like tharid laban, which is eaten with butter and sugar, or with chicken or other meat broth, upon which you put fried meat and a lot of fat. Dust it with cinnamon and serve it.

3 c semolina	~ ¼ c olive oil
⅔ c water	

Knead 2 c of semolina with the water for about 10 minutes, until smooth. Roll out to about 12"x12". Spread with about 2 t oil, sprinkle on 2-3 T semolina. Fold in half, roll up, mash together. Repeat about five more times, until all the last cup of semolina is used up.

Roll out to about 12"x10". Bake in 300° oven on an ungreased cookie sheet for about 50 minutes, until baked but not crisp (except thin parts).

For a recipe for the "tharid like fatir" that is to be made with this, see page 102.

Meat with Sauce or Stew

Palace Chicken with Mustard
Andalusian p. A-35

Cut up the chicken and place in a pot with salt and onion pounded with cilantro, oil, coriander seed, pepper and caraway; put it on the fire until it boils, and when it has boiled gently, add cilantro juice, vinegar, and murri, and let the vinegar be more than the murri; when it has cooked, pound peeled almonds fine and stir with egg and some pepper, green and dried ground coriander and a spoon of prepared mustard; pour all this into the pan and add three cracked eggs and take it to the hearthstone to rest for a while, and serve, God willing.

2 ½ lb chicken	2 T olive oil
1 ⅜ lb onion	2 T murri (see p. 5)
¼ c cilantro	3 T vinegar
3 T cilantro juice	¼ lb blanched almonds
(from ¼ c cilantro)	1 egg
1 t salt	¼ t more pepper
2 t coriander	2 T more cilantro
¾ t pepper	4 t mustard powder
2 t caraway	3 more eggs

Cut up chicken into separate joints; chop onion. Make cilantro juice (p. 8). Cook the chicken, etc. in oil over medium high heat 10-15 minutes. Add murri, vinegar, and cilantro juice, reduce heat to medium and cook 20 minutes. Grind almonds in food processor almost to flour. Mix in a bowl ground almonds, egg, and the rest of the spices. Stir into the pot, mixing well, and turn heat to low; crack eggs on top of sauce, cover, and let sit until eggs are poached (about 10-15 minutes).

Chicken Covered with Walnuts and Saffron
Andalusian p. A-43

Cut chicken in two, put in the pot, throw in onion pounded with cilantro, salt, spices, a spoon of vinegar and half a spoon of murri; fry until it smells good; then cover with water and cook till almost done; make meatballs from the chicken breast, and throw in the pot; dot with egg yolks and cover with the whites and pounded walnuts and saffron; ladle out and sprinkle with pepper and cinnamon and serve, God willing.

	for meatballs:
5 lbs chicken	2 cloves garlic
½ lb onion	3 T flour
1 c cilantro	½ t salt
2 T vinegar	½ t pepper
2 t olive oil	1 T vinegar
½ t cinnamon	*topping*: 4 eggs
¼ t cumin	1 c walnuts
¼ t coriander	16 threads saffron
½ t salt	⅛ t cinnamon
1 T murri (see p. 5)	⅛ t pepper

Remove the breast meat from the chicken, cut chicken in half. Chop onion and cilantro and pound together in a mortar. Heat the frying pan to medium high, add oil. Put in the chicken, onion and cilantro, vinegar, spices, and murri; fry at medium high. (This soon becomes something more like a simmer as the chicken and onion produce liquid.)

While the chicken is cooking, take the breast (about 15 ounces), process it in a food processor or pound in a mortar until it is sufficiently mashed to make meat balls out of. Crush garlic, add it and remaining meatball ingredients and mix thoroughly. Form meatballs about 1" to 1.5" in diameter.

After 15 minutes of frying, add 4 c water to the pot. Simmer 10 minutes, without a lid, then add the meatballs to the pot.

Pound the saffron to powder, add it to the walnuts, and pound the walnuts until you have something like walnut flour with pieces of walnut in it (walnuts tend to disintegrate when pounded or chopped); a food processor would also work for this.

When the pot has simmered for another 40 minutes, separate the eggs, putting the white with the pounded walnut and dropping the yolks into the pot. Stir the walnuts and the egg white together into a uniform paste and use it to cover the top of the pot. Cover the pot with a lid, simmer for about another 10 minutes, until the topping is hard. Sprinkle with the pepper and cinnamon and serve.

There is a fair amount of liquid, which is good over rice. One could try it with about half as much water, although this will make it somewhat harder to get the chicken cooked, since it will not be entirely covered.

Another Dish [Andalusian Chicken]
al-Andalusi p. C-4

Get a fat hen, cut off the head, clean it and cut it into small pieces; the legs in two, the breast in two and the same the wings. Put in a pot with salt, oil, murri, pepper, dried coriander, and oregano; fry it without water until it is gilded. Meanwhile, get onions and green cilantro and squeeze out their water into the pot, in a quantity sufficient to cover the meat, leaving it to bubble one hour. After get a little grated bread crumbs, beat them with two or three eggs, with pepper and saffron, and embellish with it the pot; leave it on the embers that the grease comes out and eat it.

1 T oil	2 t fresh oregano
1 t salt	*or* 1 t dried
2 t murri (see p. 5)	¼ c onion juice
1 chicken, 3 ½ lb	1 c cilantro
½ t pepper	3 eggs
1 t coriander	12 threads saffron
¼ t more pepper	½ c bread crumbs

Heat oil with salt, murri, etc. in large pot and fry cut-up chicken for 10 minutes over medium high heat, stirring occasionally. Make onion juice (p. 8). Make about ½ c of cilantro juice (p. 8). Add onion and cilantro juice and cover; simmer 40 minutes on low heat, stirring occasionally; be careful or it will stick. Beat eggs, crush saffron with a little of the egg and add, add bread crumbs and pepper; stir into the meat; cook about 5 minutes on low and remove from heat. The dish as we make it is a little spicy; if you are serving it for people with conservative tastes you might want to reduce the amount of pepper.

Muthallath with Heads of Lettuce
Andalusian p. A-47

Take meat from a young, fat sheep and cut it in small pieces and put it in a pot with salt, a piece of onion, pepper, coriander seed, clove, saffron and oil. Put it on a moderate fire and when it is almost done, take heads of lettuce and their shoots without leaves, peel and cut up and add to the meat in the pot, and when the lettuce is done, add good vinegar and finish cooking it. Cover it with beaten egg, saffron and spikenard and take it to the hearthstone.

1 lb lamb (or mutton)	⅓ c olive oil
¼ medium onion	1 bunch leaf lettuce
¼ t salt	¼ c vinegar
¼ t pepper	5 eggs
½ t coriander	8 threads more saffron
¼ t cloves	¼ t spikenard
8 threads saffron	

Cut up meat and chop onion, and put in a pot with salt, spices and oil. Cook on medium 20 minutes, until the meat is almost done. Wash lettuce and slice in ½" strips, add to meat and mix; when the lettuce is wilted (5-10 minutes), add vinegar and cook another 5 minutes. Beat eggs, add saffron and spikenard and spread on top of meat mixture, with heat turned all the way down. Let sit half an hour, until the eggs set.

Preparing Asparagus with Meat Stuffing
Andalusian p. A-41

Take asparagus, the largest you have, clean and boil, after taking tender meat and pounding fine; throw in pepper, caraway, coriander seed, cilantro juice, some oil and egg white; take the boiled asparagus, one after another, and dress with this ground meat, and do so carefully. Put an earthenware pot on the fire, after putting in it water, salt, a spoon of murri and another of oil, cilantro juice, pepper, caraway and coriander seed; little by little while the pot boils, throw in it the asparagus wrapped in meat. Boil in the pot and throw in it meatballs of this ground meat, and when it is all evenly cooked, cover with egg, breadcrumbs and some of the stuffed meat already mentioned and decorate with egg, God willing.

1 lb asparagus	¼ t salt
½ lb ground lamb	½ T murri (see p. 5)
⅛ t pepper	1 T oil
¼ t caraway	⅛ t pepper
⅛ t coriander	¼ t caraway
⅔ c cilantro	⅛ t more coriander
½ T oil	3 eggs
1 egg white	1 c breadcrumbs

Make cilantro juice (p. 8); use half for the first batch and half for the second. See A Baqliyya of Ziryab's (p. 88) for another dish with egg/meat/bread topping.

Dish of Eggplant
Andalusian p. A-49

Cut up mutton and put in the pot with salt, pepper, coriander, cumin, thyme, two spoons of murri naqî' and three of oil; take to the fire and cook and when the meat is done, add eggplants cut in quarters and boiled separately. When it has boiled, grind up white bread crumbs beaten with the right quantity of eggs in coriander juice; cover the pot with this and then take it to the hearthstone.

1 ½ lb eggplant	1 t cumin
¾ lb lamb	½ t ground thyme
2 t murri (see p. 5)	1 T oil
¾ t salt	2 T bread crumbs
1 t pepper	2 eggs
1 t coriander	2 T cilantro juice (p. 8)

Quarter eggplant, simmer in water for about 20 minutes. Cut lamb in bite sized pieces (1" to ½" on a side). Mix lamb with murri and spices and saute in oil 5-10 minutes. Drain eggplant, skin, add to meat, mashing a little, simmer together about 5-10 minutes. Mix the cilantro juice with eggs and bread crumbs, stir it into the pot, simmer briefly (about 5 minutes) to get the eggs cooked, serve.

Dish Prepared With Fried Eggplant
Andalusian p. A-40

Take meat and cut it up small, then put it in the pot and throw in half a spoon of vinegar, one of murri and another of fresh oil, and pepper, coriander and cilantro, both pounded fine, and salt. Bring the pot to a full boil until the meat and the spices are cooked, and don't throw in water. When the meat has browned and is done, remove it, stir it and throw in enough water, but do not let it cover the meat, and boil again. Then boil the eggplant separately, after salting it and removing its water, and then cut in thirds and quarters and remove the peel. Dust with good white flour and fry in the pan with some fresh oil, then throw it in the pot and cover the contents of the pot with two eggs and crumbs of leavened bread and draw off the grease to the oven. Boil moderately, take off the fire for a while and serve.

Translator's note: When I translate "removing its water," I'm reading the incomprehensible "dhâ'uhâ" as "mâ'uhâ," "its water." "Draw off the grease to the oven" is a strange instruction, not found elsewhere. The instruction to boil and take off the fire indicates that the pot itself does not go to the oven. (Charles Perry)

½ lb lamb	1 t salt
1 T oil	1 medium eggplant
½ T vinegar	½ c flour
1 T murri	⅓ c more oil
½ t pepper	½ c water
½ t ground coriander	2 eggs
4 T cilantro	⅓ c breadcrumbs

Cut the lamb up small, fry it in the oil with vinegar, murri, and seasonings about 10-15 minutes (until the meat is cooked). Add the water and simmer about another 20 minutes, until most of the water is gone.

Meanwhile, peel the eggplant and boil it 10 minutes in salted water, take it out and slice it. Lay it on paper towels or something similar for ten or fifteen minutes to let some of the juice come out. Pat it dry, smother in flour, fry in oil in a second frying pan for about 5-10 minutes. Then add it to the first pan. Stir in the beaten eggs, mix in the breadcrumbs, remove from the heat and serve.

A Baqliyya of Ziryab's
Andalusian p. A-48

Take the flesh of a young fat lamb, put in the pot with salt, onion, coriander seed, pepper, caraway, two spoons of oil and one of murri naqî'; put on a moderate fire and then take cabbage, its tender "eyes"; take off the leaves and chop small with the heads, wash, and when the meat is almost done, add the cabbage. Then pound red meat from its tender parts and beat in the bowl with eggs and the crumb [that is, everything but the crust] of bread, almonds, pepper, coriander and caraway; cover the pot with this little by little and leave on the coals until the sauce dries and the grease comes to the top and serve.

2 lb cabbage	1 T murri (p. 5)
1 lb lamb for stew	5 oz ground lamb
⅜ lb onion	2 eggs
1 t salt	½ c breadcrumbs
½ t coriander	¼ c blanched almonds
¼ t pepper	⅛ t pepper
½ t caraway	¼ t more coriander
2 T oil	⅛ t more caraway

Wash and chop cabbage. Put cut-up lamb, onion, salt, first set of spices above, oil, and murri in a pot and cook over middling high heat, stirring frequently, for 10 minutes. Stir in cabbage and cook covered for 20 minutes; the cabbage will yield a lot of liquid. Meanwhile, grind remaining lamb and mix with remaining ingredients. Add this mixture to pot by spoonfuls until the top is mostly covered. Cook covered until the topping is cooked through, then uncovered until most of the liquid is gone, about an hour in all on low heat.

Note: Ziryab was the famous arbiter of elegance during the caliphate of 'Abd al-Rahman II, in Cordoba; 'Abd al-Rahman II became Caliph in 822.

Preparing a Dish of Cardoons with Meat
Andalusian A-41

Take meat and cut it up, put in the pot with water, salt, two spoons of murri, one of vinegar and another of oil, pepper, caraway and coriander seed. Put on the fire, and when it is cooked, wash the cardoons, boil, cut up small and throw over the meat. Boil a little, and cover the contents of the pot with two eggs and bread crumbs, and sprinkle pepper on it in the platter, God willing.

10 oz. cardoons	4 ½ t murri (see p. 5)
1 T salt	½ t coriander
1 t vinegar	½ t caraway
10 oz lamb	¼ t pepper
1 c water	1 T vinegar
½ t salt	2 eggs
1 T olive oil	½ c bread crumbs

additional pepper to sprinkle on at the end

Use a vegetable peeler to strip out the fibers from the cardoon stalks. Cut them in 2 long pieces. Bring a gallon of water with 3 t salt, 1 t vinegar to a boil, add cardoons. Cook for 35 minutes. Drain and chop each piece in half.

Trim off the lamb fat and cut the meat in half inch cubes. Combine with water, salt, oil, murri spices and vinegar, bring to a simmer, simmer 25 minutes with lid on. Add cardoons. Simmer with lamb 15 minutes uncovered.

Mix eggs and bread crumbs, use to cover the liquid in the pot, simmer 7-8 minutes with lid on. Serve, with pepper sprinkled on to taste.

Anjudhâniyyah of Yahya b. Khalid al-Barmaki
Translated by Charles Perry from al-Warraq

Cut meat in strips, chop onion and fresh spices, and throw in a pot. Put in best quality oil, and when the pot boils and the meat browns, add pepper, cumin, caraway and a little murri, and throw in as much milled asafoetida [anjudhân] as you need. Break eggs over it and let it cool as needed, God willing.

Note: asafoetida is called Hing in Indian grocery stores. It comes in different mixtures; what we used is called L.G. Compounded Asafoetida Powder.

1 ½ lb lamb or beef	1 t cumin
1 large onion (12 oz)	½ t caraway seeds
1 ½ t cinnamon	4 t murri (see p.5)
¾ t coriander	¼ t asafoetida
¼ c olive oil	5 eggs
1 t pepper	

Put sliced meat, onion, cinnamon, coriander, and oil into pot, cook over moderately high heat about 5 minutes. Add remaining ingredients except for eggs, cook covered over low heat about 20 minutes. Break eggs on top and simmer until eggs are poached, about 5-10 minutes.

Another possible interpretation is to stir the eggs into the hot liquid, in which case the final cooking takes only a minute or two.

A Sicilian Dish
Andalusian p. A-46

Take fat meat from the chest, the shoulder, the ribs, and the other parts, in the amount of a ratl and a half. Put it in a pot with a little water and salt and some three ratls of onions. Then put it on a moderate fire, and when the onion is done and the meat has "returned," throw in four spoonfuls of oil, pepper, cinnamon, Chinese cinnamon, spikenard, and meatballs. Finish cooking it and when the meat is done, cover it with eggs beaten with saffron, or you might leave it without a covering, as you wish, [and cook it either] in the oven or at home.

3 lbs onions	½ t true cinnamon (p. 4)
1 ½ lbs lamb	¼ t spikenard
½ c water	4 T oil
½ t salt	4 eggs
½ t pepper	12 threads saffron
½ t cinnamon	

+meatballs from ½ pound to a pound of meat (see p. 8)

Slice onions, cut up meat into bite sized pieces. Put meat, onions, water and salt in a pot and cook covered 20 minutes, until onions are limp and meat is brown on outside. Add spices, oil, and meatballs, and simmer, covered, 40 minutes. Beat eggs, crush saffron into some of the egg and mix with the eggs. Pour this over meat mixture and simmer 15 minutes.

The Dish Mukhallal
Andalusian p. A-2

Take the meat of a plump cow or sheep, cut it small, and put it in a new pot with salt, pepper, coriander, cumin, plenty of saffron, garlic peeled and diced, almonds peeled and split, and plenty of oil; cover it with strong, very pure vinegar, without the slightest bit of water; put it on a moderate charcoal fire and stir it, then boil it. When it cooks and the meat softens and it reduces, then put it on the hearthstone and coat it with much egg, cinnamon and lavender; color it with plenty of saffron, as desired, and put in it whole egg yolks and leave it on the hearthstone until it thickens and the broth evaporates and the fat appears. This dish lasts many days without changing or spoiling; it is called "wedding food" in the West [or the Algarve], and it is one of the seven dishes cited as used among us at banquets in Cordoba and Seville.

1 lb beef or mutton	⅓ c olive oil
6 cloves garlic	¾ c vinegar
¼ t salt	6 eggs
¼ t pepper	¾ t cinnamon
½ t coriander	¼ t lavender
½ t cumin	8 threads more saffron
8 threads saffron	2 whole egg yolks
½ c blanched slivered almonds	

Cut up meat, chop garlic. Mix them with salt and the first set of spices, almonds, and oil in a pot, cook over medium high 11 minutes, turn way down. Mix eggs, lavender, cinnamon, remaining saffron, pour evenly over what is in the pot to form a layer on top. Put egg yolks on top and cook half an hour without stirring until yolks are cooked.

Preparing Tuffâhiyya (Apple Stew) with Eggplants
Andalusian p. A-49

Take three ratls of lamb, cut up and put in the pot with onion, salt, coriander, pepper, ginger, cinnamon and four ûqíyas of oil, let it evaporate in the pot on the fire, until it gives up its water; then cover with juice pressed from apples and cook; when the meat is done, put in eggplants peeled and boiled separately and whole peeled apples without cutting them up and prepared meatballs; then add some of the meat, pounded and "dissolved," and some eggs and cover it [masculine verb; this may mean that only the added meat is covered] with them, or leave [feminine verb, meaning leave the pot] without covering [khamira, the word meaning "dough"], and leave it to rest on the hearthstone.

(This is for ¼ the recipe given in the original.)

1 to 2 lb eggplants	1 ½ t cinnamon
12 oz lamb	1 oz olive oil
1 onion (4 oz)	2 c apple juice
1 t salt	1 ½ lb apples
¾ t coriander	6 oz ground lamb
¾ t pepper	3 eggs
¾ t ginger	

Meatballs:

½ lb ground lamb	½ t pepper
1 egg	½ t coriander
1 t murri (see p. 5)	½ t cinnamon
1 t onion juice	2 t olive oil

Peel the eggplants and put in a saucepan with about 5 c water and ½ t salt; boil 15 minutes and remove. Let stand ½ hour or more, and drain off the liquid that comes from them. Meanwhile, mix and knead together all meatball ingredients except the oil. Make into 25-30 meatballs. Fry them in the oil and their own fat for about 20 minutes over medium heat. In a large pot, put lamb, cut into bite sized pieces, onion, salt, spices, and oil; cook over medium heat about 5-10 minutes. Add apple juice and cook about 5 minutes more. Add whole eggplants, peeled whole apples, meatballs. Cook about 5 minutes. Meanwhile, mix the rest of the ground lamb with the eggs, stir into the liquid in the pot as a thickener. Cook with cover on over a low heat until apples are done (about another 40 minutes).

Note: The meatball recipe is loosely based on several other recipes in the same cookbook. Alternative ingredients include minced garlic instead of onion juice, white flour or egg white as a binder instead of eggs, vinegar, saffron, cumin, lavender, cloves, oil, salt, and meat fat.

Tuffahiya
al-Baghdadi p. 37

Take fat meat and cut into small strips: throw into the saucepan with a little salt and dry coriander, and boil until almost cooked. Remove and throw away the scum. Cut up onions small and throw in, with cinnamon-bark, pepper, mastic and ginger ground fine, and a few sprigs of mint. Take sour apples, remove the pips, and pound in a stone mortar, squeezing out the juice: put in on top of the meat. Peel almonds and soak in water, then throw in. Kindle the fire under it, until the whole is done: then leave over the fire to settle. If desired, add a chicken, cutting it into quarters, and letting it cook with the meat. Then remove.

¼ c blanched almonds	½ t cinnamon
1 ½ lb lamb	½ t pepper
1 t salt	½ t ginger
1 t coriander	2 sprigs fresh mint
6 oz onion	1 lb cooking apples
¹⁄₁₆ t mastic	

Put almonds to soak. Cut meat into strips ⅛"-¼" thick. Combine meat, salt, and coriander and cook about 15 minutes covered, until the meat is browned. Chop onions and grind mastic; add onions, cinnamon, pepper, mastic, ginger and mint to pot, and simmer another 10 minutes. Peel and core apples, chop very small (looks almost like apple sauce) in food processor. Dump apples and almonds on top. Cook another 10 minutes and serve.

Green Isfidhbaja by Ibrahim bin al-Mahdi
al-Warraq p. 283

Take 4 ratls meat of a sheep in its third year, and cut it up into bite-sized pieces. Put the meat in a pot with a piece of cassia, 1 ratl chopped onion, ⅓ ratl olive oil, salt as needed, and water enough to cover the meat.

Place the pot on nafikh nafshi or kanun ajlan [two kinds of slow burning stoves]. When meat is half done, add to the pot, 4 pieces of cheese, each weighing 5 dirhams [15 g]. When meat is almost done, add to the stew ½ ratl juice of cilantro and parsley. Add as well, a handful of ground coriander seeds, 1 dirham [3 grams] black pepper, and ½ dirham [1.5 g] cassia.

Let the pot simmer in the remaining heat then take it away from the stove and serve it, God willing.

(¼ recipe)

½ c parsley	1 t salt
½ c cilantro	1 c water
1 lb mutton or lamb	½ ounce parmesan
¼ lb onion	1 t coriander
2 ⅔ T olive oil	¼-½ t pepper
1 stick cinnamon	¼ t ground cinnamon

("Cassia" is what is normally sold as cinnamon in the U.S.)

Combine parsley, cilantro, and 1 T of water in the food processor, squeeze through cheesecloth to give ~¼ c juice.

Combine meat, onion, olive oil, 1 stick of cinnamon, salt and water, bring to a boil, simmer slowly for about 35 minutes, then add the cheese. In another 20 minutes add the juice and spices. Leave another 15 minutes on very low heat, then serve.

We have not tried doing it with mutton from as old an animal as the recipe specifies; that might require longer cooking.

Preparing Tabâhaja of Burâniyya
Andalusian p. A-42

Take of small eggplants fifteen, and boil gently with the skin on, whole, without peeling or splitting; then take them out of the pot and put in another pot; throw in as much salt and oil as are needed and boil on a slow fire until it is entirely done; take a ratl of mutton and slice it up, as told earlier; put in the pot with one quarter ratl of oil and some water, boil until the water disappears and then fry in the oil until the meat is browned and is done, and put in this the fried eggplants and throw in one quarter ratl of good vinegar and fry, until the vinegar is done; then throw over it a third of a ratl of murri and improve it with three dirhams weight of caraway, the same amount of coriander seed and a dirham and a half of pepper; then fry until done and leave it rest for a while, dish up and serve.

7 ½ lbs small eggplants	½ c vinegar
1 lb lamb	⅔ c murri (p. 5)
½ c oil	3 ½ t caraway seeds
1 t salt	2 T ground coriander
2 T oil	2 ¼ t pepper

Wash eggplants, cut off stem end, put into boiling water, cook 10 minutes and drain; let cool. Bone meat and cut into bite-sized pieces; put in pot with ½ c oil and 1 c water and cook uncovered 30 minutes. Peel and slice eggplants, put with salt and 2 T oil and 2 c water and simmer 25 minutes. Drain eggplants, combine them with meat, add vinegar and cook 15 minutes. Add murri and spices, cook 5 minutes, stirring, remove from heat, let sit 10 minutes and serve.

Buraniya
al-Baghdadi p. 191

Cut up fat meat small: melt tail and throw out sediment, then place the meat in it together with a little salt and ground dry coriander, and fry lightly until browned and fragrant. Then cover with water, adding green coriander leaves and cinnamon-bark; when boiling, skim off the scum. When little liquor is left, throw in a few halved onions, a dirham of salt, and two dirhams of dry coriander, cumin, cinnamon, pepper, and mastic, all ground fine. Mince red meat as described above and make into light cabobs, then add to the pot. Take eggplant, cut off the stalks, and prick with a knife: then fry in fresh sesame oil, or melted tail, together with whole onions. When the meat is cooked, a little murri may be added if desired. Color with a pinch of saffron. Put the fried eggplant in layers on top of the meat in the pan, sprinkle fine ground dry coriander and cinnamon, and spray with a little rose water. Wipe the sides of the saucepan and leave over the fire an hour to settle, then remove.

1 lb fat meat	¼ t pepper
lamb fat for "tail" (p. 4)	¼ t mastic
½ t salt	1 lb ground red meat
½ t coriander	1 medium eggplant
½ t cilantro	sesame oil for frying
2 sticks cinnamon	3 more small onions
2 small onions	[1 T murri (p. 5)]
½ to 1 t salt	1 pinch saffron
½ t more coriander	¼ t more coriander
¼ t cumin	¼ t more cinnamon
¼ t cinnamon	1 T rose water

Cut up the meat, render the fat and fry the meat in it along with salt and ½ t ground coriander. When it is browned, add enough water to cover along with cilantro and the stick cinnamon. When most of the water is boiled away, add two halved onions, salt, ½ t coriander, cumin, ¼ t cinnamon, pepper and mastic. Form the ground meat into small meat balls and add them. Slice the eggplant, fry it in sesame oil or more rendered fat, along with the remaining three onions. Add murri if you like, and saffron. Layer the eggplant on the meat, mix the final ¼ t of coriander and cinnamon, sprinkle on, along with the rose water. Remove from heat, let sit a while, and serve.

Jazariyyah
Ibn al-Mabrad p. 18

Meat is boiled with a little water. Carrots, garlic cloves and peeled onions are put with it, then crushed garlic is put with it. Some people put spinach with it also; some make it without spinach. Walnuts and parsley are put in.

2 lb lamb	6 cloves garlic
[1 t cinnamon]	5 oz onions
[½ t pepper]	2 cloves crushed garlic
[¾ t coriander]	2 c spinach = 5 oz
[¾ t salt]	¼ c walnuts
1 lb carrots	¼ c parsley

Cut the lamb up small and put it in 1 ½ c water with cinnamon, pepper, coriander and salt. Simmer 10 minutes. Add carrots cut up, whole garlic cloves, and small onions. Simmer 10 minutes. Add crushed garlic. Simmer 20 minutes. Add spinach. Simmer 10 minutes. Garnish with walnuts and parsley. The spices are based on similar recipes in al-Bagdadi.

Safarjaliyya, a Quince Dish
Andalusian p. A-34

Take meat and cut it in pieces which then throw in the pot and throw on it two spoons of vinegar and oil, a dirham and a half of pepper, caraway, coriander seed and pounded onion; cover it with water and put it on the fire, clean three or four quinces or five and chop them up with a knife, as small as you can; cook them in water and when they are cooked, take them out of the water and when the meat is done throw in it this boiled quince and bring it to the boil two or three times; then cover the contents of the pot with two or three eggs and take it off the fire, leave it for a little while, and when you put it on the platter, sprinkle it with some pepper, throw on a little saffron and serve it.

2 ½ lb lamb	1 ¼ t coriander
1 ¼ lb quinces	¾ lb onions
1 T vinegar	[1 t salt]
1 T oil	1 egg
1 ¼ t pepper	⅛ t+ more pepper
1 ¼ t caraway	12 threads saffron

Bone meat and chop it into bite sized pieces. Core quinces and chop them finely in a food processor. Bring the quince to a boil in 1 ½ c water and cook about 25 minutes covered. Meanwhile, combine meat with vinegar, oil, spices, onion (ground in food processor), salt and 1 c water and cook uncovered 15 minutes. Drain quinces and add to meat, bring back to a boil and boil about 5 minutes uncovered over medium to medium high heat. Stir in beaten egg, remove from heat. Let stand 10 minutes. Grind pepper (at least ⅛ t–more if you like pepper) and saffron together, sprinkle on, and serve. Good over rice.

Note: These spice quantities assume that it means a dirhem and a half of each of pepper, caraway, and coriander. If you interpret it as a total of a dirhem and a half, the recipe comes out much less strongly spiced; we prefer it this way. One could read "a dirhem and a half" as applying to the ground onion as well, which would imply much less than we use.

Safarjaliyya, a Dish Made With Quinces
Andalusian p. A-48

This is a good food for the feverish, it excites the appetite, strengthens the stomach and prevents stomach vapors from rising to the head. Take the flesh of a young fat lamb or calf; cut in small pieces and put in the pot with salt, pepper, coriander seed, saffron, oil and a little water; put on a low fire until the meat is done; then take as much as you need of cleaned peeled quince, cut in fourths, and sharp vinegar, juice of unripe grapes [verjuice] or of pressed quince, cook for a while and use. If you wish, cover with eggs and it comes out like muthallath.

1 lb lamb	1 T water
½ t salt	1 quince = ¾ lb
¼ t pepper	1 T wine vinegar
1 t coriander	¼ c verjuice
~4 threads saffron	[2 or 3 eggs]
2 t oil	

Cut up meat into bite-sized pieces, put in a pot with salt, spices, oil, and water, and cook over low heat about 10 minutes, stirring periodically. Meanwhile, peel and core quince and cut into eighths. Add quince, vinegar, and verjuice to pot and cook covered about 30-40 minutes, until quince is tender when poked with a fork. If adding eggs, stir them in and cook, stirring continuously for about 3 minutes.

We have also done it using quince juice instead of verjuice: to make ½ c quince juice from 1 quince, put quince through food processor with ⅙ c water, squeeze through cloth.

Fresh Beans With Meat, Called Fustuqiyya
Andalusian p. A-45

Take the flesh of a young sheep or lamb, preferably from the forelegs, the durra, the jaus and the 'anqara and after washing put in the pot with two spoons of fresh oil and water to cover the meat; put on the fire and then take a handful of fresh beans which have been shelled from their pods and throw over the meat; when it is done, take out the meat and knead the beans vigorously with a spoon until none of them is left whole; then pour in the pot a spoon of vinegar, another of fish murri and some salt, however much is enough; then throw the meat in the pot and fry a little; then take it to the embers until its face appears, dish up and use.

1 ⅓ c fresh fava beans	1 ½ c water
1 ⅓ lb lamb stew meat	1 T vinegar
2 T oil	1 T murri (p. 5)

Shell beans; it will take about 19 oz of beans in pod. Put meat, oil, and water in pot and bring to a boil, then add beans. Simmer uncovered 40 minutes, then remove meat. Mash beans with a spoon, add vinegar and murri, put meat back in and cook over low heat about 5 minutes, making sure it does not stick on the bottom.

Charles Perry, the translator, notes that Fustuqiyya (pistachio dish) is a poetical or fantasy name: the green fava beans are compared to pistachios.

Himmasiyya (a Garbanzo Dish) [Good]
Andalusian p. A-44

Cut the meat in proportionate pieces and put in the pot, with water to cover and enough oil; do not throw in salt at first, for that would spoil it; put in all the spices. And let the amount of water in this dish be small as you will substitute vinegar; then put the pot on the fire, then grind the garbanzos, sieve them, clean them and throw them on the meat, and when it is all done, grind up a head of garlic and beat with good vinegar and put in the pot; then put in the salt and stir so that all parts are mixed together, and when the pot is done, take it off the fire and leave it to cool and clarify; then sprinkle with fine spices and serve. It is best, when preparing the garbanzos for this dish, to begin by soaking them in fresh water overnight; then peel and throw in the pot, and when they have cooked, take them out of the pot and grind them in the mortar, then return them to the pot and finish cooking, God willing.

1 ¼ lb lamb	1 oz garlic (6 cloves)
15 oz can garbanzos	5 T vinegar
½ c water	¼ t salt
¼ t pepper	*fine spices*
½ t coriander	¼ t cinnamon
½ t cinnamon	⅛ t pepper
¼ c olive oil	½ t cumin

Cut meat into ¼ inch bits. Peel the garbanzos. Put meat, water, spices, oil and garbanzos in the pot. Bring to a boil, reduce heat and simmer. After ten minutes, remove the garbanzos, mash them in a mortar, and return them to the dish. Continue simmering, uncovered. Mash the garlic in the mortar, mix it with the vinegar, add it when the dish has been cooking for about 20 minutes. Stir. Add the salt, cook an additional 5 minutes, remove from the heat, sprinkle on the fine spices, and serve.

This corresponds to the "best" version of dealing with the garbanzos suggested in the original recipe. Peeling chickpeas is a pain, but seems to have been considered important in period Islamic cooking. An alternative approach is to simply mash the chickpeas in a mortar or food processor, try to sieve out the skins as best you can, and add the chickpeas at some point during the cooking. If you are not picky and are making large quantities, you could just forget about dealing with the skins—but don't tell anyone I suggested it.

Naranjiya
al-Bagdadi p. 40

Cut fat meat in middling pieces and leave in the saucepan, covered with water, to boil: when boiling, remove the scum. Add salt to taste. Cut up onions and leeks, washing in salt and water: scrape carrots, cut into strips four fingers long, and throw into the pot. Add cummin, dry coriander, cinnamon-bark, pepper, ginger and mastic, ground fine, with a few sprigs of mint. Mince red meat well with seasonings, and make into middle-sized cabobs. Take oranges, peel, remove the white pulp, and squeeze: let one person peel, and another do the squeezing. Strain through a sieve, and pour into the saucepan. Take cardamom-seeds that have been steeped in hot water an hour: wash, and grind fine in a stone mortar, or a copper one if stone is not procurable. Extract the juice by hand, strain, and throw into the pot. Rub over the pan a quantity of dry mint. Wipe the sides with a clean rag, and leave over the fire to settle: then remove.

5 seeds cardamom	1/16 t mastic
1 lb lamb	1 large sprig fresh mint
2 c water	3 oranges (¾ c juice)
½ t salt	1 lb lamb for meatballs
⅝ lb onion	*seasonings for meatballs:*
⅝ lb leeks	1 clove garlic (⅕ oz)
¾ lb carrots	¼ t pepper
¼ t cumin	¼ t coriander
½ t coriander	¼ t cumin
½ t cinnamon	1 t murri (see p. 5)
⅛ t pepper	½ t salt
¼ t ginger	½ T dry mint

Put cardamom seeds to soak in hot water. Cut up meat and bring to a boil in water with salt; turn down and simmer, covered. Cut up onions and leeks and add; cut carrots into 2.5" pieces and cut lengthwise into strips and add, by which time the meat has been going about 20 minutes. Add spices and mint. Juice oranges, add juice to pot; simmer uncovered. Make meatballs by buzzing lamb in food processor with seasonings and squeezing into balls; add to pot. Take cardamom seeds out of water, grind in mortar, and add juice to pot. Let simmer a while more, about 1 hour 15 minutes from the beginning, sprinkle dry mint over the dish, and serve.

The oranges should be sour oranges, but you may not be able to find any.

Mishmishiya
al-Bagdadi p. 40

Cut fat meat small, put into the saucepan with a little salt, and cover with water. Boil, and remove the scum. Cut up onions, wash, and throw in on top of the meat. Add seasonings, coriander, cummin, mastic, cinnamon, pepper and ginger, well-ground. Take dry apricots, soak in hot water, then wash and put in a separate saucepan, and boil lightly: take out, wipe in the hands, and strain through a sieve. Take the juice, and add it to the saucepan to form a broth. Take sweet almonds, grind fine, moisten with a little apricot juice, and throw in. Some colour with a trifle of saffron. Spray the saucepan with a little rose-water, wipe its sides with a clean rag, and leave to settle over the fire: then remove.

30 fresh *or* dried apricots	1/16 t mastic
(2 lb pitted or 7 oz dried)	1 t cinnamon
2 lb lamb	¼ t pepper
1 ⅓ c water	½ t ginger
1 t salt	⅔ c almonds
14 oz onions	[10 threads saffron]
1 t coriander	½ t rosewater
½ t cumin	

If using dried apricots, put to soak for about 3 hours. Cut up meat to small bite-sized pieces, boil in water with salt; when it comes to a boil (~10 minutes) skim, add onions, and turn down to a simmer, covered. Add seasonings. Drain soaked dried apricots or wash fresh apricots, boil either in about 2 c water about 5 minutes, drain, and force through a strainer until nothing is left but the peel (or convert to mush in a food processor). Grind almonds very fine. After simmering meat 40 minutes, add ~¾ of the apricot mush to pot; mix rest of it with ground almonds and add that to the pot. Crush saffron into a little water and add it to pot. Sprinkle a little rosewater over the surface; let sit for a few minutes over very low heat, then serve.

Raihaniya
al-Baghdadi p. 192

Cut red meat into thin slices, brown in melted tail, cover with water. When boiling skim, add a little salt, ground coriander, cummin, pepper, mastic, cinnamon. Mince red meat with seasoning and make into light cabobs, add. Take two bundles of spinach, cut off the roots, chop small, and grind in a mortar. Then throw into the pot. When cooked and dry add peeled ground garlic with a little salt and cummin. Stir, let settle over the fire an hour. Sprinkle with dry coriander and cinnamon, remove.

1-2 oz lamb fat	½ lb ground lamb
½ lb lamb	3 c spinach packed
1 ½ c water	2 cloves garlic
1/16 t mastic	¼ t more salt
¼ t cumin	¼ t more cumin
¼ t coriander	⅛ t salt
¼ t pepper	½ t more coriander
½ t cinnamon	¾ t more cinnamon

cabob seasonings (not given in recipe):

¼ t coriander	¼ t cinnamon
¼ t pepper	½ large clove garlic
¼ t salt	2 T onion

Put the lamb fat, substituting for "tail" (p. 4) in a pot over medium heat, fry until there is 1-2 T or so of oil melted out. Remove the solid, keep the rendered-out fat. Brown the sliced meat in it for about 5-10 minutes. Add water, mastic, ¼ t each of cumin, coriander, and pepper, ½ t cinnamon. Simmer 40 minutes. Make the ground lamb and cabob seasonings into about 30 cabobs, crushing the garlic and finely chopping the onion, add to the pot. Meanwhile, wash the spinach, removing stems. Mash in a mortar or pulverise in a food processor. When the cabobs have simmered for about 25 minutes, add the spinach. Simmer 30 minutes, add crushed garlic, salt, and another ¼ t cumin and ⅛ t salt. Simmer on the lowest available heat another 20 minutes, sprinkle on the final ½ t of coriander and ¾ t cinnamon, serve over rice.

Simple White Tafâyâ, Called Isfîdhbâja
Andalusian p. A-21 (Good)

This is a dish of moderate nutrition, suitable for weak stomachs, much praised for increasing the blood, good for the healthy and the scrawny; it is material and substance for all kinds of dishes.

Its Recipe: Take the meat of a young, plump lamb. Cut it in little pieces and put it in a clean pot with salt, pepper, coriander, a little juice of pounded onion, a spoonful of fresh oil and a sufficient amount of water. Put it over a gentle fire and be careful to stir it; put in meatballs and some peeled, split almonds. When the meat is done and has finished cooking, set the pot on the ashes until it is cooled. He who wants this tafaya green can give it this color with cilantro juice alone or with a little mint juice.

2 lb lamb	½ T oil
1 t salt	2 ½ c water
½ t pepper	[4 T cilantro or mint juice]
1 t coriander	¼ c blanched almonds
2 t onion juice	

meatballs:

1 lb ground lamb	¾ t murri (see p. 5)
1 egg	3 cloves garlic
1 t onion juice	¼ t pepper
2 T flour	½ t coriander
1 t vinegar	¼ t cumin
	¼ t cinnamon

Cut lamb into bite-sized pieces and put in pot with salt, pepper, coriander, onion juice, oil, and water, simmer uncovered about 40 minutes. Mix all ingredients for meatballs, chopping the garlic fine. (Note that this is one possible guess for meatballs; see p. 8 for sources and another interpretation.) If you want to do the green version, make a couple of tablespoons of cilantro juice (p. 8). When meat has cooked, take lumps of meatball mixture, squeeze together, and drop into pot. Add almonds. Simmer about another 10 minutes, add cilantro or mint juice if desired, and serve.

Making Baqliyya with Eggplants
Andalusian p. A-41

Take the breast of a sheep and its ribs, cut small, to the size of three fingers, cut onion in round slices and then take cilantro and pound coriander seed, caraway, and Chinese cinnamon; cut up the eggplants in round pieces and the same with the gourds; then take a pot and put a little oil in its bottom then arrange a layer of meat and eggplant and a layer of gourd and put some spices between each layer and the next; then put the pot on the fire, after putting in it an adequate quantity of meat, and do not add water; cook until done God willing.

2 t caraway seed	2 T oil
2 t coriander seed	1 lb lamb breast
2 t cinnamon	1 lb lamb chops
½ c cilantro	8 oz onion
1 ¼ lb opo gourd (p. 4)	[t salt]
1 lb eggplant	

Grind or pound the caraway seed, combine with other ground spices and chopped cilantro. Peel the gourds. Arrange ingredients as described, including the onion slices in with the gourd layer, in a gallon or larger pot. Cover tightly and bake 1 hr 20 min at 350°.

A Recipe for a Tasty Maghmuma by Ishaq bin Ibrahim al-Mawsili
al-Warraq p. 311

Take some fatty meat and cut it into thin slices, the thinnest you can get them. Take some round onions (basal mudawwar) and slice them thinly crosswise into discs like dirhams [coins].

Now prepare a clean pot of soapstone (burma). Spread its bottom with a layer of the [prepared] meat; sprinkle it with black pepper, coriander, and caraway; and spread a layer of the onion slices. Put another layer of the [sliced] meat and fat, sprinkle it with spices and salt then another layer of onion.

Cover [the layered meat and vegetables] with a round of bread (raghif). Cook the pot on a slow-burning fire until meat is cooked. Invert the pot onto a wide and big bowl (ghadara) and serve it, God willing.

1 lb lamb	2 t coriander
½ lb onions	1 T caraway
½ t pepper	1 loaf pita

Slice meat and onion thin, layer it as described, sprinkling on the spices and top with the pita. Cook at low to medium low for about an hour, then invert the pot into a suitable bowl.

A Recipe for Soused Poultry
al-Warraq, p. 194

Scald good quality chickens and clean and wash them thoroughly. Next, disjoint them and boil them lightly in water to which you have added salt, olive oil, a piece of galangal, and a piece of cassia.

Choose whichever you like of the chicken pieces and press them and dry them very well. Layer them in a barniyya (a wide-mouthed jar) and sprinkle each layer with the herbs [and spices] mentioned in the soused fish recipe above. Make sure to use salt.

Pour vinegar all over the chicken and set it aside [for future use].

You may add seeds of sesame and nigella, and mahrut (asafedtida root); but this is optional.

(Herbs and spices mentioned in the recipe above: parsley, cilantro, rue, bruised coriander seed, galangal, cassia.)

4 1/2 lb chicken, cut up	2 T parsley
6 c water	2 T cilantro
½ t salt	1 T rue
1 T olive oil	½ t coriander
1 oz fresh galangal	2 T more salt
3" stick cinnamon	3 c wine vinegar

Put the chicken in a pot with the water (enough to cover), salt, oil, galangal, and stick cinnamon; simmer covered 18 minutes. While it cooks, chop herbs and beat the coriander seed a little in a mortar—herbs are measured chopped and packed down. Remove chicken from broth, spread out on paper towels and press dry with more paper towels, let cool a little. Slice the galangal root from the broth and break up the stick cinnamon. Put a layer of chicken in a ceramic crock, top with some of the herbs, pieces of galangal and cinnamon, and salt, repeat until all is layered, packing the chicken in as tightly as possible. Pour the vinegar over it and refrigerate.

When you want to use it, fry the pieces for a few minutes each. Tasty, but you need to like vinegar.

Preparing Covered Tabâhajiyya [Tabahajiyya Maghmuma]
Andalusian p. A-43

Take a ratl and a half of meat and cut in slices as told earlier; pound a ratl of onion and take for this three dirhams' weight of caraway and one of pepper; put in the pot a layer of meat and another of onion until it is all used up and sprinkle flavorings between all the layers; then pour on a third of a ratl of vinegar and a quarter ratl of oil; put a lid on the pot and seal its top with paste [dough] and fry over a slow fire until done; then take from the fire and leave for a while, skim off the fat and serve.

1 ½ lb lamb	⅔ c vinegar
1 lb onion	½ c oil
1 t pepper	flour and water (for dough)
1 ½ t caraway	

Slice meat, mince onion. In a pot put a layer of sliced meat, cover with onion, and sprinkle over some of the pepper and caraway; repeat until it is all used up. Pour over vinegar and oil. Mix flour and water to make a long ribbon of dough and put around the edge of the pot; jam the lid onto this, sealing it. Cook over low heat about an hour, uncover, skim off excess oil, and serve.

Recipe for Mu'allak
Andalusian p. A-57

Take fat young mutton, clean it and cut the meat into big pieces. Put it in the earthenware pot and add pepper, onion, oil and coriander. Cook until the meat is done, then remove it and set it aside. Strain the bones from the broth and return it to a quiet fire. When it has boiled, put in crumbs made from thin bread which was made from wheat dough and add soft, rubbed cheese, as much as the crumbs. Blend with a spoon until it makes one mass and when its broth has dried up, pour on fresh milk and leave it until its foam is dispersed. Then return the meat that was removed and when it has formed a mass, take it off the fire, leave it a little and use it.

10 oz onion	1 ½ c water
1 ⅜ lb mutton or lamb	1 c breadcrumbs
½ t pepper	½ c = 4 oz ricotta
1 ¼ t coriander	½ c milk
1 T oil	

Slice onions. Cut meat in large chunks. Put meat with onions, pepper, coriander, and oil into a heavy pot, cover and bring to a boil. Simmer 2 hours (if you are using lamb reduce time to 45 minutes). Strain out meat and onions. Bring broth back to a boil, add breadcrumbs, simmer while stirring 2 minutes. Add cheese, simmer another 5 minutes while stirring constantly. Add milk and bring back to a simmer; add meat and onions and heat, stirring, about 2-3 minutes.

Labaniya
al-Bagdadi p. 42

Cut up the meat and throw it into the saucepan with a little salt and water to cover, and boil until almost done. When the meat has fried in its own oil, and most of the juice has dried, throw in chopped onions and leeks, after washing them: split egg-plant well, half-boil in a separate saucepan, and then add to the rest, with dry coriander, powdered cummin, mastic, cinnamon-bark, and some sprigs of mint. Boil in what remains of the juices until completely cooked. Add Persian milk to which ground garlic has been added. Rub over the pan a few sprigs of dry mint: wipe the sides with a clean rag. Leave over the fire for an hour to settle: then remove.

1 lb eggplant	½ t cumin
1 lb lamb	1/32 t mastic
½ t salt	~ 1 t stick cinnamon
¾ c water	1 T chopped fresh mint
10 oz leek	2 c yogurt
10 oz onion	5 cloves garlic = ¾ oz
1 t coriander	1 t dried mint

Bring 3 c of water to a boil; peel eggplant and slice to ½" slices, put in the water, and boil 10 minutes. Remove, let drain. Cut up meat to bite-sized pieces, aprox ½" cubes, put in pot with salt and water, bring to a boil and boil over moderate heat uncovered until the liquid is mostly gone, about 35 minutes. Wash leek thoroughly to get the dirt out from under the leaves, then chop leek and onion. When the meat has been cooking for 35 minutes, add onion, leek, seasonings and eggplant; cover, cook over low heat another 25 minutes. Add yogurt and crushed garlic (from a garlic press). Stir together. Sprinkle dried mint over the pot; turn heat down low, leave covered another half hour or so (we are told that the phrase translated "an hour" actually means "a while").

Madira
al-Baghdadi p. 41

Cut fat meat into middling pieces with the tail; if chickens are used, quarter them. Put in the saucepan with a little salt, and cover with water: boil, removing the scum. When almost cooked take large onions and leeks, peel, cut off the tails, wash in salt and water, dry and put into the pot. Add dry coriander, cummin, mastic and cinnamon, ground fine. When cooked and the juices are dried up, so that only the oil remains, ladle out into a large bowl. Take Persian milk, put in the saucepan, add salted lemon and fresh mint. Leave to boil: then take off the fire, stirring. When the boiling has subsided, put back the meat and herbs. Cover the saucepan, wipe its sides, and leave to settle over the fire [i.e. at a low heat], then remove.

3 ½ lb chicken *or*	⅛-¹⁄₁₆ t mastic
2 ½ lb boneless lamb	½ T cinnamon
1 T salt	4 c yogurt
2 leeks	½ lemon
4 medium onions	1 T salt
1 t ground coriander	½ c fresh mint
1 t cumin	

Chicken version: Put chicken in a pot with 1 T salt and enough water to cover and cook about 30 minutes. If you want to serve it boned (not specified in the recipe, but it makes it easier to cook and to eat–we have done it both ways), remove it from the water, let cool enough to handle, bone, and put the meat back in the pot. Add leeks, onions and spices. Cook away the rest of the water, remove meat and vegetables, and add yogurt, lemon, another T salt and mint; mint is chopped and lemon is quartered and each quarter sliced into two or three times with a knife. Let come to a simmer and put back the meat and vegetables. Heat through, not letting it boil, and serve. Use proportionately less water if you expand the recipe substantially.

We have a recipe for salted lemon in a modern North African cookbook and plan to try using that next time.

Buran
al-Baghdadi p. 191 (Good)

Take eggplant, and boil lightly in water and salt, then take out and dry for an hour. Fry this in fresh sesame-oil until cooked: peel, put into a dish or a large cup, and beat well with a ladle, until it becomes like kabis. Add a little salt and dry coriander. Take some Persian milk, mix in garlic, pour over the eggplant, and mix together well. Take red meat, mince fine, make into small cabobs, and melting fresh tail, throw the meat into it, stirring until browned. Then cover with water, and stew until the water has evaporated and only the oils remain. Pour on top of this the eggplant, sprinkle with fine-ground cumin and cinnamon, and serve.

1 lb eggplant	2 cloves garlic
1 lb ground lamb	1 c yogurt
3 T sesame oil	½ t cumin
½ t salt	1 t cinnamon
¼ t coriander	

Cut eggplants in thick slices (approximately 1 ½"), put in boiling salted water (6 c water + 6 T salt) for 7 minutes. Remove, let stand 1 hour. Make lamb into 30-40 small meatballs (add cinnamon etc. if you wish). Fry in melted lamb fat ("tail," p. 4). When browned, cover with water and simmer until only the oil is left. Then fry eggplant in sesame oil until cooked, peel, mash, add salt and coriander. Crush garlic, add to yogurt, mix with eggplant. Put the meatballs on top, sprinkle with cumin and cinnamon, and serve.

Gharibah
Ibn al-Mabrad p. 21

Meat is boiled, then you take off most of its broth and put with the remainder vegetables such as onion, gourd and aubergine. You dissolve yoghurt in what you took off and you put it with it. Then you garnish with walnut and parsley.

¾ lb lamb	½ c yogurt
2 c water	2 c chopped onion
[1 stick cinnamon]	3 lbs gourd
[¼ t cumin]	1 lb eggplant
[½ t coriander]	½ c chopped walnuts
[½ t+ salt]	2 T chopped parsley

Cut up the lamb small, removing most of the fat. Simmer it in water for about ½ hour with the spices. Remove ½ of the broth, mix with yogurt. Put the vegetables (cut up in small pieces) and the yogurt-broth mixture back in the pot with the lamb. Simmer for 1 hour. Garnish with walnuts and parsley.

Note: the spicing is based on similar dishes in al-Baghdadi. The cookbook this recipe is from is very terse; cinnamon is never mentioned, nor, I think, salt, and dry coriander only once. I assume they are simply omitted in the recipe and left to the cook's judgement. See p. 143 for a discussion of gourd, squash, and similar vegetables.

Recipe for White Karanbiyya, a Cabbage Dish
Andalusian p. A-47

Take young, fat meat; cut it into a pot with salt, onion, pepper, coriander seed, caraway and oil. Put it on a moderate fire and when it is nearly done, take a coarse cabbage, throw away the outside and take the heart and surrounding parts, and clean it of its leaves. Stick a knife between the "eyes" and throw away the rest of the leaves until it remains white like the turnip. Peel it and cut it in regular pieces and throw them into the pot, after boiling them, as has been indicated. When it is done, put it on the hearthstone and squeeze over it some coriander juice. He who wants this dish as a muthallath, let him add vinegar and saffron.

1 lb cabbage	½ t coriander
1 lb lamb	½ t caraway seed
½ t salt	⅓ c olive oil
1 medium onion	~ 3 T cilantro, packed
½ t pepper	

Cut off outer leaves, parboil cabbage heart 10 minutes and drain. Mix all ingredients and bring to a boil, cook 10 minutes covered and 5 minutes uncovered. Make cilantro juice (p. 8), add to dish and let simmer a couple of minutes.

Rutabiya
al-Baghdadi p. 195

Cut red meat into small, long, thin, slices: melt fresh tail, and throw out the sediment, then put the meat into the oil, adding half a dirham of salt and the same quantity of fine-brayed dry coriander. Stir until browned. Then cover with lukewarm water, and when boiling, skim. Put in a handful of almonds and pistachios peeled and ground coarsely, and color with a little saffron. Throw in fine-ground cumin, coriander, cinnamon and mastic, about 2.5 dirhams in all. Take red meat as required, mince fine, and make into long cabobs placing inside each a peeled sweet almond: put into the saucepan. Take dates: extract the stone from the bottom with a needle, and put in its place a peeled sweet almond. When the meat is cooked and the liquor all evaporated, so that only the oils remain, garnish with these dates. Sprinkle with about ten dirhams of scented sugar and a danaq of camphor; spray with a little rose water. Wipe the sides of the saucepan with a clean rag, and leave to settle over the fire for an hour: then remove.

1 lb lean lamb	¼ t cinnamon
"tail" (lamb fat: p. 4)	⅛ t mastic
½ t salt	1 lb ground lamb
¼ t coriander	25 whole almonds
⅓ c ground almonds	15 dates
⅓ c pistachios	1 T "scented sugar"?
⅛ t saffron	⅔ g camphor
¼ t cumin	2 T rosewater
½ t cilantro	

(Judging from the Khushkananaj recipes, "scented sugar" could have rose water, edible camphor, and (now unobtainable) musk.)

Jannâniyya (the Gardener's Dish)
Andalusian p. A-52

It was the custom among us to make this in the flower and vegetable gardens. If you make it in summer or fall, take saltwort, Swiss chard, gourd, small eggplants, "eyes" of fennel, fox-grapes, the best parts of tender gourd and flesh of ribbed cucumber and smooth cucumber; chop all this very small, as vegetables are chopped, and cook with water and salt; then drain off the water. Take a clean pot and in it pour a little water and a lot of oil, pounded onion, garlic, pepper, coriander seed and caraway; put on a moderate fire and when it has boiled, put in the boiled vegetables. When it has finished cooking, add grated or pounded bread and dissolved [sour] dough, and break over it as many eggs as you are able, and squeeze in the juice of tender coriander and of mint, and leave on the hearthstone until the eggs set. If you make it in spring, then [use] lettuce, fennel, peeled fresh fava beans, spinach, Swiss chard, carrots, fresh cilantro and so on, cook it all and add the spices already indicated, plenty of oil, cheese, dissolved [sour] dough and eggs.

Spring version

¼ lb lettuce	1 c water
1 oz fennel leaves	½ c oil
3 oz spinach	¼-½ t pepper
¼ lb chard	½ t ground coriander
or beet leaves	¼ t caraway seeds
4 T cilantro	½ c bread crumbs
2 carrots, sliced	2 eggs
½ c fresh fava beans	1 t more cilantro
4 c water + ¼ t salt	1 t more mint
½ lb onions	3 oz grated cheese
2 large cloves garlic	

Chop greens, slice carrots, put with beans into boiling salted water for about 5 minutes, and drain. Slice onion and pound in a mortar, or buzz in a food processor, and crush garlic. Mix water, oil, onion, garlic, and seasonings in clean pot, boil about 10 minutes and add greens. Mash 1 t each of cilantro and mint to juice. Cook about 3 minutes and add bread crumbs, eggs, cilantro and mint juice, and cheese. Cook over low heat until egg sets and cheese melts. Use a lower proportion of water for the second cooking if you are making this in a much larger quantity.

Preparation of Plain Liftiyya Also
Andalusian p. A-47

Take tender, fat meat and cut it. Put it in a pot with salt, onion, pepper, coriander seed and a little cumin. Cook it and when it is almost done, take the turnip and peel it in big pieces. If you boil it by itself, it will be better and the same for the vegetables. Add them to the meat and leave them until they finish cooking. Then put it on the hearthstone and if you squeeze over it cilantro juice, it will be much better.

1 ⅜ lb lamb	¾ t coriander
10 oz onion	¼ t cumin
½ t salt	1 ⅜ lb turnips
¼ t pepper	2 T cilantro juice (p. 8)

Cut meat to bite-sized pieces, put in pot with onion and seasoning, and simmer covered 45 minutes. Meanwhile peel and cut turnips to ½" cubes and set turnips to boil in separate pot for 25 minutes. Drain turnips and add to pot with meat. Cook another 5 minutes or so, add cilantro juice, and serve.

Zirbaya
Andalusian p. A-6

Take a young, cleaned hen and put it in a pot with a little salt, pepper, coriander, cinnamon, saffron and sufficient of vinegar and sweet oil, and when the meat is cooked, take peeled, crushed almonds and good white sugar, four ounces of each; dissolve them in rosewater, pour in the pot and let it boil; then leave it on the embers until the fat rises. It is very nutritious and good for all temperaments; this dish is made with hens or pigeons or doves, or with the meat of a young lamb.

1 chicken, 3 ½ lb *or*	20 threads saffron
2 ¼ lb boned lamb	2 T wine vinegar
1 t salt	2 T olive oil
⅝ t pepper	4 oz = ⅔ c almonds
1 ¼ t coriander	½ c sugar
2 t cinnamon	4 T rosewater

Put cut-up chicken or lamb, salt, spices, vinegar, and oil into pot. Bring to boil, cook covered over moderate to low heat 30 minutes, stirring periodically to keep the meat from sticking. Blanch and grind almonds, mix with sugar and rosewater to make a paste. Stir this in with the meat, bring back to a boil and cook about 8 minutes until sauce thickens.

Sikbaj
al-Baghdadi p. 34

Cut fat meat into middling pieces, place in the saucepan, and cover with water, fresh coriander, cinnamon bark, and salt to taste. When boiling, remove the froth and cream with a ladle, and throw away. Remove the fresh coriander, and add dry coriander. Take white onions, Syrian leeks, and carrots if in season, or else eggplant. Skin, splitting the eggplant thoroughly, and half stew in water in a separate saucepan: then strain, and leave in the saucepan on top of the meat. Add seasonings and salt to taste. When almost cooked, take wine vinegar and date juice, or honey if preferred–date juice is the more suitable–and mix together so that the mixture is midway between sharp and sweet, then pour into the saucepan and boil for a while. When ready to take off the fire, remove a little of the broth, bray into it saffron as required, and pour back into the saucepan. Then take sweet almonds, peel, split, and place on top of the pan, together with a few raisins, currants, and dried figs. Cover for a while, to settle over the heat of the fire. Wipe the sides with a clean rag, and sprinkle rosewater on top. When settled, remove.

2 lb lamb	1 t salt
3 c water	⅓ c wine vinegar
¼ oz cilantro	⅓ c honey *or*
1 stick cinnamon	date juice (dibs)
½ t salt	about 10 threads saffron
¾ lb leeks	~2 T split almonds
¾ lb carrots	2 T raisins
⅝ lb white onions	1 T currants
1 t coriander	2 T figs
½ t pepper	½ t cinnamon
1 t cumin	1 t rose water

Cut lamb in about ½" cubes. Bring to a boil with water, etc, and skim. Meanwhile chop leeks and carrots, cut onions in halves or quarters, put in boiling water, boil 10 minutes and strain. Remove cilantro from meat (it should have been simmering about 20 minutes by then), add powdered coriander, vegetables, pepper, cinnamon and cumin and simmer for half an hour. Mix vinegar and honey, add and simmer another 10 minutes. Grind saffron into ½ t of the broth, put into the pot. Sprinkle on almonds, raisins, etc., cover and let sit 15 minutes on low heat, turn off heat, sprinkle on rosewater and serve.

Fried Dishes

Recipe of Eggplant Pancakes
al-Andalusi p. C-5

Get sweet eggplant and boil it with water and salt until it becomes well cooked and is dissolved or falling apart. You should drain the water, crush and stir it on a dish with crumbs of grated bread, eggs beaten with oil, dried coriander and cinnamon; beat it until all becomes equal. Afterwards fry cakes made with this batter in a frying pan with oil until they are gilded. Make a sauce of vinegar, oil, almori, and mashed garlic; give all this a shaking and pour it over the top.

1 ¼ lb eggplant	1 ½ t cinnamon
2 qts water + 2 t salt	2 large cloves garlic
½ c bread crumbs	2 T vinegar
2-3 eggs	2 T oil
1 T oil	2 t murri (see p. 5)
1 ¼ t coriander	about 6 T oil for frying

Peel and quarter eggplant, boil 30 minutes in salted water. Drain, mash and mix with bread crumbs, eggs, oil, coriander and cinnamon. Crush garlic in a garlic press and mix with vinegar, oil and murri for the sauce. Fry in oil at medium high, about 1-2 minutes a side. Pour the sauce over pancakes before serving.

Eggplant Isfîriyâ
Andalusian A-51

Cook the peeled eggplants with water and salt until done, take out of the water and rub them to bits in a dish with grated bread crumbs, eggs, pepper, coriander, cinnamon, some murri naqi' and oil; beat all until combined, then fry thin breads, following the instructions for making isfîriyya.

3 lbs eggplants	¾ t coriander
12 c water	¼ t cinnamon
½ t salt	½ t murri
1 ½ c bread crumbs	2 t oil
2 large eggs	oil for frying
¼ t pepper	

Trim and peel eggplants and cut them into ¾" slices. Put in boiling water with salt and cook about 15 minutes until soft, then drain well. Put them in a bowl, mash thoroughly, and add bread crumbs, eggs, spices, murri, and oil.

Heat 3 T oil to medium, make about 9 patties, each with about 2 ½ T of the mashed eggplant mixture. Fry several at a time for about 8 minutes each side, pressing down with spatula to ³⁄₁₆" thick, adding more oil for each batch.

Recipe for Dusted Eggplants
Andalusian p. A-51

Take sweet ones and split in strips crosswise or lengthwise and boil gently. Then take out of the water and leave to drain and dry a little. Then take white flour and beat with egg, pepper, coriander, saffron and a little murri naqi'; when it is like thick soup, put those eggplants in it and fry with oil in the hot pan; then brown them, then immerse them and do a second time and a third.

2 lb of eggplants	½ t coriander
½ c flour	6 threads saffron
4 eggs	2 T murri (see p. 5)
½ t pepper	oil to fry in

Slice eggplants ½" thick and cut into pieces between quarter and dollar size. Simmer for 10 minutes, then drain. Mix together other ingredients for the batter. Soak the saffron in a teaspoon of water to extract color and flavor. Dip eggplant pieces in the batter, fry in shallow oil until brown, drain, dip in the batter again, fry again.

Recipe for the Fried Version of the Same [Dusted Eggplant]
Andalusian p. A-51

Take sweet ones and cut, however you wish, lengthwise or crosswise, as mentioned before; boil with water and salt, then take out of the water and leave till dry and the water drains off; then dust in white flour and fry in the pan with fresh oil until brown and add to them a cooked sauce of vinegar, oil, some murri naqi' and some garlic. You might fry in the same way boiled gourd, following this recipe.

2 lb eggplant or gourd	4 T vinegar
6 c water	4 T olive oil for sauce
1 T salt	2 T murri (see p. 5)
1 c flour	8 T oil for frying
1 oz garlic	

Slice eggplant or gourd (see p. 4) crossways to about ¼"-½" thick. Boil about 4 minutes in salted water. Drain in strainer. Flour each slice on both sides. Mash garlic, simmer in vinegar, oil and murri 20 minutes. Meanwhile, heat oil in frying pan at medium high and fry slices about 3 minutes on one side, a little less on the other, until lightly browned on both sides. Drain briefly on paper towels then put on a serving plate, pour sauce over and serve.

Counterfeit (Vegetarian) Isfîriyâ of Garbanzos
Andalusian p. A-1

Pound some garbanzos, take out the skins and grind them into flour. And take some of the flour and put into a bowl with a bit of sourdough and some egg, and beat with spices until it's all mixed. Fry it as before in thin cakes, and make a sauce for them.

1 c chickpea flour	4 t cinnamon
½ c sourdough	¼ c cilantro, chopped
4 eggs	½ t salt
2 t pepper	*garlic sauce*:
2 t coriander	3 cloves garlic
16 threads saffron	2 T oil
2 t cumin	2 T vinegar

Chickpea flour can be made in a mortar and pestle or a spice grinder (a food processor would probably work too). To make it, pound or process until the dried chickpeas are broken, then remove the loose skins and reduce what is left to a powder. An easier approach is to buy the flour in a health food store or a Middle Eastern grocery. Crush the garlic in a garlic press, combine with vinegar and oil, beat together to make sauce. Combine the flour, sourdough, eggs and spices and beat with a fork to a uniform batter. Fry in about ¼ c oil in a 9" frying pan at medium high temperature until brown on both sides, turning once. Add more oil as necessary. Drain on a paper towel. Serve with sauce.

Note: The ingredients for the sauce are from "A Type of Ahrash [Isfîriyâ]" (p. 96) which is from the same cookbook. What is done with them is pure conjecture.

Maqluba al Tirrikh
al-Baghdadi p. 204 (Good)

*Take tirrikh and fry in sesame-oil: then take out, and place in a dish to cool. When cold, cut off the heads and tails, remove the spine, bone, and scale with the greatest care. Crumble and break up the flesh, and sprinkle with dry coriander, cumin, caraway and cinnamon. Break eggs, throw on, and mix well. Then fry in sesame-oil in a frying pan as *maqluba* is fried, until both sides are browned: and remove.*

½ lb perch or catfish	1 t caraway
1 T sesame oil	1 ½ t cinnamon
½ t coriander	1 egg
½ t cumin	2 T sesame oil

Fry fish in 1 T sesame oil; let it cool. Bone and crumble it. Add spices and eggs. Fry like pancakes in more sesame oil. Tirrikh is a kind of Middle Eastern freshwater fish; we do not know what other fish it is similar to.

Maqluba
al-Baghdadi p. 201

Take and slice red meat, then chop with a large knife. Put into the mortar, and pound as small as possible. Take fresh sumach, boil in water, wring out, and strain. Into this place the minced meat, and boil until cooked, so that it has absorbed all the sumach-water, though covered to twice its depth: then remove from the saucepan and spray with a little lemon-juice. Lay out to dry. Then sprinkle with fine-ground seasonings, dry coriander, cumin, pepper and cinnamon, and rub over it a few sprigs of dry mint. Take walnuts, grind coarse, and add: break eggs and throw in, mixing well. Make into cakes, and fry in fresh sesame-oil, in a fine iron or copper frying-pan. When one side is cooked, turn over on to the other side: then remove.

10 oz lamb	½ t pepper
2 T dried sumac	1 t cinnamon
½ c water	½ t dry mint
1 T lemon juice	1 ¼ c walnuts
½ t ground coriander	5 eggs
½ t cumin	2 T sesame oil

Either use ground lamb or take lamb meat, chop it with a knife, then pound in a mortar. Both ways work but give different textures.

Boil sumac in water about 2 minutes, let stand 5 minutes, then add it to the meat and simmer about 15 minutes. Drain the meat, sprinkle it with lemon juice, let dry about one hour. Mix meat with spices and mint. Grind walnuts coarsely (something between chopped fine and ground coarse). Add walnuts and eggs, fry as patties in sesame oil on a medium griddle. Best eaten hot with a little salt. This produces about 20 patties roughly 3 inches in diameter.

The instructions call for using fresh sumac, straining it, and using only the water it is boiled in. I cannot get fresh sumac, and when I used dried sumac (which you get in Iranian grocery stores) and followed the instructions it came out rather bland, so I use both the sumac and the water the sumac was boiled in.

A Type of Ahrash [Isfîriyâ]
Andalusian p. A-1

This is the recipe used by Sayyid Abu al-Hasan and others in Morocco, and they called it isfîriyâ. Take red lamb, pound it vigorously and season it with some murrî naqî', vinegar, oil, pounded garlic, pepper, saffron, cumin, coriander, lavender, cinnamon, ginger, cloves, chopped lard, and meat with all the gristle removed and pounded and divided, and enough egg to envelop the whole. Make small round flatbreads (qursas) out of them about the size of a palm or smaller, and fry them in a pan with a lot of oil until they are browned. Then make for them a sauce of vinegar, oil, and garlic, and leave some of it without any sauce: it is very good.

¼ lb lamb	½ T cinnamon
1 t murri (see p. 5)	¼ t ginger
2 t vinegar	¼ t cloves
1 t oil	1 oz lard (lamb fat)
2 cloves garlic	2 oz meat (beef)
½ t pepper	1 egg
4 threads saffron	½ c oil for frying
¾ t cumin	3 cloves garlic
1 t coriander	2 t oil
½ t lavender	1 ½ t vinegar

Cut up lamb and mash in a mortar. Then add murri etc., garlic pounded in a mortar, finely chopped lamb fat, and beef cut up and pounded in a mortar. Mix, add an egg and mush together. Fry in a pan on medium to medium high heat until brown on both sides, turning once. To make the sauce, mash the garlic in a garlic press, combine it with the additional oil and vinegar.

To Make Isfîriyâ
Andalusian p. A-39

Pound the flesh of a leg until it is like brains. Remove the sinews and throw in pepper, half a spoon of honey, a little oil, as much as is needed, and a little water. Mix all smoothly with flour and do not neglect to pound it, and do not slacken in this, because it will cool and be ruined. Grease the pan with oil or fat, make the pounded meat into flatbreads and fry in the pan; if there be with the meat almonds or walnuts or apples, it will be superb, God willing.

12 oz lamb leg meat	1 T flour
½ t pepper	[almonds]
1 t honey	[walnuts]
2 T oil	[3 T chopped apple]
2 T water	2 T oil for frying

Either pound the meat in a mortar for a long time (20-30 minutes) until it gets mooshy, almost like clay, or run it through a food processor to the same stage. Remove any sinew, membrane, etc. you can. Add remaining ingredients, including optional walnuts, almonds, or apples. Fry on medium to medum high in a frying pan. To get them thin (¼" to ½"), put a patty down, flatten it on the pan, turn it, flatten it more with the pancake turner. Fry a minute or two on each side.

Serve with the garlic, vinegar, and oil sauce from the recipe for "A Type of Ahrash [Isfîriyâ]" (p. 96).

Simple Isfîriyâ
Andalusian p. A-1

Break however many eggs you like into a big plate and add some sourdough, dissolved with a commensurate number of eggs, and also pepper, coriander, saffron, cumin, and cinnamon. Beat it all together, then put it in a frying pan with oil over a moderate fire and make thin cakes out of it, as before.

2 eggs	½ t cumin
½ c sourdough	1 t cinnamon
2 more eggs	about 4 T oil for frying
½ t pepper	*sauce*: 1 T vinegar
½ t coriander	4 t olive oil
7 threads saffron	6 cloves garlic

Mix two of the eggs with the sourdough and beat smooth, then add to the other two eggs and the spices. Beat all together—a fork is adequate for this scale. Put 2 T oil in a medium frying pan over a medium heat, fry the batter like pancakes, about a minute on the first side and half a minute on the second, adding additional oil as needed. The sauce is from a different Isfiriya recipe (see p. 95); mix vinegar with olive oil, then crush garlic and add.

Preparing the Dish Dictated by Abu Ishaq
Andalusian p. A-41

Take meat and pound smooth until it is like marrow; put in the pot and pour over it oil and salt, clean onions and chop them, then boil and stir and throw in the pot with this some coriander seed and pepper in the amount needed, soaked garbanzos and a handful of peeled almonds pounded like salt; pour in white of egg and leave until the grease runs out, God willing.

1 lb pureed meat	½ t pepper
¼ c oil	7 ½ oz canned chickpeas
1 t salt	½ c almonds
1 onion	2 egg whites
½ t+ coriander	

Another Tabâhajiyya
Andalusian p. A-37

Cut the meat up small and fry in oil and salt; throw in some pepper, cumin, salt and a little vinegar and leave for a while and fry with fresh oil until browned. Take an egg and throw over it a spoon of vinegar and another of murri and the same of cilantro; stir it all and throw over the meat in the pan, leave and stir until it is good and serve it sprinkled with pepper, rue and cinnamon.

½ lb lamb	1 egg
1 T oil	1 T vinegar
¼ t salt	1 T murri (see p. 5)
¼ t pepper	1 T cilantro
¼ t cumin	¼ t pepper
1 T salt	½ t dried rue
1 T vinegar	¼ t cinnamon
1 T more oil	

Fry 5 minutes with ¼ t of salt. After adding pepper, etc., fry another 10 minutes

Tabâhajah from the Manuscript of Yahya b. Khalid [Good]
Tr. Charles Perry from al-Warraq

Take an earthenware pot and pour in one quarter ratl of Nabataean murri, and of good honey an ûquiyah, and beat them. When they are mixed, strain with a sieve, then put with them a dirhem of coriander, one and a half dirhams of cinnamon and two dâniqs of ground pepper. Then take two ratls of tender meat and slice fine in wide strips and put them in this condiment for a while. Then put the pot on the fire and pour in four ûquiyahs of good oil. And when the oil begins to boil, throw the strips in the pot with the condiment and two dâniqs of milled salt. Then cook the meat until it is done and the condiment is dried. Then take it off the fire and cut up on it some cilantro, and rue, and some green mustard, and serve. And it [can be] a Tabâhajah with asafoetida, if you wish. [for units see p. 6.]

¼ c murri (see p. 5)	2 ½ T cilantro
4 t honey	1 T rue
scant ½ t coriander	3 T mustard greens
⅝ t cinnamon	[asafoetida]
⅛ t pepper	⅓ c olive oil
1 lb trimmed lamb	⅛ t salt

Beat murri and honey in a bowl, add spices and stir well. Cut meat into thin strips, removing most fat, mix into the marinade and let sit for an hour and a half. Chop herbs, removing stems. Heat oil in frying pan on high heat until a few bubbles start to come up, put in meat and marinade, and add salt. Let come to a boil and turn down to medium/medium high heat. Cook, stirring, about 15 minutes, until sauce is mostly cooked down. Remove from heat and serve with herbs on top.

Note: The quantity above is half the original recipe; all quantities are specified in the original except for the herbs at the end. The Islamic measures could be either weight or volume measures; I have assumed volumes in calculating amounts.

Recipe for Fried Tafâyâ, Which Was Known in Morocco as Tâhashast
Andalusian p. A-21 (Good and simple)

Get young, fat meat and cut it in little pieces. Fry it in a clean pot with salt, pepper, coriander, a little onion, a spoonful of oil and a little water. Stir it until the water is gone, the oil hot, the meat done and browned. This is similar to the preceding.

1 lb meat (lamb)	¼ c chopped onion
⅛ t salt	2 T oil (olive)
½ t pepper	1 T water
1 ½ t coriander	

Cut meat into ½" cubes. Put in pot and heat medium low 10 minutes, then on high 5 minutes to cook off juice while stirring, cook another 3 minutes and remove from heat.

A Roast of Meat
Andalusian p. A-38 (Good)

Roast salted, well-marbled meat [cut up] like fingertips, and put in a pot spices, onion, salt, oil and soaked garbanzos. Cook until done and add the roast meat; cover the contents of the pot with cilantro and sprinkle with pepper and cinnamon; and if you add whole pine nuts or walnuts in place of garbanzos, it will be good.

1 ½ lb lamb or beef	¼ t cumin
¾ lb onion	1 t salt
2 15 oz cans chickpeas	3 T olive oil
¼ t black pepper	¼ c cilantro
½ t cinnamon	⅛ t more pepper
½ t coriander	¼ t more cinnamon

Note: an earlier recipe in the same book calls for spices and then specifies which ones: "all the spices, pepper, cinnamon, dried coriander and cumin."

Roast meat and cut into ¼" by ½" pieces. Slice onions. Put chickpeas, onion, spices, salt and oil in a pot and cook over moderate heat, stirring, for 10 minutes, turning down the heat toward the end as it gets dry; add meat and cook one minute, add cilantro and cook another minute, and turn off heat. Sprinkle with pepper and cinnamon and serve.

Cooked Fried Chicken
Andalusian p. A-3

Cut up the chicken, making two pieces from each limb; fry it with plenty of fresh oil; then take a pot and throw in four spoonfuls of vinegar and two of murri naqî' and the same amount of oil, pepper, cilantro, cumin, a little garlic and saffron. Put the pot on the fire and when it has boiled, put in the fried chicken spoken of before, and when it is done, then empty it out and present it.

1 chicken, 2 ½ lb	1 t pepper
¼ c oil	4 sprigs cilantro ~¹⁄₁₆ oz
¼ c vinegar	3 threads saffron
2 T murri (see p. 5)	¼ t crushed garlic
2 T oil	¼ t cumin

Cut up chicken and brown it in ¼ c olive oil over medium low heat for 10 minutes. Set chicken aside. Add to a large pot vinegar, murri, 2 T oil, pepper, cilantro, saffron, crushed garlic, cumin, and heat the pot on medium for 3 minutes. Add chicken and simmer on low for 25 minutes with the lid on, stirring often. Baste with the liquid five minutes before it is done.

Mufarraka
al-Baghdadi p. 201

Take chickens' livers and crops, wash, and boil in water with a little salt: then take out, and cut up small. Mix with yolks of eggs, adding the usual seasonings as required: then fry in a frying-pan in sesame-oil, stirring all the time. If desired sour, sprinkle with a little pure lemon-juice. If desired plain, use neither lemon nor egg.

¼ t salt	1 ½ t cumin
14 oz chicken gizzards	1 ½ t cinnamon
14 oz chicken livers	¾ t pepper
8 egg yolks	2 T sesame oil
1 ½ t coriander	¼ c lemon juice

Bring 3 c water to a boil with ⅛ t salt, add gizzards and simmer 50 minutes. Near the end of this time, bring another 3 c of water and ⅛ t salt to a boil and cook livers in it 3 minutes. Drain both, cut up small (½"x½" pieces), put in a bowl and mix with egg yolks and spices. Heat oil and fry mixture about 4 minutes, sprinkle with lemon juice. Serve. The spices chosen are the combination al-Baghdadi most commonly uses.

Dishes with Legumes

Cooked Dish of Lentils
al-Andalusi no. 377 (Good)

Wash lentils and put them to cook in a pot with sweet water, oil, pepper, coriander and cut onion. When they are cooked throw in salt, a little saffron and vinegar; break three eggs, leave for a while on the flame and later retire the pot. Other times cook without onion. If you wish cook it with Egyptian beans pricked into which have been given a boil. Or better with dissolved yeast over a gentle fire. When the lentils begin to thicken add good butter or sweet oil, bit by bit, alike until it gets absorbed, until they are sufficiently cooked and have enough oil. Then retire it from the flame and sprinkle with pepper.

½ lb onions	¾ t salt
1 ½ c dried lentils	12 threads saffron
2 ¼ c water	2 T vinegar
1 ½ T oil	4 eggs
⅜ t pepper	more pepper
1 ½ t coriander	[Egyptian beans]
4 T butter (or oil)	[yeast]

Slice onions. Put lentils, water, oil, pepper, coriander and onion in a pot, bring to a boil, and turn down to a bare simmer. Cook covered 50 minutes, stirring periodically. Add butter or oil and cook while stirring for about 5 minutes. Add salt, saffron (crushed into 1 t water) and vinegar, and bring back to a boil. Put eggs on top, cover pot and keep lentils at a simmer; stir cautiously every few minutes in order to scrape the bottom of the pot without stirring in the eggs. We find that if the heat is off, the eggs don't cook; if the heat is up at medium, the eggs cook but the lentils start to stick to the pot. A larger quantity might hold enough heat to cook the eggs without leaving it on the flame. When the eggs are cooked, sprinkle with a little more pepper and serve. Makes 5 ¼ c.

A Muzawwara (Vegetarian Dish) Beneficial for Tertian Fevers and Acute Fevers
Andalusian p. A-52

Take boiled peeled lentils and wash in hot water several times; put in the pot and add water without covering them; cook and then throw in pieces of gourd, or the stems [ribs] of Swiss chard, or of lettuce and its tender sprigs, or the flesh of cucumber or melon, and vinegar, coriander seed, a little cumin, Chinese cinnamon, saffron and two ûqiyas of fresh oil; balance with a little salt and cook. Taste, and if its flavor is pleasingly balanced between sweet and sour, [good;] and if not, reinforce until it is equalized, according to taste, and leave it to lose its heat until it is cold and then serve.

2 c lentils	1 t salt
5 c water	one of:
¾ t coriander	1 ½ lb gourd (see p. 4)
¾ t cumin	1 lb chard or beet leaves
1 ½ t cinnamon	1 lb lettuce
6 threads saffron	2 8" cucumbers
¼ c vinegar	melon (?)
¼ c oil	

Boil lentils about 40 minutes until they start to get mushy. Add spices, vinegar, oil and salt. Add one of the vegetables; leafy vegetables should be torn up, gourd or cucumbers are cut into bite-sized pieces and cooked about 10-15 minutes before being added to lentils. Cook lettuce or chard version for about 10 minutes, until leaves are soft. Cook gourd or cucumber version about 20 minutes. Be careful not to burn during the final cooking.

Adas
Ibn al-Mabrad p. 21

The best way of cooking lentils is to crush them and then cook them and put with them chard and taro. When it is done, sumac, fried onion, parsley, vinegar and oil are put with it.

1 c lentils	2 T parsley (chopped)
2 lb taro	1 T vinegar
½ lb chard	1 T oil
½ lb onion	¾ t salt
1 T oil	2 t dried sumac

Grind the lentils in a mortar or a spice/coffee grinder (a gadget like a miniature food processor), then simmer them in 4 ½ c water about 1 hour. Simmer the taro about 15 minutes, drain, peel, and slice. Rinse and chop the chard. At the end of the hour add the taro and chard. Simmer together about another ½ hour. Chop and fry the onion in a little oil. At the end of the half hour, add onion, parsley, vinegar, oil, salt and sumac. Stir together and serve. Taro is sometimes available in Chinese or Indian grocery stores.

Adasiya
al-Bagdadi p. 45

Cut up the meat, and dissolve the tail as usual. Put the meat into the oil, and fry lightly until browned: then throw in a little salt, cummin, and brayed dry coriander, and cover with water. When nearly cooked, add beet washed and cut into pieces four fingers long. When thoroughly boiling, add as required lentils, cleaned and washed, and keep a steady fire going until the lentils are cooked. When set smooth and definitely cooked, add as required fine-bruised garlic, stirring with a ladle. Then leave over a slow fire: and remove. When serving, squeeze over it lemon juice.

1 ½ lb lamb	1 t coriander
½ lb beet greens	2 ½ c water
"tail": 1 oz lamb fat (p. 4)	1 ¼ c lentils
¼ t salt	6 cloves garlic
½ t cumin	2 T lemon juice

Cut up meat into ½" cubes. Wash beet greens and cut into 2" pieces, including stems. Render out fat to get ~2 T melted fat for "tail" (p. 4) and fry meat for 5 minutes on medium high until brown. Add salt and spices, cover with water. Bring to a boil, cooking 8 minutes, add greens and cook 3 minutes, add lentils. Turn down to low and cook 45 minutes. Crush garlic with a garlic press and add, cook another 15 minutes. Squeeze lemon juice over the dish and serve.

Fuliyyah
Ibn al-Mabrad p. 21

Meat is boiled and fava beans are fried in fat, then you put them with the meat and broth. Then you put pounded thyme, coriander and garlic with it. Then you break an egg on it and sprinkle pepper and coriander seed on it. It is covered until it thickens and taken off.

1 c dry fava beans	1 ½ T cilantro
4-6 T fat	1 large clove garlic
¾ lb lamb	2 eggs
2 c water	½ t black pepper
2 t fresh thyme	½ t coriander
or 1 t dry	

Soak the beans overnight; they should make about 2 ½ c soaked. I expect 2 ½ c of fresh favas would work too. Render the fat from about 6 oz of lamb fat, giving 4-6 T of liquid fat; it would probably also work using olive oil. Fry beans for about 10-15 minutes in the fat (just enough time for beans to absorb most of the fat), then add to the meat, which has been boiling the same length of time in 2 c water. Put thyme, cilantro, and peeled garlic in a mortar and mash. Add to pot. Simmer for about another 45 minutes. Stir frequently, scraping the bottom, after adding the beans (medium heat at most), since otherwise it can easily scorch. Beat two eggs together and stir into the bubbling pot. Add pepper and coriander, then let sit on low flame a few minutes while the egg sets. Serve. This is good but rather spicy; those who do not like spicy dishes might try using half the quantity of pepper and garlic.

An alternative interpretation is that you are poaching an egg on top of the Fuliyyah. If you do it that way, start with only 1 ¾ c of water so that the Fuliyyah will come out thicker.

Dishes with Grains, Bread, or Pasta

Tharid
Ibn al-Mabrad p. 18

Meat is boiled and bread is moistened with the broth. Yoghurt, garlic and mint are put with it and the meat is put with it. Likewise there is a tharid without meat.

1 ½ lb meat	4 large cloves
3 ½ c water	8 sprigs mint (leaves only)
4 slices bread	½ c yogurt

Cut meat into bite-sized pieces and boil in water about 30-40 minutes, by which time the broth is down to about one cup. Crush bread into broth, chop garlic and mint, and add them and the yogurt to the bread mixture and serve the meat over it.

Tharda of Zabarbada
Andalusian p. A-42

Take a clean pot and put in it water, two spoons of oil, pepper, cilantro and a pounded onion; put it on the fire and when the spices have boiled, take bread and crumble it, throw it in the pot and stir smoothly while doing so; pour out of the pot onto a platter and knead this into a tharda and pour clarified butter over it, and if you do not have this, use oil.

2 T cilantro	¼ t pepper
4 oz onion	1 c breadcrumbs
2 c water	2 T ghee or oil
2 T oil	

Wash and chop cilantro. Slice onion and pound in a mortar (or run through the food processor). Put water, oil, pepper, cilantro, and onion in pot and bring to a boil. Add breadcrumbs, stirring constantly, and heat for 5 minutes, then pour onto platter. Top with oil or ghee; most people preferred ghee.

This is a fairly plain dish, rather like bread stuffing. If you particularly like cilantro, you may want to double it. For more elaborate thardas or tharids with meat, see nearby recipes.

White Tharîdah of al Rashid
Tr. Charles Perry from al-Warraq

Take a chicken and joint it, or meat of a kid or lamb, and clean it and throw it in a pot, and throw on it soaked chickpeas, clean oil, galingale, cinnamon sticks, and a little salt. And when it boils, skim it. Take fresh milk and strain it over the pot and throw in onion slices and boiled carrots. And when it boils well, take peeled almonds and pound them fine. Break over them five eggs and mix with wine vinegar. Then throw in the pot and add coriander, a little pepper and a bit of cumin and arrange it and leave on the fire, and serve, God willing.

2 ¾ lb lamb	1 c milk
or 2 ½ lb chicken	1 ¼ lbs onion
2 15 oz cans chickpeas	5 oz almonds
2 T olive oil	5 eggs
¾ t galingale	1 ½ T wine vinegar
1 oz stick cinnamon	1 t coriander
1 T salt	1 ¾ t pepper
~5 c water or less	1 ¼ t cumin
1 ¼ lbs carrots	

Cut up lamb or chicken, put it, chickpeas (with liquid), oil, galingale, cinnamon sticks and salt in a large pot with as little water as will cover, boil 15 minutes. Meanwhile boil carrots separately; drain them. Add milk, sliced onion and carrots to the pot, boil another 15 minutes. Grind almonds, combine with eggs, and vinegar; add this mixture and spices to the pot. Cook another five minutes, serve.

An alternative interpretation of the recipe omits the water, so that the meat is cooked in the oil until partially cooked, then the milk, onions, and carrots are added.

Tharids are normally made with bread or breadcrumbs, and there is a Tradition that tharid was the Prophet's favorite dish. Bread may have been good enough for the Prophet, but not for Haroun al Rashid; this version uses ground almonds instead.

Al-Ghassani's Tharda
Andalusian A-42

Take fat meat and cut it up, arrange in a large pot and throw in coriander seed, chopped onion, cilantro, caraway, pepper, soaked garbanzos, three whole eggs and enough water to cover the meat and salt; when the meat is done, reduce the fire below it and throw in two dirhams of saffron; when you see that it is colored, remove part of the sauce, leaving enough to cover the meat; boil the meat with the saffron and then take off the fire, strain the sauce and leave in the pot, take one kail of sauce and three of honey, then take the pot to the fire and bring it to the boil three times with the honey and the sauce. Then take best white bread, crumble it and sieve the crumbs, cover the pot with them and put in it fat and pepper; pour into the platter over bread soaked in the broth and serve, God willing.

18 oz lamb	1 ⅝ c water
1 lb onion	½ t salt
½ t coriander	⅛ t saffron
2 T cilantro	6 T honey
½ t caraway	¼ lb bread
½ t pepper	3 T melted lamb fat
2 15 oz cans chickpeas	½ t+ pepper
3 eggs	11 slices bread

Cut lamb in 1" cubes; combine lamb, onion, etc, in pot, breaking the eggs in whole to poach in the pot. Simmer about 30 minutes (until the lamb is cooked), mostly uncovered, stirring occasionally. Lower heat, add saffron, simmer 10 minutes, stir a little to spread the saffron. Turn off the heat, remove 2 T of sauce, mix it with honey and return the mixture to the pot. Bring back to a boil, then convert ¼ lb of bread to crumbs—you may find a food processor useful—run them through a strainer and stir them in. Add fat and pepper. Arrange sliced bread, toasted if you like, on a large platter (10-12"). Spoon liquid part of the broth onto the bread, then ladle everything on top.

Tharid that the People of Ifriqiyya (Tunisia) Call Fatîr
Andalusian p. A-55

It is one of the best of their dishes. Among them this fatir is made with fat chicken, while others make it with the meat of a fat lamb. Take whatever of the two you have on hand, clean and cut up. Put it in the pot with salt, onion, pepper, coriander seed and oil, and cook it until it is done; then take out the meat from the pot and let the broth remain, and add to it both clarified and fresh butter, and fry [or boil] it. Then fabricate crumbs of a fatir that have been prepared from well-made layered thin flatbread cooked in the tajine with sourdough, and repeatedly moisten the dish [evidently, the dish in which the crumbs are] until it's right. Then spread on it the meat of that chicken, after frying it in the pan with fresh oil or butter and dot it with egg yolks, olives and chopped almonds; sprinkle it with cinnamon and serve it.

2 ¼ lbs chicken	¼ c almonds
or lamb	2 T ghee
1 c water	2 T butter
½ t salt	½ recipe "folded bread"
½ lb onion	(p. 76)
½ t pepper	or ½ lb pita
1 t coriander	3 T more oil or butter
2 T oil	olives
4 eggs	½ t cinnamon

Combine meat, water, salt, sliced onion, pepper, coriander, and oil in a pot, simmer about an hour. Hard boil eggs and remove the yolks, chop almonds coarsely. Take the meat out, add 2 T each ghee and butter to the broth, boil about 5 minutes. Crumble the flatbread, line the bottom of a pot with it, gradually add about 1 ½ - 2 c of the broth mixture—as much as the crumbs will absorb.

The chicken at this point is falling off the bones; let it. Put the meat in a frying pan over a medium heat and fry in butter, using a total of about 3 T. Put the meat on top of the crumbled flatbread, dot it with yolks from hard boiled eggs and olives, sprinkle on chopped almonds, sprinkle with cinnamon, serve.

Tharîda in the Style of the People of Bijaya (Bougie, a city in Algeria) Which They Call the Shâshiyya of Ibn al-Wadi'.
Andalusian p. A-55

Take the meat of fat spring lamb, from its flanks, its chest and its fat part; cut it up and put it in a pot with salt, onion, pepper and coriander seed; put it on a moderate fire and when it is almost done, add to it lettuce, spinach, fennel "eyes" and tender turnips. When all is ready, add peeled green fava beans and fresh cilantro; when it is finished cooking, moisten with it the tharid and arrange on it that meat, the vegetables and the beans; put on top of the tharid, on the highest part, a small amount of butter that will pour down the sides among the vegetables. For that reason it has been likened to the shashiyya of Ibn al-Wadi, as if that white butter were the cotton [tassel] of the shashiyya,[a fez with a white tassel, characteristic of southern Morocco in our times (CP)] that falls all over.

Comments from other recipes in this book on how to make the tharid itself: "and moisten with it a tharid crumbled from white bread crumbs and leavened semolina well kneaded and baked." "A tharid of the crumb of leavened bread..." "Then crumble enough clean white bread and moisten it with the sauce until it soaks it up."

1 ¼ lb lamb	¼ c spinach
¼ lb onion	¼ c lettuce
2 ½ c water	1 t fennel
1 ½ t salt	¼ c green fava beans
½ t pepper	1 ½ t cilantro
1 ½ t coriander	8 slices bread = ~7 oz
6 oz turnips	2 T butter

Cut meat into 1" to 1 ½" cubes, chop onion. Boil meat, onion, salt and spices together over moderate heat until meat is tender. Peel and chop turnips, add to meat and cook until about three quarters done. Tear or chop spinach and lettuce, chop fennel finely, add to meat, cook. Shell beans, chop cilantro and add. Tear up bread, mix with the broth from the meat, put on platter and serve meat and vegetables over it, and put butter on top. Total cooking time 1 hour 45 minutes, more or less.

Tharda of Isfunj with Milk
Andalusian p. A-27

Make isfunj from white flour and make it well, and fry it. Add to it while kneading as many eggs as it will bear. When you are finished making it and frying it, cook as much fresh milk as is needed and beat in it eggwhites and fine white flour, and stir carefully until cooked. Then cut the isfunj into small pieces with scissors and moisten with the milk until saturated. Then melt butter and throw on the tharid, and sprinkle with sugar and use, God willing. [see quotes from isfunj recipe p. 119]

⅛ c sourdough	2 c milk
⅜ c water	3 T more flour
2 c flour	3 egg whites
1 ½ eggs	¼ lb butter
oil for frying	2 T sugar

Dissolve sourdough in water and stir it into the flour, then add eggs, stir and knead to a reasonably uniform dough. Let it rise four hours in a warm place. Make into thick patties about 3" in diameter and ½" thick; fry in about ½" of hot oil. Cut patties up into small pieces with shears.

Put the milk on a medium heat, stir in flour and beaten egg white with a whisk. Beat frequently as you bring it slowly to a simmer, simmer for about 5 minutes. Stir in the cut up isfunj, add melted butter, sprinkle on sugar, and serve.

Tharda of Lamb with Garbanzos
Andalusian p. A-31

Cut up lamb in large pieces and put with it spices, soaked garbanzos, oil and salt. When it has fried, pour in enough water to cover. And when it is about done, throw in orach [a leafy vegetable related to spinach]. When it is done, throw in fresh cheese cut up in pieces like fingertips, and break eggs into it and crumble bread in it, and sprinkle it with pepper and cinnamon, God willing.

⅞ lb lamb	1 c water
"spices":	orach: 1 lb spinach
¼ t pepper	14 oz fresh cheese
½ t cinnamon	3 eggs
¼ t cumin	1 c bread crumbs
15 oz can chickpeas	⅛ t pepper
¼ t salt	¼ t cinnamon
2 T oil	

Note: the cheese we used for this was a "sweet cheese" (i.e. not salty) fron an Iranian grocery.

Saute the lamb, spices, drained chickpeas and salt in the olive oil about 10 minutes, until the meat is browned. Add water and cook about 20 minutes. Rinse spinach and cut in half. Add the spinach, cook about 5 minutes, stirring enough to get spinach down into water so that it wilts. Cut the cheese into small rectangles (about ¾"x¼"), add cheese, eggs and bread crumbs. Cook a few minutes, long enough to melt cheese, sprinkle pepper and cinnamon on top, and serve.

Tharîda with Lamb and Spinach, Moist Cheese and Butter
Andalusian p. A-55

This used to be made in Cordoba in the spring by the doctor Abu al-Hasan al-Bunani, God have mercy on him and pardon us and him. Take the meat of a fat lamb, cut it and put it in the pot with salt, onion juice, pepper, coriander seed, caraway and oil; put it to the fire and when it has finished, put in it chopped and washed spinach in sufficient quantity, rubbed moist cheese and butter. When it has finished, take the pot off the fire and moisten with butter. Let there be crumbs of bread moderately leavened, and put your meat on them, and if he (God have mercy on him) lacked lamb meat, he would make a tharîda of spinach, moist cheese, butter and the previously mentioned spices and eggs instead of meat.

1 lb lamb	1 T olive oil
¼ t salt	10 oz spinach
2 t onion juice	½ lb fresh cheese
¼ t pepper	1 T butter
1 t coriander	3 7" pita breads (6 oz)
½ t caraway	1 T more butter

Cut lamb to bite sized pieces. Put it in the pot with salt, onion juice, spices, and oil, heat through, turn down to a simmer, and cook for 15 minutes covered. Turn up heat and cook another 5 minutes uncovered, stirring periodically to cook off most of the liquid. While the lamb is cooking, wash and chop spinach, crumble cheese. Add spinach, cheese, and 1 T butter to the lamb and cook 10 minutes. Tear up bread and put on a serving platter. Add remaining butter to lamb, pour it over the bread, and serve.

We used fresh cheese from an Iranian grocery; other fresh crumbly cheeses, such as queso fresco or some kinds of farmer's cheese should also work, although how salty the cheese is will affect how much salt you want to put in.

White Tharîda with Onion, called Kâfûriyya (Camphor-White)
Andalusian p. A-55

This tharid is made with mutton or with chicken and much clarified butter. Take young fat meat, cut it up and put it in the pot with salt, pepper, coriander seed, oil, mild clarified or fresh butter. When it has fried in its fat and its spices, throw into it some juice of pounded, squeezed onions, about a ratl or more, so that the meat is covered abundantly and finishes cooking; when it is done, break the necessary amount of whole eggs and soak with them a tharid of crumbs of white leavened bread or leavened semolina, and with clarified butter kneaded in it like ka'k (p. 75) dough, and don't beat it much. When the tharida absorbs and is level, put its meat on top of it and serve it. There are those who make it with pounded cut large onions.

1 lb boneless chicken thighs	1 T butter
1 t salt	1 lb onion
⅜ t pepper	⅜ lb bread
⅜ t coriander	2 eggs
2 T oil	5 T ghee

Cut up chicken in pieces an inch or two across, combine with salt, pepper, coriander, oil and butter, cook at medium high for 5-10 minutes until chicken appears cooked. Chop onion and process to mush in a food processor, strain out the juice and add juice to the pot, simmer for about 25 minutes. Use a pot small enough so that the onion covers the meat—for this quantity a 1 quart pot works.

Tear up the bread then process it in a food processor, stir in the beaten eggs, knead in melted ghee, spread out in the serving dish. Dump on it the solids from the pot, serve.

Harisah
Ibn al-Mabrad p. 22

Meat is boiled, then wheat is put on it until it gives up its starch. Then the meat is plucked off the bones and pounded [and returned to the porridge]. Some add milk.

½ lb lamb	1 c milk
2 c water	[1 ½ T lamb fat]
[½ stick cinnamon]	[¼ t cumin]
[¾ t salt]	[½ t cinnamon]
5 oz of cracked wheat	[½ T lemon]

Cut lamb into a few large pieces, put it and the water in a pot, add stick cinnamon and salt. Bring to a boil. Add the cracked wheat. Cook about ½ hour. Remove the lamb (that is why it is in only a few pieces). Cut the lamb up, pound in a mortar almost to a paste, then put it back in. Add milk. Cook another hour at a low temperature.

Render out lamb fat ("tail" in the original; see p. 4), sprinkle it, cumin, cinnamon, and lemon over the harisa when you serve it (this is an addition from the al-Baghdadi version of the dish; Ibn al-Mabrad gives very little information on spicing).

Rishta
al-Baghdadi p.45 (Good)

Cut fat meat into middling pieces and put into the saucepan, with a covering of water. Add cinnamon-bark, a little salt, a handful of peeled chickpeas, and half a handful of lentils. Boil until cooked: then add more water, and bring thoroughly to the boil. Now add spaghetti (which is made by kneading flour and water well, then rolling out fine and cutting into thin threads four fingers long). Put over the fire and cook until set to a smooth consistency. When it has settled over a gentle fire for an hour, remove.

1 lb lamb	6 T canned chickpeas
4 c water	3 T lentils
½ stick cinnamon	2 c flour
1 t salt	⅜-½ c water

Cut up meat, combine it with water, cinnamon, salt, chickpeas, and lentils, simmer about half an hour. Mix flour with about ½ c cold water (just enough to make an unsticky dough). Knead thoroughly, roll out, cut into thin strips. Add to pot, simmer another ½ hour being careful not to let it stick to the bottom and scorch, serve. A favorite of ours.

Salma
Ibn al-Mabrad p. 20

Dough is taken and twisted and cut in small pieces and struck like a coin with a finger, and it is cooked in water until done. Then yoghurt is put with it and meat is fried with onion for it and mint and garlic are put with it.

1 c flour	½ c plain yogurt
about ¼ c water	1 T mint
¼ lb onion	2-4 cloves crushed garlic
5 oz lamb	[½ t salt]
½ oz lamb ("tail" p. 4)	

Knead flour and water to a smooth dough. Divide it in about 8 equal portions. Roll each portion between your palms into a string about ½ inch in diameter, twist it a little, then cut it in about ¼" slices. Dump slices in a little flour to keep them from sticking. Squeeze each between your fingers into a flat, roughly round, coin shaped piece. Boil in 1 quart slightly salted water about 10 minutes.

About the same time you put the pasta on to boil, fry the onions and lamb, both cut small, in the tail (i.e. lamb fat—p. 4) or other oil. Drain the pasta, combine all ingredients, and serve.

Shushbarak
Ibn al-Mabrad p. 20

You take minced meat and stuff it in dough rolled out like cut tutmaj. It is cooked in water until done. Then take it off the fire and put yoghurt, garlic and mint with it.

about 1 lb meat (lamb)	4 oz yogurt
2 c flour	1 clove garlic
¼ c water	1 sprig mint
3 eggs	

We tried both ground and minced meat; both worked. Knead together flour, water and eggs for the dough, roll it out thin and make the shushbarak like ravioli, stuffing them with the meat, then boil 5-10 minutes. For sauce, blend together the yogurt, garlic, and mint in a food processor; a mortar and pestle would also work. As an experiment, we tried mixing ⅓ c of minced lamb with ¼ t cinnamon, ⅛ t ginger, and ⅛ t coriander as filling; that also came out well.

Shurba
al-Baghdadi p. 44

Cut fat meat into middling pieces. Dissolve fresh tail, and throw away the sediment. Put the meat into the oil, and stir until browned. Cover with lukewarm water, and add a little salt, a handful of peeled chickpeas, small pieces of cinnamon-bark, and some sprigs of dry dill. When the meat is cooked, throw in dry coriander, ginger and pepper, brayed fine. Add more lukewarm water, and put over a hot fire until thoroughly boiling: then remove the dill from the saucepan. Take cleaned rice, wash several times, and put into the saucepan as required, leaving it over the fire until the rice is cooked. Then remove from the fire. Do not leave so long that the rice becomes hard set. If desired, add some cabobs of minced meat.

2 T lamb fat	3 3" sticks cinnamon
2 lb boneless lamb	2 t dry coriander
3 c water	½ t ginger
2 t dry dill	1 t pepper
2 t salt	9 c more water
15 oz can chickpeas	4 ½ c rice

meatballs (optional):

¾ lb ground lamb	¼ t ginger
1 t cinnamon	½ t coriander

If you want to make it with meatballs, mix the ground lamb and spices and make small meatballs. Put fat (the "tail" of the original recipe—p. 4) in pot and render out about 2 T. Cut up meat and brown it (and the meatballs) in fat about 5 minutes, then cover with 3 c water. Tie the dill up in a little piece of cheesecloth; put salt, chickpeas, cinnamon, and dill in with the meat and simmer 10 minutes. Add coriander, ginger, pepper, and remaining water and bring to a boil. Remove dill. Add rice, bring back to a boil, turn down to a simmer and cook covered 20 minutes, stirring occasionally.

Labaniyyah
Ibn al-Mabrad p. 22

Meat is boiled, then leeks are put in and yoghurt is dissolved and rice is put with it. Some people put the yoghurt first, then the meat then the rice.

¾ lb boned lamb	1 ¼ c rice
1 ¾ cup of water	[2 t cumin]
2 leeks = 2 c sliced	[2 t coriander]
1 ¼ c yogurt	[1 t cinnamon]
½ t salt	

Cut meat into bite-sized pieces. Boil meat for 15 minutes in water at low heat, covered. Add leeks, yogurt and salt. Add rice and spices. Simmer (again covered) until rice is done (about an hour). The spices are based on similar recipes in al-Bagdadi, one of which is on page 96 above.

Rizz Hulw
Ibn al-Mabrad p.19

Rice is put in boiling water until it swells and is nearly done. Then a sweet ingredient is put with it until it thickens, and it is sprinkled with ginger and taken off the fire.

¾ c rice
1 ¼ c water
3 T honey
¼ t ginger

Cook rice in water about 15 minutes then add honey, cook another 15 minutes. Add ginger.

A Recipe for Rice Porridge (Harisat al-Aruzz)
al-Warraq p. 256

Wash fat meat and put it in a pot. Pour water on it and then add some salt. Let it cook until meat disintegrates and falls off the bones. Put the pot off the heat. Take meat out of the pot and pound it in a mortar and pestle if it is still chunky.

Next, pick over white rice and wash it three times. Pour strained milk on the meat broth and bring it to a boil. Add the rice and continue cooking until it is done. Return the pounded meat and keep on stirring until rice grains are crushed. Pour into it butter, clarified butter, a mixture of equal parts of rendered fat and sesame oil, or milk.

Beat the mixture continuously until it is completely crushed. Keep on stirring until it looks like natif (p. 122) and meat looks like threads integrated into the rice.

Serve the porridge with a bowlful of murri, God willing.

1 lb lamb
5 ½ c water
t+ salt
2 ½ c rice
1 c milk
6 T butter

Wash meat in lukewarm water, put it to simmer in 5 ½ c of water with a pinch of salt, simmer 2 hrs 25 minutes, cut up, then simmer another five minutes. Remove meat from broth, mush it in a mortar for about 5-10 minutes.

Cook the rice for half an hour in 4 c of the broth from the meat plus 1 c of milk, adding the meat after about 15 minutes, then later the butter and salt. Stir forcibly to mush the rice and meat together. Serve with murri for your guests to add. We have not tried the other versions.

(There is a harisa recipe on p. 105.)

Preparation of Rice Cooked Over Water [a double boiler method]
Andalusian A-56

Take rice washed with hot water and put it in the pot and throw to it fresh, pure milk fresh from milking; put this pot in a copper kettle that has water up to the halfway point or a little more; arrange the copper kettle on the fire and the pot with the rice and milk well-settled in it so that it doesn't tip and is kept from the fire. Leave it to cook without stirring, and when the milk has dried up, add more of the same kind of milk so that the rice dissolves and is ready; add to it fresh butter and cook the rice with it; when the rice is done and dissolved, take off the pot and rub it with a spoon until it breaks up; then throw it on the platter and level it, dust it with ground sugar, cinnamon and butter and use. With this same recipe one cooks itriyya, fidaush and tharid al-laban [milk tharid].

1 c rice
3 ½ c milk
2 T butter
2 T more butter
½ t cinnamon
1 ½ T sugar

Bring water in the bottom of double boiler to a boil. Wash rice in hot water. Combine rice with 1 c milk in the top of the double boiler. Cook for about two to two and a half hours, gradually adding more milk as the milk in it is absorbed. When the last addition has been absorbed and the rice is soft, add 2 T butter, stir it in, and continue cooking for another ten minutes. Remove from heat, and stir vigorously to reduce the rice to something close to a uniform mush. Melt remaining butter; mix cinnamon and sugar. Spread the rice flat on a plate, pour the melted butter over it and sprinkle with cinnamon sugar.

Oven Dishes and Roasting

The making of Badî'i, the Remarkable Dish
Andalusian p. A-9

Take the meat of a very plump lamb and cut it in small pieces and put them in a pot with a little salt, a piece of onion, coriander, lavender, saffron and oil, and cook it halfway. Then take fresh cheese, not too soft in order that it will not fall apart, cut it with a knife into sheets approximately the size of the palm, place them in a dish, color them with saffron, sprinkle them with lavender and turn them until they are colored on all sides. Place them with the cooked meat in the pot or in a tajine and add eggs beaten with saffron, lavender and cinnamon, as necessary, and bury in it whole egg yolks and cover with plenty of oil and with the fat of the cooked meat. Place it in the oven and leave it until the sauce is dry and the meat is completely cooked and the upper part turns red [the translator suggests the alternative "browns" but it turns red in our experience]. Take it out, leave it a while until its heat passes and it is cool, and then use it.

1 lb lamb	6 oz cheese
½ t dried lavender	½ t lavender
4 threads saffron	3 threads saffron
¼ t salt	½ t more lavender
½ small onion (2 oz)	2 beaten eggs
½ t ground coriander	½ t cinnamon
2 T olive oil	4 whole egg yolks
6 more threads saffron	2 T olive oil

Cut lamb into ½" cubes. Grind ½ t lavender and 4 threads saffron in a mortar. Combine lamb, salt, onion, coriander, lavender, saffron and oil and simmer in 1 c water for 10 minutes. Grind the second lot of saffron (6 threads) in a mortar, adding 1 T water. Cut cheese—we used mozzarella—in slices, paint them with the saffron water, sprinkle with ½ t more lavender. Drain meat and separate the fat from the broth. Put meat in the pot, cover with cheese slices. Grind 3 threads saffron and ½ t lavender in a mortar, beat with eggs and cinnamon. Pour eggs over meat and cheese. Place whole egg yolks on top, pour over everything the fat (I had about 3 T) plus the second 2 T of oil. Bake at 350° for 45 minutes, by which time the top should have turned reddish brown. Let cool, then serve.

Recipe for Thûmiyya, a Garlicky Dish
Andalusian p. A-8

Take a plump hen and take out what is inside it, clean that and leave aside. Then take four ûqiyas of peeled garlic and pound them until they are like brains, and mix with what comes out of the interior of the chicken. Fry it in enough oil to cover, until the smell of garlic comes out. Mix this with the chicken in a clean pot with salt, pepper, cinnamon, lavender, ginger, cloves, saffron, peeled whole almonds, both pounded and whole, and a little murri naqî'. Seal the pot with dough, place it in the oven and leave it until it is done. Then take it out and open the pot, pour its contents in a clean dish and an aromatic scent will come forth from it and perfume the area. This chicken was made for the Sayyid Abu al-Hasan and much appreciated.

5 oz of garlic	1 t ginger
1 hen	¼ t cloves
6 T oil	15 threads saffron
½ t salt	½ c whole almonds
½ t pepper	⅞ c crushed almonds
1 t cinnamon	¼ c murri (see p. 5)
2 t lavender	~1 c flour + water

Crush garlic. Fry garlic and giblets from chicken in oil on medium heat for about 15 minutes. Put all ingredients except dough in the pot, crushing the saffron into a few T of water to extract flavor and color. Mix flour and water to make the dough, roll it into a strip, put it on the edge of the dish and jam the lid onto it to seal the lid on the pot. Bake at 350° for 1 hour.

Charles Perry, who translated this, notes that four ûqiyas of garlic (⅓ of a pound) works out pretty close to the 40 cloves called for in a famous Provençal dish. "Leave out the spices and the almonds, and you'd about have poulet à 40 gousses d'ail."

Mahshi, a Stuffed Dish
Andalusian p. A-9

It is made with a roast hen, or with young pigeons or doves, or small birds, or with the meat of a young lamb. Take what you have of this, clean it, cut it up and put it in a pot with salt, a piece of onion, pepper, coriander, cinnamon, saffron, some murri naqi' and plenty of oil. Put this on the fire and when it is done and the broth has formed, take out the meat from the pot and leave it aside. Take as much as necessary of grated white breadcrumbs and stir them in a tajine with the remaining chicken fat and sauce. Tint it with plenty of saffron and add lavender, pepper and cinnamon. When the breadcrumbs have come apart, break over it enough eggs to cover ["flood"] it all and sprinkle it with peeled, split almonds. Beat all this until it is mixed, then bury the pieces of chicken in this so that the chicken is hidden in the stuffing and whole eggyolks, and cover this with plenty of oil. Then place in the oven and leave it until it is dry, thickened and browned and the top of the tajine is bound. Then take it out and leave it until its heat passes and it cools, and use it.

4 ¼ lb chicken	⅔ c bread crumbs
½ t salt	20 threads more saffron
2 oz onion	1 t lavender
½ t pepper	½ t more pepper
½ t coriander	1 t more cinnamon
1 t cinnamon	6 eggs
20 threads saffron	¾ c slivered almonds
2 T murri (see p. 5)	½ c more oil
¼ c oil	[hard boiled egg yolks]

Wash the hen, roast it to an internal temperature of 160° (about 1-1 ½ hrs at 350°), separate the drippings into fat and broth, cut up the hen. Put the hen and broth in a pot with the first bunch of ingredients. Cook, covered, over a low to medium heat about 20 minutes. Remove the chicken, add bread crumbs, chicken fat, second batch of saffron, lavender, pepper and cinnamon.

Cook another five minutes or so, then break in the eggs, sprinkle over the almonds and stir it all together. Put the chicken back in and cover it as best you can with the egg/almond etc mixture. If you wish add egg yolks. Add the additional oil, bake at 350° for 30 minutes.

The Recipe of ibn al-Mahdi's Maghmûm
Andalusian p. A-8

Take a plump hen, dismember it and put it in a pot, and add coriander of one dirham's weight, half a dirham of pepper and the same of cinnamon, and of ginger, galingale, lavender and cloves a quarter dirham each, three ûqiyas of vinegar, two ûqiyas of pressed onion juice, an ûqiya of cilantro juice, an ûqiya of murri naqi', and four ûqiyas of fresh oil. Mix all this in a pot with some rosewater, cover it with a flatbread and put a carefully made lid over the mouth of the pot. Place this in the oven over a moderate fire and leave it until it is cooked. Then take it out and leave it a little. Let it cool and invert it onto a clean dish and present it; it is remarkable.

1 chicken (2-3 lb)	⅜ c vinegar
1 T coriander	¼ c onion juice
1 t pepper	2 T cilantro juice (p. 8)
1 ½ t cinnamon	2 T murri (see p. 5)
½ t ginger	½ c olive oil
½ t galingale	2 t rosewater
1 T lavender	2 medium pita breads
½ t cloves	

Mix everything in a pot, put in the chicken. Put two medium pita on top, put on lid, bake at 350° about 1 hour, let settle about 15 minutes, invert into a bowl, and serve. Would be good over rice or additional bread.

A Hen Roasted in the Oven
Andalusian p. A-14

Clean a plump, young, tender hen, salt it with salt and thyme, peel four or five cloves of garlic and place them between the thighs and in the interior. Pound pepper and coriander, sprinkle them over the hen, rub with murri and oil and a little water, and send it to the oven, God willing.

4 lb whole chicken	½ t coriander
¼ t salt	1 T murri
¼ t thyme	1 T oil
5 cloves garlic	~ 1 t water
⅛ t pepper	

Rub chicken with salt and thyme and put in garlic as described above. Sprinkle with pepper and coriander. Mix murri, oil and water and rub over chicken. Put in baking dish and bake in preheated oven at 375° for about 1 ½ hours (until meat thermometer shows 180°).

Hen Roasted in a Pot at Home
Andalusian p. A-3

Take a young, plump, cleaned hen; slice it on all sides and then make for it a sauce of oil, murri naqî', a little vinegar, crushed garlic, pepper and a little thyme. Grease all parts of the hen with this, inside and out; then put it in the pot and pour over it whatever remains of the sauce, and cook it; then remove the fire from beneath it and return the cover to it and leave it until it smells good and is fried. Then take it out and use it.

¾ oz garlic (~5 cloves)	2 T murri (p. 5)
1 T fresh thyme	½ t pepper
½ c oil	5 ½ lb hen
¼ c vinegar	

Peel the garlic and put it through a garlic press, or chop it very fine. Strip thyme leaves from stem, chop. Combine garlic, thyme, oil, vinegar, murri, and pepper in a bowl, stir. Wash the hen in cold water and drain well. With a sharp knife, cut about fifty shallow slits all over it, top and bottom. Smear mixture over chicken, inside and outside. Put chicken in a heavy pot, pour on the remaining mixture. Cover the pot and cook on medium low until the internal temperature of the chicken gets to 190°; it should take about an hour and a half. Remove from heat, leave covered for another ten minutes, then serve.

Another Kind of Lamb Breast
Andalusian A-5

Get the breast of a plump lamb, pierce it between the meat and the ribs, so that the hand and fingers can fit in; then get a large handful each of peeled almonds and hazelnuts, and a dirham each of Chinese cinnamon, lavender, cloves, saffron and pepper, and a little salt; pound all this and mix it with breadcrumbs and knead it with oil, and knead until it thickens and can be used as a stuffing. When it is stuffed, sew up the breast with clean gut and hang it in a tannur, and set under it an earthen pot into which what melts from the breast can drip, and when it is done take it out.

2 lb lamb breast	½ t saffron
¼ c blanched almonds	1 t pepper
¼ c hazelnuts	¼ t salt
½ t stick cinnamon	½ c breadcrumbs
1 gram fresh lavender	¾ c olive oil
½ t cloves	

Slice between the meat and the bone of the ribs so as to make a pocket for the stuffing. Pound nuts in the mortar. Add the spices, breadcrumbs and oil. Stir all together. Stuff the pocket, sew it up with cotton thread, put it in a pot supported by pieces of wood. Bake at 350° until the meat thermometer in the stuffing shows 180°, about 55 minutes.

Meat Roasted Over Coals
Andalusian p. A-42 (Good)

Cut the meat however you wish and throw on a spoon of oil and another of murri, salt, coriander seed, pepper and thyme; leave for a while until it has absorbed the spices, prepare without smoke and roast on a spit and watch it.

meat: 2 lb lamb	1 t coriander
¼ c oil	½ t pepper
¼ c murri (see p. 5)	½ t thyme
½ t salt	

Mix all ingredients except meat to make a marinade. Cut meat into 2 ½ ounce pieces (about 2"-3" across) and stir into marinade. Let sit 2 ½ hours. Put on a spit or skewer and roast over coals or in a baking pan under the broiler at high for 15 minutes or so, basting two or three times with the marinade.

Recipe for the Barmakiyya
Andalusian p. A-9 (Good)

It is made with a hen, pigeons, doves, small birds or lamb. Take what you have of them, after cleaning, and cut up and put in a pot with salt, an onion, pepper, coriander and lavender or cinnamon, some murri naqî', and oil. Put it on a gentle fire until it is nearly done and the sauce is dried. Take it out and fry it in fresh oil without overdoing it, and leave it aside. Then take fine flour and semolina, make a well-made dough with leaven, and if it has some oil it will be more flavorful. Then roll out from it a flatbread and put inside it the fried and cooked meat of these birds, cover it with another flatbread and stick the ends together. Put it in the oven, and when the bread is done, take it out. It is very good on journeys. You might make it with fish and that can be used for journeying too.

Note: The Barmecides were a family of Persian viziers who served some of the early Abbasid Caliphs, in particular Haroun al-Rashid, and were famed for their generosity.

1 lb boned chicken *or* lamb	3 T olive oil
	3 T more olive oil
10 oz onion	1 ½ c white flour
1 t salt	1 ½ c semolina
½ t pepper	[1 t salt in dough]
1 t coriander	3 T more olive oil
1 ½ t lavender *or* cinnamon	¾ c water
	½ c sourdough
1 T murri (see p. 5)	

Cut the meat fairly fine (approximately ¼" slices, then cut them up), combine in a 3 quart pot with chopped onion, 1 t salt, spices, murri, and 3 T oil. Cook over a medium low to medium heat about an hour. Cover it at the beginning so it all gets hot, at which point the onion and meat release their juices; remove the cover and cook until the liquid is gone, about 30 minutes. Then heat 3 T more oil in a large frying pan on a medium high burner, add the contents of the pot, fry over medium high heat about five minutes.

Stir together flour, semolina, 1 t salt. Gradually stir in 3 T oil. Combine ¾ c water, ½ c sourdough. Stir this into the flour mixture and knead to a smooth dough (which should only take a few minutes). If you do not have sourdough, omit it; since the recipes does not give the dough much time to rise, the sourdough probably does not have a large effect on the consistency of the dough.

Divide the dough in four equal parts. Take two parts, turn them out on a floured board, squeeze and stretch each (or use a rolling pin) until it is at least 12" by 5". Put half the filling on one, put the other on top, squeeze the edges together to seal. Repeat with the other two parts of the dough and the rest of the filling. Bake on a lightly oiled cookie sheet at 350° for 40 minutes.

For the fish version, start with 1 ¼ lb of fish (we used salmon). If it is boneless, proceed as above, shortening the cooking time to about 35 minutes; it is not necessary to cut up the fish fine, since it will crumble easily once it is cooked. If your fish has bones, put it on top of the oil, onions, spices etc., in the largest pieces that will fit in the pot, cover the pot, and cook for about 10-15 minutes, until the fish is almost ready to fall apart; in effect, it is being steamed by the liquid produced from the onions and by its own liquid. Take out the fish, bone it, return to the pot, and cook uncovered about 30 minutes until the liquid is mostly gone. Continue as above.

Relishes & Dips

Badinjan Muhassa
Ibn al-Mahdi's cookbook in al-Warraq translated by Perry. (9th-10th c.) (Good)

Cook eggplants until soft by baking, boiling or grilling over the fire, leaving them whole. When they are cool, remove the loose skin, drain the bitter liquor and chop the flesh fine. It should be coarser than a true purée. Grind walnuts fine and make into a dough with vinegar and salt. Form into a patty and fry on both sides until the taste of raw walnut is gone; the vinegar is to delay scorching of the nuts. Mix the cooked walnuts into the chopped eggplant and season to taste with vinegar and ground caraway seed, salt and pepper. Serve with a topping of chopped raw or fried onion.

¾ lb eggplant	⅛ t salt
1 c walnuts	1 t caraway seed
2 T vinegar	1 ½ T vinegar (at the end)
½ t salt	¼ c chopped raw onion
⅛ t pepper	

Simmer the eggplant 20 to 30 minutes in salted water (½ t salt in a pint of water). Let it cool. Peel it. Slice it and let the slices sit on a colander or a cloth for an hour or so, to let out the bitter juice.

Grind the walnuts, add vinegar and salt to make a dough. Make patties about ½" thick and put them on a frying pan at medium to medium high heat, without oil. In about half a minute, when the bottom side has browned a little, turn the patty over and use your pancake turner to squash it down to about ¼" (the cooked side is less likely to stick to your implement than the uncooked side). Continue cooking, turning whenever the patty seems about to scorch. When you are done, the surface of the patty will be crisp, brown to black–and since it is thin, the patty is mostly surface. If the patties start giving up lots of walnut oil (it is obvious–they will quickly be swimming in the stuff) the pan is too hot; throw them out, turn down the heat and make some more.

Chop up the eggplant, mix in the nut patties (they will break up in the process), add pepper, salt, caraway (ground in a spice grinder or mortar), and vinegar. Top with onion. Eat by itself or on bread.

Zabarbada of Fresh Cheese
Andalusian p. A-42

Take fresh cheese, clean it, cut it up and crumble it; take cilantro and onion, chop and throw over the cheese, stir and add spices and pepper, stir the pot with two spoons of oil and an equal quantity of water and salt, then throw this mixture in the pot and put on the fire and cook; when it is cooked, take the pot from the fire and cover with egg and some flour and serve.

8 oz farmer's cheese	½ t pepper
1 c chopped cilantro	2 T oil
6 oz onion	1 T water
1 t ground coriander	½ t salt
1 t cumin	1 egg
1 t cinnamon	2-3 T flour

Mix together cheese, cilantro, onion, and spices. Put oil, water and salt in a large frying pan or a dutch oven; shake to cover the bottom. Put in the cheese mixture and cook on medium-high to high about 3 minutes, stirring almost constantly, until the mixture becomes a uniform goo. Remove from heat, stir in egg, sprinkle on flour and stir in, serve forth. It ends up as a sort of thick dip, good over bread. It is still good when cold.

We have also used cheddar, feta, mozzarella and ricotta; all came out well, although with the feta it was a little salty, even with the salt in the recipe omitted. Some cheeses will require more flour to thicken it; the most we used was ½ cup.

Baid Masus
al-Baghdadi p. 202

Take fresh sesame-oil, place in the saucepan, and boil: then put in celery. Add a little fine-brayed coriander, cummin and cinnamon, and some mastic; then pour in vinegar as required, and colour with a little saffron. When thoroughly boiling, break eggs, and drop in whole: when set, remove.

½ lb celery	1/16 t mastic
2 T sesame oil	1 ½ T vinegar
½ T coriander	12 threads saffron
1 t cumin	6 eggs
½ t cinnamon	

Trim celery and cut into ¼" bits. Heat oil. Saute celery in oil over moderate heat for 7 minutes, adding spices just after putting in the celery. Stir vigorously. Crush saffron into vinegar; pour vinegar into pan with celery. Immediately crack in whole eggs and let cook, covered, until egg white is set.

Some people like this; others do not like anything that has enough mastic to taste.

Isfanakh Mutajjan
al-Baghdadi p. 206

Take spinach, cut off the lower roots, and wash: then boil lightly in salt and water, and dry. Refine sesame-oil, drop in the spinach, and stir until fragrant. Chop up a little garlic, and add. Sprinkle with fine-ground cumin, dry coriander, and cinnamon: then remove.

1 lb spinach	¼ t cumin
1 clove garlic	⅛ t coriander
1 T sesame oil	½ t cinnamon

Boil spinach in salted water about 2 minutes. Chop garlic. Fry spinach in oil briefly; add garlic and fry a bit more. Add spices and serve.

Another Recipe for Dressed Eggplant by Him (ibn al-Mahdi) Too
al-Warraq p. 227

Boil eggplant and chop it into fine pieces. Take a platter, and pour on it a little vinegar, white sugar, ground almonds, saffron, caraway seeds, cassia, [and mix]. Spread the [chopped] eggplant and fried onion all over the sauce. Drizzle some olive oil on the dish and serve it, God willing.

1 ¾ lb eggplant
½ lb onion
2 T olive oil
¼ c vinegar
2 T sugar
½ c ground almonds
8 threads saffron
2 t caraway seeds
2 t cinnamon
3 T olive oil

Boil eggplants for about half an hour, remove, skin, chop. Chop onion, fry in 2 T olive oil until limp and beginning to brown, about 10 minutes. Combine all other ingredients except oil, stir together to a paste, spread thinly on the plate, dump on chopped eggplant and chopped onion, drizzle over 3 T olive oil.

A Recipe for Soused Eggplants
al-Warraq p. 228

At the end of their season [i.e. late summer], cut the calyxes of the eggplants and cook them in vinegar until done. Take them out, drain them well, and set them aside.
Finely chop some round onion, along with cilantro, rue, and parsley. Fry them in olive oil until browned. Pour vinegar on them and add some spices (abzar).
Arrange the eggplants in wide mouthed jars and pour on them the vinegar which has been seasoned with the herbs and spices. Let it cover the eggplants.
Store away the jars. The eggplant will stay good for a whole year. Whenever you wish to eat it, take some out and put them in a bowl, garnish them with chopped rue, and serve them, God willing.

2 lb eggplant
4 c vinegar
3 oz onion
¼ c more vinegar
1 T cilantro
1 t rue
1 T parsley
1 T olive oil
¾ c more vinegar
Abzar:
1 t pepper
1 t coriander
1 T caraway seeds
1 t cinnamon

Simmer eggplants in 4 c of vinegar for about half an hour, drain. Fry the onion etc. in olive oil about ten minutes. Add ¼ c vinegar plus spices. Put eggplants in a jar, pour onion etc. over them, add ¾ c vinegar to cover.

Keeps for months. Very vinegary. I like it on bread.

Deserts

A recipe for Judhaba of Bananas by Ibn al Mahdi
al-Warraq p. 375

Peel the bananas and set them aside. Spread a ruqaqa [thin round of bread] in the pan and spread a layer of bananas over it. Sprinkle the banana layer with pure sugar, and spread another ruqaqa all over it. Repeat the layering of banana, sugar, and ruqaqa until the pan is full. Pour enough rose water to drench the layered ingredients, [put the pan in a hot tannur,] suspend a fine chicken over it, [and let it roast] God willing.

10 oz Iranian lavash
3 ¼ lb bananas
½ c sugar
1-4 T rose water
4-5 lb chicken

Oil the bottom of your pot. Line the pot with lavash—an Iranian thin bread that is the closest equivalent to ruqaqa we know of. Cover that with sliced (or mashed) bananas. Sprinkle over them 2 T of sugar. Cover with another layer of lavash. Repeat until you run out of banana, then put on a final covering of lavash. Sprinkle the rose water over that—4 T will leave a very strong taste of rose water, which some may not like.

Arrange your chicken so it is suspended above the layers. I did it by running a hardwood skewer lengthwise through the chicken and laying it across the top edge of my pot.

Bake the chicken until done—roughly 20 minutes a pound at 350°, to an internal temperature of about 190°—letting the drippings fall on and soak into the layered bread and bananas.

Preparation of Qursas
Andalusian p. A-70

Take very white flour and knead it with milk, salt and yeast. And when you have kneaded it considerably, leave it until it rises. Then take one egg or several, according to the quantity of the dough. Break them in a bowl and beat them. Moisten the dough with them little by little and knead it until it slackens. Take a new frying pan and shower it with clarified butter or fresh oil. Take a handful of the dough and spread it in the pan. Put over it a layer of almonds and pistachios, or whichever one you have. When the almonds cover the dough, put another dough on the almonds, and so on, layer on layer. In this way you fill the frying pan up to two fingers [from its rim]. Put it in the oven with the bread and when it is done, prick it with a knife and take it out as it is. Heat honey and clarified butter and pour over, and when it has soaked them up, throw it on a platter and sprinkle over it Chinese cinnamon and cinnamon and serve it, if God wishes.

<u>Yeast version</u> *(Different from the sourdough version in other ways as well)*

2 t yeast	more flour
¼ c warm water	1 egg
1 ¼ c milk	1 t olive oil
4 c flour	10 T honey
½ t salt	10 T ghee
½ to 1 c more flour	¼ t cinnamon
2 c chopped almonds and/or pistachios	

Combine yeast and warm water and let sit until it gets bubbly, then mix with the milk. Mix 4 c flour and salt, then stir the liquid ingredients into the dry ingredients and knead smooth. Knead in up to another cup of flour, continuing until you have a dough that doesn't tend to stick to you. Cover with a damp cloth and leave about an hour to rise.

When it has risen, chop the nuts and grease an 8 ½" diameter frying pan with the olive oil. Get a small bowl with flour in it. You do these things before the next step, because after the next step your hands will be covered with sticky dough.

Beat one egg and gradually knead it into the dough. Take about one eighth of the dough. Flour it so that it isn't too sticky to handle. Press it between your hands to a disk about 6" across. Put it in the middle of the frying pan. Spread about ¼c+ of chopped nuts on it, as evenly as you can. Take another, similar handful of dough. Flour it. Repeat. You may want to press each sheet of dough down a bit on the one before, which will spread the whole thing a little, so that by the time you are finished it will just about fill the frying pan. You may also find, if you are having a hard time getting the handfuls into wide enough disks, that it helps to stick one edge of a not quite large enough disk to the layer below and then stretch it so that you can fasten the rest of its edge to the rest of the edge of the layer below.

<u>Sourdough version</u>

1 c milk	2 eggs
1 ¼ c sourdough	2 T ghee
1 t salt	¾ c honey
4 c white flour	½ c ghee
⅔ c pistachios	¼ t cinnamon
⅔ c almonds	¼ t true cinnamon (p. 4)

Mix milk, sourdough and salt. Stir into flour, knead smooth, leave to rise 2 ½ hours. Chop the nuts coarsely. Beat the eggs briefly and gradually knead into the dough. Grease an 8 ½" frying pan with 2 T ghee. Take about one sixth of the dough, spread it over the bottom of the frying pan, sprinkle over it about a fifth of the nuts. Repeat until you have five layers of dough and nuts, with a sixth layer of dough above—you may end up with a layer or two more or less, which is fine.

(Both Versions) Bake for 50 minutes at 350°. Remove from oven. Cut lots of slits with the point of a sharp knife—in ornamental patterns if you are feeling ambitious. Heat the honey and ghee (use butter if you can't find ghee), mix them, pour them over the loaf, letting them soak in through the top and the bottom. Let stand a little so it can absorb the honey and butter. Remove from the pan, sprinkle with cinnamon, and serve.

Stuffed Qanânît, Fried Cannoli
Andalusian p. A-70

Pound almond and walnut, pine nuts and pistachio very small. Knead fine white flour with oil and make thin breads with it and fry them in oil. Pound [sugar] fine and mix with the almond, the walnut and the rest. Add to the paste pepper, cinnamon, Chinese cinnamon and spikenard. Knead with the necessary amount of skimmed honey and put in the dough whole pine nuts, cut pistachio and almond. Mix it all and then stuff the qananit that you have made of clean wheat flour.

Its Preparation: Knead the dough well with oil and a little saffron and roll it into thin flatbreads. Stretch them over the tubes (qananit) of cane, and you cut them [the cane sections] how you want them, little or big. And throw them [into a frying pan full of oil], after decorating them in the reed. Take them out from the reed and stuff them with the stuffing and put in their ends whole pistachios and pine nuts, one at each end, and lay it aside. He who wants his stuffing with sugar or chopped almond, it will be better, if God wishes.

Translator's note: The general discussion in the beginning, which is the only place where the stuffing is described, must have dropped the word sugar, as the recipe section omitted the instruction to fry the tubes. "Qanânît" is the plural of "qanut"—canes or cylinders. (Charles Perry)

½ c almonds	¼ c whole pine nut
½ c walnuts	¼ c pistachios
½ c pine nuts	¼ c almonds
½ c pistachios	3 c flour
1 t pepper	½ c oil
1 T cinnamon	½ c water
1 T true cinnamon (p. 4)	oil for frying
1 t spikenard	one per cylinder of:
¼ c sugar	whole pistachios
¾ c honey	whole pine nuts

Grind fine ½ c each of almonds, walnuts, pine nuts and pistachios. Combine with spices, sugar, and honey and knead together. Chop the additional ¼ c each of almonds and pistachios and add them along with ¼ c of whole pine nuts. Knead flour, oil and water together and refrigerate 20 minutes. Form dough into cylinders ~2" long on ¾" wooden dowels and deep-fry them in hot oil while on the dowel. (They had to be fried on the dowels, since they would not remain as cylinders otherwise.) Remove each cylinder from its dowel, stuff it with filling, stop one end with a whole pistachio and the other with a whole pine nut.

The Making of Dafâir, Braids
Andalusian, p. A-25

Take what you will of white flour or of semolina, which is better in these things. Moisten it with hot water after sifting, and knead well, after adding some fine flour, leavening, and salt. Moisten it again and again until it has middling consistency. Then break into it, for each ratl of semolina, five eggs and a dirham of saffron, and beat all this very well, and put the dough in a dish, cover it and leave it to rise, and the way to tell when this is done is what was mentioned before [it holds an indentation]. When it has risen, clean a frying pan and fill it with fresh oil, then put it on the fire. When it starts to boil, make braids of the leavened dough like hair-braids, of a handspan or less in size. Coat them with oil and throw them in the oil and fry them until they brown. When their cooking is done, arrange them on an earthenware plate and pour over them skimmed honey spiced with pepper, cinnamon, Chinese cinnamon, and lavender. Sprinkle it with ground sugar and present it, God willing. This same way you make isfunj, except that the dough for the isfunj will be rather light. Leave out the saffron, make it into balls and fry them in that shape, God willing. And if you wish stuffed dafâir or isfunj, stuff them with a filling of almonds and sugar, as indicated for making qâhiriyât.

Note: the recipe calls for a dirham of saffron = 3.8 grams, which is a lot of saffron. If this is a scribal error for a danaq it would be .6 grams, which is how we do it. Feel free to substitute 3.8 grams if you really like saffron.

1 c water	1 T lavender
1 lb semolina = 2 ⅜ c	1 c honey
1 c sourdough	½ t pepper
¾ c flour	1 t cinnamon
1 t salt	~1 T oil to brush on
.6 gram saffron	oil for frying
3 eggs	1 ½ t sugar
¾ c more flour	

Add water to semolina ⅛ c at a time, mixing, until all the semolina is barely moistened. Add sourdough, ¾ c flour, and salt, and knead until it is a smooth elastic dough. Crush saffron into 2 t water; add it and eggs to dough and knead in. The dough being too soppy for braiding, add another ¾ c flour. Leave to rise in a warm place until doubled, about an hour and a half. While the dough rises make the sauce: grind the lavender and add to the honey with pepper and cinnamon; boil honey and spices about 10 minutes on medium heat. Flour a cutting board, take small lumps of dough (about 2 tablespoons), roll into 6" strings, and braid three together into braids 6" long. Let rise half an hour. Brush with oil. Heat about ½" of oil in a frying pan at medium high heat (275°) and fry the braids a few at a time, so that there is room to turn them over as they fry, until puffed up and light brown on both sides: about 2-3 minutes total. Drain braids on paper towels, put on a plate, drizzle with the sauce and sprinkle with sugar. Makes 15 braids.

Khushkananaj
al-Baghdadi p. 212 (Good)

Take fine white flour, and with every ratl mix three uqiya of sesame-oil [one part oil to four of flour], kneading into a firm paste. Leave to rise; then make into long loaves. Put into the middle of each loaf a suitable quantity of ground almonds and scented sugar mixed with rose water, using half as much almonds as sugar. Press together as usual, bake in the oven, remove.

2 c white flour	1 c almonds
1 c whole wheat flour	1 ½ c sugar
½ c sesame oil	1 T rose water
¾ to ⅞ c cold water *or*	more flour
½ c water, ½ c sourdough	

We originally developed the recipe without leavening, but currently use sourdough, which is our best guess at what the original intended (and also seems to work a little better). The two versions are:

Without leavening: Mix the flour, stir in the oil. Sprinkle the water onto the dough, stir in. Knead briefly together.

Sourdough: Mix the flour, stir in the oil. Mix the water and the sour dough starter together. Add gradually to the flour/oil mixture, and knead briefly together. Cover with a damp cloth and let rise about 8 hours in a warm place, then knead a little more.

We also have two interpretations of how the loaves are made; they are:

Almost Baklava: Divide in four parts. Roll each one out to about 8"x16" on a floured board. Grind almonds, combine with sugar and rose water. Spread the mixture over the rolled out dough and roll up like a jelly roll, sealing the ends and edges (use a wet finger if necessary). You may want to roll out the dough in one place and roll it up in another, so as not to have bits of nuts on the board you are trying to roll it out on. You can vary how thin you roll the dough and how much filling you use over a considerable range, to your own taste.

Long thin loaves: Divide the dough into six or eight parts, roll each out to a long loaf (about 16"), flatten down the middle so that you can fill it with the sugar and almond mixture, then seal it together over the filling. You end up with a tube of dough with filling in the middle.

Bake on a lightly oiled pan at 350° about 45-50 minutes.

Notes: At least some of the almonds should be only coarsely ground, for texture. Be sure to use middle Eastern (or health food) sesame oil, from untoasted sesame seeds (see p. 4). The following recipe gives us some idea of what scented sugar contained, but for this one we just add rose water.

A Recipe for Khushkananaj Shaped Like Crescents
al-Warraq p. 419

Take 4 ratls fresh almonds, taste them for bitterness, shell them then dry them in a big copper pot set on the fire. Grind them finely. Pound 8 ratls refined tabarzad sugar (white cane sugar), and mix it with the almonds.

Take 2 ratl pith (brick-oven thick bread), dry it in the tannur, and as soon as you take it out, sprinkle it with ½ ratl rose water. Crumble the pith on a plate and dry it. Finely crush it with some camphor and musk then mix them well. Add the breadcrumbs to the almond-sugar mixture and sift them in a sieve so that they all mix well.

Take 15 ratl excellent-quality fine samīdh flour (high in starch and bran free). Knead it with ¼ ratl fresh yeast dissolved in water, and 2 ½ ratls fresh sesame oil. Mix them all together then knead and press and rub the dough vigorously. Keep on doing this while gradually feeding it with water, 5 dirhams at a time until it is thoroughly kneaded. The [final] dough should be on the stiff side.

Divide the dough into portions, whether small or big is up to you. Take a portion of the dough, roll it out on a (wooden low table) with a rolling pin. Let it look like a tongue, wide in the middle and tapered towards both ends. Spoon some of the filling and spread it on part of the dough, leaving the borders free of the filling. Fold the dough on the filling [lengthwise]. Press out air so that the dough and the filling become like one solid mass. If any air remains inside, the cookie will tear and crack while baking in the tannur. Bend the two ends of the piece to make it look like a crescent. Arrange the finished ones on a tray and cover them with a piece of cloth.

Light fire in the tannur and wait until the coals look white. Wipe the inside walls of the tannur with a wet piece of cloth after you brush it with a broom. Gather all the embers in the middle, and shape them like a dome. Now, transfer the tray closer to the tannur and put a bowl of water next to the top opening of the oven.

When ready to bake, take the filled pastries from the tray one by one, wipe their backs with water, enough to make them sticky, and stick them all to the inner wall of the tannur, taking care not to let them fall down. When you see that all the pieces are sealed well at the seams, cover the [top opening of the] tannur, and close the (bottom vent hole) for a short while to create moisture in the oven.

When the cookies start to take on color, open the bottom vent hole, remove the oven's top lid, and start scraping off the browned ones as they are done with a spatula held in one hand and a huge iron scoop [held in the other hand to receive the scraped cookies].

You should have prepared a bowl of gum Arabic dissolved in water. Wipe the khushkananaj tops with the gum solution [to give them a nice gloss], and stow the cookies away in a wicker basket, God willing.

(One tenth of the original recipe)

3 c semolina	⅞ c bread crumbs
½ c sesame oil	1 ½ T rose water
1 T sourdough	1.6 c sugar
¾ c water	1 t gum arabic
1 ¼ c almonds	in ½ c water
⅓ gram edible camphor	

Combine semolina and sesame oil, stir in sourdough dissolved in water. Leave about 5 hours to rise. Grind almonds. Grind camphor in mortar, combine with bread crumbs and rose water, spread out to dry for fifteen minutes or so. Add sugar and bread crumbs to almonds, mix. Take a ball of dough about 1 ¼ inches in diameter, press and roll out to an oval about 5"x4", put T+ of filling in the middle, fold along the long axis as a crescent, press out the air.

Put a baking stone in the oven and a pie pan or something similar on another shelf, heat oven to 350°. Brush each crescent with water, put wet side down on baking stone, pour a cup of hot water into the pie pan to make the oven steamy. Bake about 25-30 minutes until they start to brown. Remove, brush with gum arabic solution, let dry.

We have not yet found an adequate substitute for musk.

Ka'k Stuffed with Sugar
Andalusian p. A-70

Knead the amount that you want of fine flour and knead a long time. Leave it until it rises and then pound almonds very fine until they are like brains. Grind with an equal amount of white sugar and knead the two parts with some rosewater and perfume it with fine spices. Roll the dough out long and put on the stuffing and cover with dough. Make it round and make ka'ks with it. Send it to the oven and, if you want, fry it in the frying pan with oil and scatter sugar on top. He who wants it simple, let him omit the spices.

2 ½ c flour   1 ½ c sugar
½ c water   ½ t cinnamon
½ c sourdough   3 T rosewater
1 ¼ c blanched almonds

Mix the water and sourdough and stir the mixed liquid into the flour; we used a mix of white and whole wheat, which works, but there is no particular reason to do it that way. Knead it for 10-15 minutes, adding up to an additional ¼ c flour if necessary to keep it from being sticky. Cover with a damp cloth and leave to rise 3 hours in a warm place.

Grind the almonds about 40 seconds in a food processor (or longer in a mortar) until very finely ground. Combine with sugar and cinnamon, stir in rose water, and knead together.

Take 1 T of dough, flour it, roll between your hands to a 4" long cylinder. Flatten with your finger, making the middle lower than the edges (i.e. a depression almost 4" long down the middle of the dough). Fill with about 1 ½ t of the sugar/almond mixture. Fold the dough up over the filling, making a tube of dough filled with filling about 4" long, sealed at both ends. Bend it into a ring (small bracelet). Put on an oiled cookie sheet, bake at 300° 40 minutes.

My guess at the size and shape of the individual pieces is based on a description of something with the same name (but different structure) in a modern cookbook (by Claudia Rodin). You can also use 2 T of dough, 1 T of filling, make a cylinder 6" long. Or experiment with other sizes. You can flatten the ring either by pressing it down against the cookie sheet or by making it like a napkin ring. Experiment.

Recipe for Oven Cheese Pie, Which We Call Toledan
Andalusian p. A-62

Make dough as for musammana and make a small leafy round loaf of it. Then roll it out and put sufficient pounded cheese in the middle. Fold over the ends of the loaf and join them over the cheese on all sides; leave a small hole the size of a dinar on top, so the cheese can be seen, and sprinkle it with some anise. Then place it in the oven on a slab, and leave it until it is done, take it out and use it, as you wish.

2 c semolina flour   6 oz feta or other cheese
~ ⅝-¾ c water   ⅛ t anise, ground
¼ c = ⅛ lb butter

Make dough as in Musammana recipe (p. 121) and divide into 4 pieces. Flatten each to about 6"x 8". Put 1 ½ oz cheese in the middle of each. Sprinkle with anise. Fold the edges in and join, leaving a small space open in the center. Bake at 400° for 15 minutes

Recipe for Mujabbana (Fried Cheese Pie)
Andalusian p. A-61

Know that mujabbana isn't prepared with only one cheese, but of two; that is, of cow's and sheep's milk cheese. Because if you make it with only sheep cheese, it falls apart and the cheese leaves it and it runs. And if you make it with cow's cheese, it binds, and lets the water run and becomes one sole mass and the parts don't separate. The principle in making it is that the two cheeses bind together. Use one-fourth part cow's milk and three-quarters of sheep's. Knead all until some binds with its parts another [Huici Miranda observes that this passage is faintly written and only a few letters can be made out] and becomes equal and holds together and doesn't run in the frying pan, but without hardening or congealing. If you need to soften it, soften it with fresh milk, recently milked from the cow. And let the cheese not be very fresh, but strong without...[words missing]...that the moisture has gone out of. Thus do the people of our land make it in the west of al-Andalus, as in Cordoba and Seville and Jerez, and elsewhere in the land of the West.

Manner of Making it: Knead wheat or semolina flour with some yeast into a well-made dough and moisten it with water little by little until it loosens. If you moisten it with fresh milk instead of water it is better, and easy, inasmuch as you make it with your palm. Roll it out and let it not have the consistency of mushahhada, but firmer than that, and lighter than musammana dough. When the leaven begins to enter it, put the frying pan on the fire with a lot of oil, so that it is drenched with what you fry it with. Then wet your hand in water and cut off a piece of the dough. Bury inside it the same amount of rubbed cheese. Squeeze it with your hand, and whatever leaves and drains from the hand, gather it up [? the meaning of this verb eludes me] carefully. Put it in the frying pan while the oil boils. When it has browned, remove it with an iron hook prepared for it and put it in a dipper ["iron hand"] similar to a sieve held above the frying pan, until its oil drips out. Then put it on a big platter and dust it with a lot of sugar and ground cinnamon. There are those who eat it with honey or rose syrup and it is the best you can eat.

1 ½ c flour	4 oz feta
¼ c sourdough	2 c olive oil for frying
½ c milk	1 t cinnamon
⅔ oz ricotta	1 T sugar or honey

Mix flour, sourdough and milk; knead for a few minutes into a smooth dough. Roll out to about a 12" circle, making sure the board (or marble slab) is well floured so it will not stick when you later take it off. Let rise about 3 hours in a warm place. Mash together the cheeses—we used ricotta and feta, but you could try different cow's and sheep's cheeses—and knead them to a smooth consistency. Cut a piece of the dough, put cheese filling on top, fold dough up on all sides around it and over the cheese; squeeze to a circular, flattened patty, using a wet hand so that the dough will seal. At this point you have cheese entirely surrounded by dough. Pour the oil in a 8 ½" frying pan or dutch oven (about ½" deep), heat to about 340°. Put patties into the oil, cook until the bottom is brown (about 40-60 seconds), turn over, cook until that side is brown (about another 40 seconds), remove, drain. Eat with either cinnamon sugar or honey.

The cut pieces of rolled dough used to make the fritters ranged from about a 1.5"x1.5" square to a 2.5"x2.5". The former requires about ½ t of filling, the latter about 1 t or a little more. The former ends up, before frying, as a roughly circular patty about 1.5" in diameter and ½" thick; the latter ends as a circular patty about 2.5" in diameter and ½" or a little thicker. The recipe makes about 20-30 patties. You could probably cook them faster by using enough more oil so that the patties were entirely covered.

Recipe for Murakkaba, a Dish which is Made in the Region of Constantine and is Called Kutâmiyya
Andalusian p. A-62 (Good)

Knead a well-made dough from semolina like the "sponge" dough with yeast, and break in it as many eggs as you can, and knead the dough with them until it is slack. Then set up a frying pan of clay [hantam] on a hot fire, and when it has heated, grease it with clarified butter or oil. Put in a thin flat loaf of the dough and when the bread is done, turn over. Take some of the dough in the hand and smear the surface of the bread with it. Then turn the smeared surface to the pan, changing the lower part with the upper, and smear this side with dough too. Then turn it over in the pan and smear it, and keep smearing it with dough and turning it over in the tajine, and pile it up and raise it until it becomes a great, tall loaf. Then turn it by the edges a few times in the tajine until it is done on the sides, and when it is done, as it is desired, put it in a serving dish and make large holes with a stick, and pour into them melted butter and plenty of honey, so that it covers the bread, and present it.

[From "Making of Elegant Isfunja ("Sponge")," Andalusian: You take clear and clean semolina and knead it with lukewarm water and yeast and knead again. When it has risen, turn the dough, knead fine and moisten with water, little by little, so that it becomes like tar after the second kneading, until it becomes leavened or is nearly risen. ...]

2 ¼ c semolina flour	2 eggs
½ c water	1-2 T oil for frying
½ c sourdough	⅜ c honey
¼ c more water	½ c butter

Combine flour, ½ c water, and sourdough and knead smooth. Cover with a damp cloth and leave overnight to rise. In the morning knead in an additional ¼ c water, making it into a sticky mess, and leave another few hours in a warm place to rise. Add the eggs and stir until they are absorbed into the dough.

Heat a frying pan over medium to high heat and grease it with oil or ghee. Pour on enough batter to make a thick pancake about 7" in diameter. When one side is cooked (about 2 minutes) turn it over. Put onto the cooked side about ¼ c more batter, spreading it out to cover. When the second side is done (1-2 minutes more), turn it over, so that the side smeared with batter is now down. Cook another 1-2 minutes. Repeat. Continue until the batter is all used up, giving you about 8-10 layers—like a stack of pancakes about 3" thick, all stuck together. Turn the loaf on its side and roll it around the frying pan like a wheel, in order to be sure the edges are cooked.

Punch lots of holes in the top with the handle of a wooden spoon, being careful not to get through the bottom layer. Pour in honey and melted butter, letting it soak into the loaf. Serve.

Note: Scale the recipe up as desired to suit your ambition and frying pan. If you don't have sourdough you could use yeast instead, with shorter rising times.

Recipe for Murakkaba Layered with Dates
Andalusian p. A-62

Take the dough described under murakkaba kutamiyya [see preceeding recipe] and make of it a thin flatbread in a heated tajine, and when it is done, turn it over, and top it with dates that have been cleaned, pounded, kneaded in the hands and moistened with oil. Smooth them with the palm, then put on another flatbread and turn it over, and then another bread, and repeat this until it is as high as desired. When it is done on all sides, put it in a dish and pour over it hot oil and honey cleaned of its scum; this is how the people of Ifriqiyya make it.

2 ¼ c semolina flour	12 oz dates
½ c water	2 T oil
½ c sourdough	1-2 T oil or ghee
¼ c more water	1 c honey
4 eggs	¼ c almond oil

Combine flour, ½ c water, and sourdough and knead smooth. Cover with a damp cloth and leave overnight to rise. In the morning knead in an additional ¼ c water, making it into a sticky mess, and leave another few hours in a warm place to rise. Add the eggs, and stir until they are absorbed into the dough. Pound dates in the mortar, knead in 2 T of oil.

Heat a frying pan over a medium to high heat and grease it with oil or ghee. Pour on about ½ c batter to make a thick pancake about 7" in diameter. When one side is cooked (about 2 minutes) turn it over. Put on about ¼ c of the date paste, smearing it on so that most of the pancake is covered. Cover that with about ½ c more batter. When the second side is done (1-2 minutes more), turn it over, so that the side smeared with batter is now down. Put on another layer of dates. Continue until the batter and dates are all used up. Turn the loaf on its side and roll it around the frying pan like a wheel, in order to be sure the edges are cooked.

Briefly boil honey, removing scum as it rises. Heat ¼ c oil. Punch lots of holes with the handle of a wooden spoon (this is based on the other Murakkaba recipe, which gives more detail). Pour on honey and hot oil, letting it soak into the loaf. Serve.

Cheese and Flour Cake
al-Andalusi no. 79 (Good)

Knead the necessary quantity of flour, one time with water, another with oil, and to it add yeast and milk until it has the same consistency as the dough of fritters, and leave it until it has next risen. Next grease with oil a large earthen pot, stretch in it a piece of dough, and over it a bit of cheese, and over the cheese a bit of dough, and so a little of one, and a bit of the other until the last of the dough and cheese. Next cover it with dough as you did in the previous recipe and cook it in the same way in the oven. Afterwards, drizzle it with honey, sprinkle it with sugar and pepper and eat it.

⅓ c white flour	3 T oil
⅔ c whole wheat flour	12 oz cheese
½-¾ c water	6 T honey
3 T milk	1 T sugar
1 ½ t yeast	¼ t pepper

Knead flours and water to a very dry dough, mix warm milk and yeast, let sit five minutes, add oil to dough, knead in. Knead milk and yeast into the dough for about 5-10 minutes, until fairly uniform. Leave 45 minutes to rise in a warm place. Divide dough in about 8 equal portions, flour and pat, stretch, or roll out to size of pan (about 4"x7"); if you roll it out you can use 12 equal portions. Layer with sliced cheese. Bake 45 minutes at 350°. Drizzle the honey over it. Serve with mixed sugar and pepper for the guests to sprinkle over to taste. This should probably be done with sourdough instead of yeast, but we have not tried it that way yet.

Preparation of Musammana [Buttered] Which Is Muwarraqa [Leafy]
Andalusian p. A-60 (Good)

Take pure semolina or wheat flour and knead a stiff dough without yeast. Moisten it little by little and don't stop kneading it until it relaxes and is ready and is softened so that you can stretch a piece without severing it. Then put it in a new frying pan on a moderate fire. When the pan has heated, take a piece of the dough and roll it out thin on marble or a board. Smear it with melted clarified butter or fresh butter liquified over water. Then roll it up like a cloth until it becomes like a reed. Then twist it and beat it with your palm until it becomes like a round thin bread, and if you want, fold it over also. Then roll it out and beat it with your palm a second time until it becomes round and thin. Then put it in a heated frying pan after you have greased the frying pan with clarified butter, and whenever the clarified butter dries out, moisten [with butter] little by little, and turn it around until it binds, and then take it away and make more until you finish the amount you need. Then pound them between your palms and toss on butter and boiling honey. When it has cooled, dust it with ground sugar and serve it.

~ ⅝-¾ c water	¼ c butter at the end
2 c semolina flour	¼ c honey at the end
⅛ lb butter, melted	1 T+ sugar
¼ c ghee for frying	

Stir most of the water into the flour, knead together, then gradually knead in the rest of the water. Knead for about 5-10 minutes until you have a smooth, elastic and slightly sticky dough that stretches instead of breaking when you pull it a little. Divide in four equal parts. Roll out on a floured board, or better on floured marble, to at least 13"x15". Smear it with about 4 t melted butter. Roll it up. Twist it. Squeeze it together, flatten with your hands to about a 5-6" diameter circle. If you wish, fold that in quarters and flatten again to about a 5-6" circle. Melt about 1 T of ghee in a frying pan and fry the dough about 8 minutes, turning about every 1 ½ to 2 minutes (shorter times towards the end). Repeat with the other three parts, adding more ghee as needed. Melt ¼ c butter, heat ¼ c honey. Beat the cooked circles between your hands to loosen the layers, put in a bowl, pour the honey and butter over them, dust with sugar, and serve. If you are going to give it time to really soak, you might use more butter and honey.

For regular flour, everything is the same except that you may need slightly more water. You can substitute cooking oil for the ghee (which withstands heat better than plain butter) if necessary.

Cakes with Honey [no title in the original]
Andalusian p. A-23

Sift white flour three times, take the choicest part, mingle it with butter and knead it with egg yolk and put into the dough some saffron and salt. Put clarified butter into an earthenware frying pan, boil it and take one kail of honey and one of dough and throw them into the melted butter until it is cooked. Before it is thickened, put in blanched almonds and pine-nuts, sprinkle it with pepper and present it.

4 T butter	¼ c blanched almonds
1 c white flour	¼ c pine nuts
2 egg yolks	~ ¼ c ghee
4 threads saffron	¾ c honey
¼ t salt	¼ t pepper

Cut butter into the flour, then knead in the egg yolks with saffron (extracted in water) and salt. Chop the almonds, mix with the pine nuts. For each cake, put 1 T ghee in a small frying pan on low heat, put 3 T of dough in the form of a patty about ⅛" thick into the ghee along with 3 T of honey. Cook for 5-10 minutes, spooning honey over the patty and flipping the patty at least once. Pour 1 T of the nut mixture into it. Remove onto a plate, pouring the honey and butter mixture over top, add a pinch of pepper. This should work fine with larger batches but we haven't tried that yet.

Hulwa
Ibn al-Mabrad p.19

Its varieties are many. Among them are the sweets made of natif. You put dibs [fruit syrup], honey, sugar or rubb [thick fruit syrup] in the pot, then you put it on a gentle fire and stir until it takes consistency. Then you beat eggwhite and put it with it and stir until it thickens and becomes natif. After that, if you want almond candy you put in toasted almonds and 'allaftahu; that is, you bind them. walnuts, pistachios, hazelnuts, toasted chickpeas, toasted sesame, flour. [apparently alternative versions]. You beat in the natif until it thickens. For duhniyyah you put in flour toasted with fat. As for ... [other versions.]

Sugar version	Honey version
¼ c water	1 c honey
1 ¼ c sugar	1 egg white
1 egg white	2 ½-3 c or more nuts
1 ½ - 2 c nuts	[ground nuts or sesame seeds]

This makes 25-40 hulwa.

Sugar version: Bring the water to a boil, stir in the sugar, continuing to heat. When it is dissolved and reasonably clear, turn it down to a simmer and put the top on the pot for two or three minutes (this is to let the steam wash down any sugar on the sides of the pot). Take the top off, boil gently until the temperature reaches the hard ball stage (250° -260° F). Beat the egg white until it is just stiff enough to hold its shape. Pour the sugar syrup into the egg white, beating continuously. You now have a thick white mixture; this is the natif. Mix it with chopped nuts (we have used almonds and walnuts) or toasted sesame seeds, or some mixture thereof. Squeeze the mixture into balls and set them aside to cool. As the natif cools it gets harder and less sticky, so you have to work quickly; the hotter you get the syrup before combining it with the egg white (and hence the less water ended up in it), the faster this happens and the dryer the hulwa ends up. If you get past 260°, the syrup may crystallize on you as or before you pour it; if so, give up and start over.

Honey version: Simmer the honey gently until it reaches a temperature of 280° -290° F. From that point on, the recipe is the same as for sugar, using the boiled honey instead of the sugar syrup. Note that honey requires a higher temperature than sugar to get the same effect. Also note that natif made from honey will be stickier than natif made from sugar (maybe you can solve this by getting the honey up to 310° without burning it; I couldn't). So use a higher ratio of nuts to natif and have the nuts chopped more finely; this helps reduce the stickiness. You may want to roll the honey hulwa in sesame seeds or ground nuts, also to reduce stickiness.

Dibs version (still experimental). Stir the dibs while simmering at medium heat about ½ hour+, until it gets to about 250°. If you do not stir, it may separate out. By 250° there is some problem with scorching.

Note: Dibs is date syrup, available from some Middle Eastern grocery stores.

To toast sesame seeds, put them in a heavy iron pot over a medium to high flame. When the ones on the bottom begin to tan, start stirring. When they are all tan to brown, take them off the heat or they will burn.

Makshufa
al-Baghdadi p. 211

Take equal parts of sugar, almonds (or pistachios), honey, and sesame-oil. Grind the sugar and almonds, and mix together. Add saffron to color, mixed with rose-water. Put the sesame oil into a basin and boil until fragrant: then drop in the honey, and stir until the scum appears. Add the sugar and almonds, stirring all the time over a slow fire until almost set: then remove.

1 c+ almonds	3 T rosewater
¾ c sugar	¾ c sesame oil
10 threads saffron	½ c+ honey

Grind the almonds coarsely in a food processor, then add the sugar and grind briefly together to mix (I assume the original is using a block of sugar, which is why it has to be ground). Grind the saffron into the rose water, add, and run the food processor long enough to mix it in smoothly. Heat the oil to about 350° over a medium heat, add the honey and cook about 3 minutes on low. Foam (not very thick–like the bubbles of bubble bath, or a little thinner) will cover the top. Add the almonds and sugar. At this point it may foam up and boil over, so be careful, use a reasonably large pot, and be ready to remove it from the heat temporarily if necessary. Cook on medium to medium high, with a candy thermometer in the pot; be careful to keep the thermometer from touching the bottom.

At a temperature of about 230° the mixture becomes smooth. After cooking about 10 minutes (from the time the sugar went in) it reaches about 270°. If you stop at that point, your Makshufa will be light colored and chewy. Another 6 minutes or so gets the syrup up to about 290°, giving a darker candy, crunchier, with a slightly caramelized taste.

Remove from heat, spoon onto a buttered cookie sheet (to make lots of little candies) or else pour it on (to make a sheet of candy like peanut brittle) and let cool. Chill, remove from the cooky sheet and keep the candy refrigerated or frozen to make it less likely to stick together. It is crunchier if you serve it chilled. The recipe makes about 40-45 pieces 1 ¾" in diameter with a total weight of about 21 ounces.

Sukkariyya, a Sugar Dish from the Dictation of Abu 'Ali al-Bagdadi
Andalusian p. A-23

Take a ratl of sugar and put in two ûqiyas of rosewater and boil it in a ceramic pot until it is on the point of thickening and sticks between the fingers. Then take a third of a ratl of split almonds, fried, not burnt, and pound well and throw the sugar on them and stir it on the fire until thickened. Then spread it out on a dish and sprinkle it with ground sugar.

2 c sugar   5 oz = ⅞ c slivered almonds
5 T rosewater   1-2 T more sugar

Toast the almonds in a hot (400°) frying pan for 3-5 minutes, stirring continuously. Then crush them with mortar and pestle to something between ground and chopped. Cook sugar and rosewater mixture on medium high until it comes to a boil, reduce to medium and continue cooking to a temperature of 275°, about ten minutes. Combine syrup and nuts in a frying pan, cook at medium to medium high, stirring constantly, for another nine minutes, turn out on a plate and sprinkle with sugar. An alternative interpretation of the original recipe is that you cook the syrup and nuts together only long enough to get them well mixed; the binder is then sugar syrup rather than carmelized sugar. Both ways work.

Barad
al-Baghdadi p. 211

Take best white flour, made into a dough, and leave to rise. Put a basin on the fire, with some sesame-oil. When boiling, take in a reticulated ladle some of the dough, and shake it into the oil, so that as each drop of the dough falls in, it sets. As each piece is cooked, remove with another ladle to drain off the oil. Take honey as required, mix with rose water, and put over the fire to boil to a consistency: then take off, and while still in the basin, whip until white. Throw in the barad, and place out on a soft-oiled surface, pressing in the shape of the mould. Then cut into pieces, and serve.

½ c white flour   1 ¼ c sesame oil
½ c water   1 T rose water
½ t dried yeast   ½ c honey
or ¼ c sourdough

Make the flour and water into a smooth batter. If using yeast mix it with 2 t water, wait about 10 minutes, then add it (or the sourdough) to the flour-water mixture. Let stand 2-3 hours. Heat 1 c of the sesame oil to about 300° in a large frying pan. Pour the batter through a ladle or skimmer with small holes in it, so as to form small balls in the hot oil. Cook to a pale brown (1-3 minutes), take out, drain on paper towel. Add more sesame oil when it gets low.

Mix rose water and honey, cook to 250°. Pay close attention–you want it almost but not quite boiling over. As it cools, whip it; it eventually takes a sort of whipped butter consistency, with a light color. Mix it with the fried dough, press down on an oiled plate, press down from above with another plate or a spatula. Chill before serving.

It has some tendency to come out a bit oily; you may want to use paper towels during the pressing to absorb as much of the surplus oil as possible.

Hais
al-Baghdadi p. 214 (Good)

Take fine dry bread, or biscuit, and grind up well. Take a ratl of this, and three quarters of a ratl of fresh or preserved dates with the stones removed, together with three uqiya of ground almonds and pistachios. Knead all together very well with the hands. Refine two uqiya of sesame-oil, and pour over, working with the hand until it is mixed in. Make into cabobs, and dust with fine-ground sugar. If desired, instead of sesame-oil use butter. This is excellent for travellers.

⅓ c almonds   7 T melted butter
⅓ c pistachios   *or* sesame oil
2 c (1 lb) pitted dates   enough sugar
2 ⅔ c bread crumbs

We usually grind the nuts separately in a food processor, then mix dates, bread crumbs, and nuts in the food processor, then stir in melted butter or oil. Dates vary in hardness—fresher is better (softer, moister). If it does not hold together, add a few tablespoons of water, one at a time. For "cabobs," roll and squeeze into one inch balls. Good as caravan food (or for taking to wars). They last forever if you do not eat them, but you do so they don't.

Nuhud al-Adhra [Virgin's Breasts.]
The Description of Familiar Foods p. 422

Knead sugar, almonds, samid and clarified butter, equal parts, and make them like breasts, and arrange them in a brass tray. Put it into the bread oven until done, and take it out. It comes out excellently.

½ lb blanched almonds   ½ lb semolina
½ lb sugar   ½ lb ghee

Process almonds in food processor until quite fine. Stir together dry ingredients, melt ghee, add, stir until blended. Mold into the shape of breasts, using a small Chinese teacup or something similar, total volume of each from 1 T (small) to 4 T (large). Put on a baking sheet, bake at 350° for about 13 minutes (small) to 18 minutes (large).

Khabîsa with Pomegranate
Andalusian p. A-24

Take half a ratl of sugar and put it in a metal or earthenware pot and pour in three ratls of juice of sweet table pomegranates [rummân sufri; probably tart pomegranates were more common in cooking] and half an ûqiya of rosewater, with a penetrating smell. Boil it gently and after two boilings, add half a mudd of semolina and boil it until the semolina is cooked. Throw in the weight of a quarter dirham of ground and sifted saffron, and three ûqiyas of almonds. Put it in a dish and sprinkle over it the like of pounded sugar, and make balls [literally, hazelnuts] of this.

This is about ½ the original (this assumes the small Mudd is what is meant for the semolina; the alternative is four times as much semolina):

½ c sugar   1 t saffron, ground
3 c pomegranate juice 2 oz blanched almonds
4 t rosewater   ¼ c sugar
1.1 c semolina

Dissolve sugar in juice and rosewater, bring to a boil, simmer for about 5-10 minutes. Stir in semolina, keep stirring and cooking about ten minutes more, stir in saffron and almonds, stir together. Pour out on a plate, sprinkle with the additional 2 oz of sugar, form into balls, let cool. If you want, sprinkle some of the sugar on after the balls are formed.

Drinks

Sekanjabin

Modern Recipe: Dissolve 4 cups of sugar in 2 ½ cups of water; when it comes to a boil add 1 cup wine vinegar. Simmer ½ hour. Add a handful of mint, remove from fire, let cool. Makes 5 c of syrup, which stores without refrigeration. Dilute to taste with ice water (5 to 10 parts water to 1 part syrup).

Note: This is the only recipe in the *Miscelleny* that is based on a modern source: *A Book of Middle Eastern Food*, by Claudia Roden. Sekanjabin is a period drink; it is mentioned in the *Fihrist* of al-Nadim, which was written in the tenth century. The only period recipe I have found for it (in the Andalusian cookbook) is called "Simple Sekanjabin" (see below) and omits the mint. It is one of a large variety of similar drinks described in that cookbook–flavored syrups intended to be diluted in either hot or cold water before drinking.

Syrup of Simple Sikanjabîn (Oxymel)
Andalusian p. A-74

Take a ratl of strong vinegar and mix it with two ratls of sugar, and cook all this until it takes the form of a syrup. Drink an ûqiya of this with three of hot water when fasting: it is beneficial for fevers of jaundice, and calms jaundice and cuts the thirst, since sikanjabîn syrup is beneficial in phlegmatic fevers: make it with six ûqiyas of sour vinegar for a ratl of honey and it is admirable.

This seems to be two different recipes, for two different medical uses. The first, at least, is intended to be drunk hot. In modern Iranian restaurants, sekanjabin is usually served cold, often with grated cucumber.

Syrup of Lemon
Andalusian p. A-74

Take lemon, after peeling its outer skin, press it and take a ratl of juice, and add as much of sugar. Cook it until it takes the form of a syrup. Its advantages are for the heat of bile; it cuts the thirst and binds the bowels.

This we also serve as a strong, hot drink. Alternatively, dilute it in cold water and you have thirteenth century lemonade. All three of the andalusian syrup recipes include comments on medical uses.

Syrup of Pomegranates
Andalusian p. A-74

Take a ratl of sour pomegranates and another of sweet pomegranates, and add their juice to two ratls of sugar, cook all this until it takes the consistency of syrup, and keep until needed. Its benefits: it is useful for fevers, and cuts the thirst, it benefits bilious fevers and lightens the body gently.

Use equal volumes of sugar and pomegranate juice (found in some health food stores). Cook them down to a thick syrup, which will keep, without refrigeration, for a very long time. To serve, dilute one part of syrup in 3 to 6 parts of hot water (to taste).

Odds and Ends

The Making of Stuffed Eggs
Andalusian A-24

Take as many eggs as you like, and boil them whole in hot water; put them in cold water and split them in half with a thread. Take the yolks aside and pound cilantro and put in onion juice, pepper and coriander, and beat all this together with murri, oil and salt and knead the yolks with this until it forms a dough. Then stuff the whites with this and fasten it together, insert a small stick into each egg, and sprinkle them with pepper, God willing.

12 large eggs	5 t murri
3 t crushed cilantro	3 T olive oil
5 t onion juice	½ t salt
¼ t ground pepper	additional pepper
1 ½ t ground coriander	

Bring enough water to cover the eggs to a boil. Boil eggs 15 minutes. Drain, put in cold water, and peel under running cold water. Divide them in half lengthways with a thread (it really works).

Remove yolks, put in a bowl and crush with a fork. Add remaining ingredients, stir to a coarse paste. Fill the half egg whites and rejoin them with a toothpick. Sprinkle with pepper and serve.

A Recipe for Conserving Quince
al-Warraq p. 486

Quarter and core quince, put it in a pot with honey, and pour water on it. Let the pot come to a boil then drain the quince, return it to the pot and add honey to it. Do not use water this time. Cook the quince again until it is well done.

1 lb quince   ½ c honey   1 ½ c honey

Core and quarter the quince(s). Dissolve ½ c honey in 1 ½ c of water. Put the quince in the liquid, bring it to a boil, then drain off the liquid, return the quince to the pot along with 1 ½ c honey. Bring the honey to a boil and cook for about an hour. Put the quince and boiled honey in a jar, seal it.

Mint Paste
Andalusian A-76

Take a ratl of green mint leaves and crush them gently; add three ratls of honey, cleaned of its foam, and blend it until it takes the form of a paste. Then season it with an ūqīya of flower of cloves per ratl. Its benefits: it eases and aids against heaviness of the body and mind, aids in eardrum [? tabli: from the word for drum] dropsy, dissolves phlegm in the various parts of the body, strengthens the urine, and cuts vomit; it is good with sweet grains of anise, eaten with them or after them. It is beneficial, God willing.

2 oz mint leaves   2 ⅔ t cloves
½ c honey

Strip the leaves from the stalks, wash them, crush them in a mortar. Add honey, mush all together for a while. Add cloves. Put in a container. Good for what ails you.

Indian Dishes
Harisa
Ain I Akbari no. 17

Harisa: 10 s. meat; 5 s. crushed wheat; 2 s. ghee; ½ s. salt; 2 d. cinnamon: this gives five dishes.

Note: For units, see p. 6. These *Ain I Akbari* "recipes" give quantities but no instructions; for another harisa recipe, with instructions on how to make it, see p.105.

1 lb meat (leg of lamb)   ½ t cinnamon
3 c water   ½ lb cracked wheat
1 T+ salt   3 oz ghee

Cut lamb in strips, then boil about 20 minutes in water, take out, cool, and shred. Put it back in the pot with the salt, cinnamon and cracked wheat, and simmer, stirring often so that it will not scorch on the bottom. When the cracked wheat is done, add ghee and serve out.

This is quite salty, as is consistant with the other dishes from this source.

Another Recipe, For The Method Of Kedgeree
Nimatnama p. 15

Put three parts of mung dal and one part of rice into sweet-smelling ghee which has been flavored with fenugreek, and fry it well. Add water and salt, cook it well and serve it.

1 c dry mung beans   ⅔ c rice
2 c water   1 c water
½ c ghee   ½ t salt
¼ t fenugreek

Combine the beans with 2 c water, bring to a boil, turn off the heat, leave several hours (or soak in cold water overnight).

Melt ghee, add fenugreek, fry ten minutes until fenugreek seeds are dark. Add beans and rice, fry for ten minutes. Add water and salt, cook 25 minutes, let stand 5 minutes.

Khichri
Ain i Akbari no. 3

Khichri: Rice, mung dal, and ghee 5 s. of each; ⅓ s. salt; this gives seven dishes. [see p. 6 for units]

¾ c dried mung beans   1 ⅓ t salt
¾ c rice = 5 oz   2-4 T ghee
3 oz ghee (6 T)

Note: This source gives ingredients by weight, but no instructions; we are going by a khichri recipe in a modern Indian cookbook.

Put the beans and rice in to soak separately, using about 1 c of water each. After 45 minutes, drain the beans. Melt 3 oz of ghee in a sauce pan, add the drained beans, cook about 5 minutes. Add 2 ¼ c water. Simmer about ½ hour. Drain the rice, add it, salt, and another 1 c water. Simmer about ½ hour. Melt the remaining ghee, stir in, serve.

Note: The use of the remaining ghee is entirely conjectural, based on the fact that a modern Khichri recipe serves melted ghee on the side (with onion fried in it). The result would not be very different if all the ghee were used initially.

(Presumably a different version of the same dish as the previous recipe.)

Qaliya Rice
Nimatnama p. 15

Put ghee into a cooking pot and when it has become hot, flavour it with asafoetida and garlic. When it has become well flavored, put the meat, mixed with chopped potherbs, into the ghee. When it has become marinated [!mistranslation!], add water and add, to an equal amount, one sir of cow's milk. When it has come to the boil, add the washed rice. When it is well cooked, take it off. Cook other rice by the same recipe and, likewise, do not make it with cow's milk but put in four sirs of garlic and whole peppers, and serve it.

3 cloves garlic   1 ¼ c whole milk
⅓ c ghee   1 ¼ c water
⅛ t asafoetida   1 ½ c rice
1 ¼ lb lamb   [½ t salt]
10 oz spinach

Slice garlic, melt ghee, add asafoetida, fry garlic in ghee about 20 minutes. Add meat and spinach, fry about ten minutes. Add milk and water, bring to a boil (about 8 minutes). Add washed rice, salt, cook about 25 minutes, let sit five minutes, serve.

Bread
Ain i Akbari chapter 25

There is a large kind, baked in an oven, made of 10 s. flour; 5 s. milk; 1 ½ s. ghi; ¼ s. salt. They make also smaller ones. The thin kind is baked on an iron plate. One ser will give fifteen, or even more. There are various ways of making it; one kind is called chapati, which is sometimes made of khushka; it tastes very well when served hot.
[see p. 6 for units]

⅜-½ c ghee   1 c milk
3 ½ c flour   ½ T salt

Melt the ghee, stir it into the flour with a fork until there are only very small lumps. Stir in the milk until thoroughly mixed, knead briefly. Put the ball of dough in a bowl covered by a damp cloth and leave for at least an hour. Then knead the dough until it is smooth and elastic, adding a little extra flour if necessary. Either:

Take a ball of dough about 2" in diameter, roll it out to about a 5" diameter circle. Cook it in a hot frying pan without grease. After about 2 minutes it should start to puff up a little in places. Turn it. Cook another 2 minutes. Turn it. Cook another 2 minutes. It should be done. The recipe should make about 11 of these.

Or ...

Take a ball of dough about 3" in diameter. Roll it down to a circle about 7" in diameter and ¼" thick. Heat a baking sheet in a 450° oven. Put the circle of dough on it in the oven. Bake about 6 minutes; it should be puffing up. Turn it over. Bake about 4 minutes more. Take it out. The recipe should make about 5 of these.

Qima Shurba
Ain I Akbari no. 16

Qima [Kheema] Shurba: 10 s. meat; 1 s. rice; 1 s. ghee; ½ s. gram, and the rest as in the Shulla: this gives ten full dishes.

Shulla: 10 s. meat, 3 ½ s. rice; 2 s. ghee; 1 s. gram; 2 s. onions; ½ s. salt; ¼ s. fresh ginger; 2 d. garlic, and round pepper, cinnamon, cardamons, cloves, 1 d. of each: this gives six dishes.

Note: For units, see p. 6. For a shurba recipe with instructions, see page 106.

¼ c ghee	¼ stick cinnamon
1 lb lamb	1 T fresh ginger
3 oz onions	½ t pepper
½ clove garlic	½ t cardamon
1 T salt	½ t cloves
2 T canned chickpeas	3-4 T rice

Melt the ghee, put it in a pot. Brown the meat, onions, and garlic in it for about 5 minutes on a medium heat. Add 1 ¼ c of lukewarm water, salt, chickpeas, cinnamon. Simmer about another 10 minutes, then add peeled chopped ginger, pepper, cardamom and cloves. Add the rice and another ½ c of water. Simmer another ½ hour. Serve. Somewhat salty, which seems to be typical of recipes from this source.

Kashk
Ain I Akbari no. 18

10s. meat; 5 s. crushed wheat; 3 s. ghee; 1 s. gram; ¼ s. salt; 1 ½ s. onions; ½ s. ginger; 1 d. cinnamon; saffron, cloves, cardamons, cumin seed, 2 m. of each: this gives five dishes.

Note: Since the source gives ingredients with quantities but without instructions, the recipe below is a guess based on modern Indian cooking. For units see p. 6. The recipe given below is for one twentieth of the original.

5 oz ghee	⅓ t cumin
2 T fresh ginger	2 ½ oz onions
⅜ t cinnamon	1 lb lamb
½ g saffron:	¼ c canned chickpeas
(1 t loosely packed)	1 ⅓ t salt
⅛ t cloves	1 ½ c cracked wheat
3 cardamom seeds	

Melt ghee, put in spices, cook for 5 minutes. Add onions, cook 10 minutes, add meat, cook 20 minutes. Add chickpeas, salt and wheat, cook 15 minutes, add 1 c water, cook another 20 minutes. Serve.

Qutab or Sanbusa
Ain I Akbari no. 20

Qutab, which the people of Hind call sanbusa: This is made in several ways. 10 s. meat; 4 s. fine flour; 2 s. ghee; 1 s. onions; ¼ s. fresh ginger; ½ s. salt; 2 d. pepper and coriander seed; cardamons, cumin seed, cloves, 1 d. of each; ¼ s. of summaq. This can be cooked in twenty different ways, and gives four full dishes.

Andalusian version of Preparation of Sanbûsak:

Take meat of the innards or any meat you wish and pound fine, and pick out its tendons, and put cut-up fat with it, about a third the amount of the meat, and throw upon all many spices, and increase the pepper, onion juice, cilantro, rue and salt, and mix well, and throw in oil and a little water until wrinkled. Take semolina and knead well with clarified butter and a little pepper, and take an amount of the dough the size of a walnut, and roll it out as large as half a hand-span, and take a piece of stuffing as large as a walnut and put it in the middle of the dough, and wrap up the edges over it, and fry it in fresh oil, and dispose of it as you wish, God willing.

(Compare to modern samosa)

½ c white flour	½ t pepper
½ c whole wheat flour	¼ t cloves
4 T ghee	¼ oz fresh ginger
10 oz meat	¼ t cardamon
1 oz onion	¼ t cumin
½ t coriander	2 t salt
¼ oz sumac	

Mix the flours, cut in the ghee. Sprinkle on about 4 T water and knead to a smooth dough.

Cut up meat, combine it and all remaining ingredients in a food processor. Process a minute or two, until it is all cut finely together. Roll out the dough to about 12"x14", and cut into 2"x2" pieces. Put a little more than a teaspoon of the filling in each, using up all the filling. Wrap the filling in the dough. Alternatively, press thin a little less than a teaspoon of dough, put a little more than a teaspoon of filling in the middle, and stretch the dough to completely cover the filling.

Put about 3 c of cooking oil in a pot, heat to between 350° and 390°, fry the Sanbusa about 2-3 minutes each, drain, serve.

(People who do not like salt should probably cut it in half. Almost all of the dishes from this source come out quite salty).

Sag
Ain I Akbari no. 9

Sag: It is made of spinach, and other greens, and is one of the most pleasant dishes. 10 s. spinach, fennel, etc., 1 ½ s. ghee; 1 s. onions; ½ s. fresh ginger; 5 ½ m. of pepper; ½ m. of cardamons and cloves; this gives six dishes. [for units see p. 6]

⅔ oz fresh ginger	1/20 t cloves
10 oz spinach	½ t pepper
3 oz fennel	1/20 t cardamon
1 ⅓ oz onions	4 T ghee

Peel and chop ginger. Wash and chop the greens and onion, put them in a pot with everything else except the ghee, plus ¼ c water. Cook about 35 minutes on medium heat, stirring occasionally. Add ghee. Cook another few minutes, stirring occasionally.

We have no cooking instructions for this dish, only ingredients and quantities, so are going by a recipe for Saag in a modern Indian cookbook. An alternative interpretation is that the greens etc. are fried in the ghee. The recipe refers to "other greens": cabbage, sorrel, and mint are mentioned in the *Ain I Akbari*.

Chinese Dishes

Carp Another Way
Ni Tsan no. 28

Cut into chunks. Boil some fragrant oil. In another pan use the oil to cook fresh ginger and chinese pepper. Let them fry a little while. Remove them and save in a container. Add the fish in while the oil is still hot. When the fish is fried till it colors [begins to brown], add the ginger and pepper mixture and let them cook a while. Turn off the fire before adding soy sauce. Then proceed as with the previous method.

1 ¾ lbs boned carp	½ t whole peppercorns
3 T fresh ginger	¼-⅜ c dark soy sauce
⅜ c Chinese sesame oil	

Bone the carp and cut into pieces about 1" cubed or smaller. Peel and chop the ginger. Heat the oil to medium high, cook ginger and pepper in it for about 3 minutes, remove them, and set aside. Add fish and cook for about 5 minutes, then put ginger and pepper back in, cook another 3 minutes. Add the soy sauce, turn off the heat and cover the pan, let sit about another ten minutes and serve over rice.

Barbecued Pork
Ni Tsan no. 47

Wash the meat. Rub spring onion, chinese pepper, honey, a little salt, and wine on it. Hang the meat on bamboo sticks in the saucepan. In the pan put a cup of water and a cup of wine. Cover. Use moist paper to seal up the pan. If the paper dries out, moisten it. Heat the pan with grass bunches; when one is burned up, light another. Then stop the fire and leave for the time it takes to eat a meal. Touch the cover of the pan; if it is cold, remove the cover and turn the meat over. Cover it again and seal again with the moist paper. Heat again with one bunch of grass. It will be cooked when the pan cools again.

1 T spring onion	1 T wine
½ t Chinese pepper	15 oz pork tenderloin
1 T honey	1 c rice wine
½ t salt	1 c water

Mix chopped onion, pepper, honey, salt and 1 T wine. Rub them on the pork. Let stand one hour. Put 1 c rice wine and 1 c water in a pot. Arrange skewers so the pork tenderloin can lie on them and you can still put the lid on; I did it by putting a lower pan inside the pot with the skewers lying across it. Put on the lid, sealing with wet paper towels. Simmer about 1 hour 25 minutes. Take off heat, let cool about an hour. Turn over the pork. Reseal. Bring back to a boil, simmer five minutes, remove from the heat, let sit another half hour or so. Slice.

Mastajhi [Mastic] Soup
A Soup for the Qan p. 275

Mutton (leg; bone and cut up), tsaoko cardamoms (five), cinnamon (2 ch'ien), chickpeas (one-half sheng; pulverize and remove the skins).

Boil ingredients together to make a soup. Strain broth. [Cut up meat and put aside.] Add 2 ho of cooked chickpeas, 1 sheng of aromatic non-glutinous rice, 1 ch'ien of mastajhi. Evenly adjust flavors with a little salt. Add [the] cut-up meat and [garnish with] coriander leaves.

[These quantites are for about 40% of the amount in the original recipe]

7 T canned chickpeas	.8 c jasmine rice
1 lb 2 oz lamb	$\frac{1}{40}$ t mastic
2 cardamoms	1 t salt
$\frac{1}{20}$ t cinnamon	1 T cilantro
3 ½ T canned chickpeas	

Peel 7 T chickpeas and mash. Put the lamb in a pot with 6 c water, cardamom, cinnamon and mashed chickpeas. Boil for 1 hour 10 minutes. Boil remaining chickpeas for about 15 minutes.

Remove meat and strain everything else, forcing the chickpea mush through the strainer. Return the liquid to the pot, add rice, mastic, and cooked chickpeas, and boil for another 20 minutes. Cut meat up in pieces. Return it to the pot, add salt, sprinkle chopped cilantro on top, and serve.

[This is from a Chinese cookbook/health manual written for a Mongol emperor of China; some of the recipes show Mongol or Middle Eastern influence, this being one of the latter.]

Index of Recipes

A Food of Hens	28
A Good Filling	61
A Pottage of Quinces	60
A Recipe for Rice Porridge	107
A Tart with Plums	49
Adas	100
Adasiya	100
Ahrash [Isfîriyâ]	96
Almond Butter	72
Almond Fricatellae	31
Almond Milk	7
Alows de Beef or de Motoun	39
An Apple Tart	49
Andalusian Chicken	77
Anjudhâniyyah of Yahya b. Khalid	80
Another Crust with Tame Creatures	44
Another Kind of Lamb Breast	110
Another Pottage of Coriander	67
Arbolettys	73
Armored Turnips	11
Asparagus with Meat Stuffing	78
Autre Vele en Bokenade	35
Badî'i, the Remarkable Dish	108
Badinjan Muhassa	111
Baid Masus	112
Baqliyya of Ziryab's	79
Baqliyya with Eggplants	88
Barad	123
Barbecued Pork	129
Barmakiyya	110
Beef Hash	38
Beef y-Stewed	32
Benes Yfryed	18
Berenjenas a la Morisca	15
Blamaunger in Lenten	21
Blank Desure	67
Boiled Meats Ordinary	31
Bourbelier of Wild Pig	38
Brawn en Peuerade	35
Brawune Fryez	39
Brazzatelle of Milk and Sugar	9
Bread	
Ain-i-Akbari	127
Folded, from Ifriquiyya	76
Loaf Kneaded with Butter	75
of Abu Hamza	75
Platina	11
Qursas	114
Bruet of Savoy	33
Bruette Saake	29
Buen Membrillate	60
Buran	90
Buraniya	83
Byzantine Murri	5
Caboges	13
Cakes with Honey	121
Cameline Sauce	66
Canisiones	47
Capons Stwed	26
Cardoons with Meat	80
Carp Another Way	129
Caudell	65
Cazuela de Carne	34
Cazuela de Salmon— Salmon Casserole	19
Chare de Wardone	61
Chawettys	42
Chebolace	12
Cheese and Flour Cake	120
Cheesecakes	52
Chicken Covered with Walnuts and Saffron	77
Chicken Tart	42
Chicones in Mose	30
Chisan	20
Chopped Liver	40
Chykens in Hocchee	25
Cinnamon Bruet	27
Cold Sage Chicken	29
Condoignac	73
Conserving Quince	126
Conyng, Hen, or Mallard	30
Cooked Dish of Lentils	99
Cooked Fried Chicken	98
Corat	40
Cormarye	33
Counterfeit (Vegetarian) Isfîriyâ	95
Covered Tabâhajiyya	89
Cow's Meat	34
Creme Boylede	53
Cress in Lent with Milk of Almonds	13
Cressee	71
Creteyney	26
Cretonnée of New Peas	24
Crustade	43
Crustade Gentyle	45
Cryspes	58
Cuskynoles	59
Custard Tart	52
Custarde	51

Dafâir, Braids	115
Darioles	52
Dish Dictated by Abu Ishaq	97
Dish Prepared with Fried Eggplant	79
Douce Ame	29
Dressed Eggplant	113
Eggplant Isfîriyâ	94
Eggplant Pancakes	93
Eggplant, Dish of	78
Egredouncye	37
Excellent Boiled Salad	18
Excellent Cake	47
Excellent Small Cakes	46
Fine Powder of Spices	41
Flampoyntes Bake	44
Flathonys	53
Flaune of Almayne	50
Flesh of Veal	39
Fricassee of Whatever Meat You Wish	37
Frictella from Apples	56
Fried Broad Beans	17
Fried Gourd	14
Fried Tafâyâ	98
Fried Version of the Same	94
Fritter of Milk	57
Fritur þat Hatte Emeles	55
Froys	36
Froyse out of Lentyn	37
Frumente	71
Frytour Blaunched	56
Frytour of Erbes	55
Fuliyyah	100
Funges	17
Fustuqiyya	85
Fylettes en Galentyne	35
Galantine for Carp	21
Garbage	30
Garlic Sauce with Walnuts or Almonds	66
Garlic Sauce, a More Colored	67
Gaylede	60
Gharibah	91
Gingerbrede	62
Gnochi	68
Golden Morsels	58
Gourd in Juice	14
Gourdes in potage	38
Green Broth of Eggs and Cheese	24
Green Isfidhbaja by Ibrahim bin al-Mahdi	82
Green Pesen Royal	16
Hais	124
Harisa	126
Harisah	105
Hen Roasted in a Pot at Home	110
Hen Roasted in the Oven	109
Herbelade	45
Himmasiyya (a Garbanzo Dish)	85
Hippocras	64
Hulwa	122
Ibn al-Mahdi's Maghmûm	109
Icelandic Chicken	25
Isfanakh Mutajjan	112
Isfîriyâ	96
Isfîriyâ, Simple	96
Iumbolls	48
Jance	65
Jannâniyya	92
Jazariyyah	83
Judhaba of Bananas	113
Ka'k made for Abu 'Ata Sahl bin Salim	75
Ka'k Stuffed with Sugar	117
Kashk	128
Kedgeree	126
Khabîsa with Pomegranate	124
Khichri	127
Khushkananaj	116
Khushkananaj Shaped like Crescents	116
Koken van Honer	44
Labaniya	89
Labaniyyah	106
Lange Wortys de Chare	16
Leek Pottage	19
Lemon Dish	68
Lente Frytoures	56
Lenten Foyles	13
Lesagne	70
Limonada	68
Longe Frutours	57
Longe Wortes de Pesone	15
Lord's Salt	74
Losenges Fryes	56
Losyns	68
Macrows	70
Madira	90
Mahshi, a Stuffed Dish	109
Makke	17
Makshufa	122
Malaches of Pork	41
Malaches Whyte	43
Manjar Lento o Suave	55
Manjar Principal	54
Maqluba	95
Maqluba al Tirrikh	95
Marmelade of Quinces or Damsons	62
Mastajhi [Mastic] Soup	130
Maumenye Ryalle	27
Meat Casserole	34
Meat Roasted over Coals	110
Meatballs	8

Mete of Cypree	36
Milkemete	54
Mincebek [or, Funnel Cakes]	58
Mint Paste	126
Mirause of Catelonia	28
Mirrauste de Manzanas	66
Mirrauste of Apples	66
Mishmishiya	86
Moorish Chicken	28
Moorish Eggplant	15
More Colored Garlic Sauce	67
Mortrewys of Flesh	38
Mu'allak	89
Mufarraka	98
Mujabbana (Fried Cheese Pie)	118
Mukhallal	81
Murakkaba	119
Murakkaba Layered with Dates	120
Murri	5
Musammana [Buttered]	121
Mushroom Pastries	41
Mustard	67
Mustard Greens	11
Muthallath with Heads of Lettuce	78
Muzawwara (Vegetarian Dish)	99
Naranjiya	86
Nourroys Pies	43
Nuhud al-Adhra	124
On Preparing Lettuce	14
Onion Juice	8
Otro Potaje de Culantro Llamado Tercio	67
Oven Cheese Pie, Which We Call Toledan	118
Oysters in Bruette	21
Palace Chicken with Mustard	76
Papyns	54
Para Hazer Tortillon Relleno	10
Payn Ragoun	63
Perre	16
Pescoddes	73
Picadinho de Carne de Vaca	38
Pie Crust	7
Pine Kernels	63
Pipefarces	55
Plain Liftiyya	92
Pork Doucetty	44
Pot Torteli	70
Potage from Meat	22
Potage of Beans Boiled	24
Potage of Onions	18
Potage with Turnips	22
Potaje de Fideos	69
Potaje de Porrada	19
Pottage of Noodles	69
Pottage with Whole Herbs	32
Preparing Carrots and Parsnips	11
Prince-Bisket	46
Principal Dish	54
Puffy Fricatellae	57
Puree with Leeks	19
Pynade	63
Qaliya Rice	127
Qima Shurba	128
Quince Marmalade	73
Quinces in Pastry	48
Qursas	114
Qutab or Sanbusa	128
Raihaniya	87
Rapes in Potage	22
Rastons	9
Ravioli	69
Rice Cooked over Water	107
Rice Fricatellae	57
Rishta	105
Rizz Hulw	106
Roast Chicken	25
Roast of Meat	98
Russian Cabbage and Greens	12
Rutabiya	91
Ryschewys Closed and Fried	59
Ryse of Fische Daye	71
Safarjaliyya, a Dish Made with Quinces	84
Safarjaliyya, a Quince Dish	84
Saffron Broth	23
Sag	129
Salma	105
Salmon Roste in Sauce	20
Savoury Tosted or Melted Cheese	65
Sawgeat	73
Sekanjabin	125
Sesame Candy	63
Short Paest for Tarte	45
Shurba	106
Shushbarak	106
Sicilian Dish	80
Sikanjabîn, Syrup of Simple	125
Sikbaj	93
Simple White Tafâyâ, Called Isfîdhbâja	87
Slow or Smooth Dish	55
Small Mead	64
Soup Called Menjoire	23
Sourdough	7
Soused Eggplants	113
Soused Poultry	88
Spinach Tart	41
Strawberye	60
Stuffed Eggs	72, 125
Stuffed Qanânît, Fried Cannoli	115
Stuffed Tortillon	10

Sturgeon pour Porpeys	20
Stwed Mutton	32
Sukkariyya, a Sugar Dish	123
Syrup of Lemon	125
Syrup of Pomegranates	125
Tabâhaja of Burâniyya	83
Tabâhajah from the Manuscript of Yahya	97
Tabâhajiyya, Another	97
Tart de Bry	52
Tart on Ember Day	40
Tarte of Beans	46
Tarte of Spinage	17
Tarte of Strawberries	49
Tartlettes	70
Tarts owte of Lente	42
Tartys in Applis	48
Tasty Maghmuma by Ishaq al-Mawsili	88
Taylours	61
Tharda of Isfunj with Milk	103
Tharda of Lamb with Garbanzos	103
Tharda of Zabarbada	101
Tharda, Al-Ghassani's	102
Tharid	101
Tharid that the People of Ifriqiyya (Tunisia) Call Fatîr	102
Tharîda in the Style of the People of Bijaya	103
Tharîda with Lamb and Spinach	104
Tharîdah, White of al Rashid	101
Thûmiyya, a Garlicky Dish	108
Torta from Gourds	51
Torta from Red Chickpeas	51
Torta of Herbs in the Month of May	50
Tostee	62
Tuffahiya	82
Tuffâhiyya (Apple Stew) with Eggplants	81
Variants on Platina Soups	23
Veal, Kid, or Hen in Bokenade	27
Virgin's Breasts	124
Vyaunde de Cyprys in Lent	21
Weak Honey Drink	64
White Karanbiyya, a Cabbage Dish	91
White Pudding	74
White Tharîda with Onion	104
White Torta	53
Zabarbada of Fresh Cheese	112
Zanzarella	23
Zirbaya	93

Additional Material on Period Cooking

Cooking from Primary Sources: Some General Comments

One definition of what the Society is about is "studying the past by selective recreation." Period cooking is one of the few activities that really lets us do this, in a sense of "study" that goes substantially beyond merely learning things that other people already know. There are thousands of pages of period source material available, and I would guess that most of the dishes have not been made by anyone in the past three hundred years. As with many things, the best way to learn is to do it; the following comments are intended to make the process a little easier.

When working with early English recipes, remember that the spelling has changed much more than the language and is often wildly inconsistent; one fifteenth century recipe contains the word "Chickens" four times with four different spellings, of which the first is "Schyconys." It often helps to try sounding out strange words, in the hope that they will be more familiar to the ear than to the eye.

Recipes rarely include quantities, temperatures, or times. Working out a recipe consists mostly of discovering that information by trial and error. You may find a modern cookbook useful in doing so. The idea is not to adapt a modern recipe but to use the modern recipe for information on how long a chicken has to be boiled before it is done or how much salt is added to a given volume of stew. That gives you a first guess, to be used the first time you try the dish and modified accordingly.

It is sometimes asserted that real medieval food would be too highly flavored for modern palates. Thomas Austin, the 19th-century editor of *Two Fifteenth Century Cookery Books,* mentions a Cinnamon Soup as evidence that medieval people preferred strongly seasoned food. But since his reference is not to a recipe but only an item in a menu, the fact that he took it as evidence may tell us more about 19th c. English cooking than medieval English cooking.

Our experience with recipes that do contain information on quantities suggests that the assertion is not true. For many years we made Hippocras from the recipe in *Le Menagier de Paris* (p. 64), using about half the ratio of sugar and spices to wine specified in the original, because otherwise it came out too sweet for our tastes. Eventually Jeremy de Merstone (George J. Perkins) pointed out to us that, while the pound and ounce used in Paris in 1391 were approximately the same as the modern pound and ounce, the quart was equal to almost two modern U.S. quarts–which implied that, by modifying the recipe to taste, we had gotten back to almost exactly the proportions of the original. The same conclusion–that medieval food, although hardly bland, was not extraordinarily spicy–is suggested by our experience with other recipes. One exception is a collection of dishes from 16th century India for which we have ingredient lists with quantities but without instructions; many of them turn out too salty for modern tastes. I am told that the same is true of modern Indian cooking in India.

Along with the idea that medieval food was overspiced one finds the claim that the reason it was overspiced was to hide the taste of rotten meat, due to the lack of modern refrigeration. We have found no evidence to support that claim and quite a lot to oppose it. Chiquart's description of how to put on a large feast, for example, makes it clear that he expects to slaughter animals on site. Other sources show medieval cooks concerned with the risk of spoiled meat and taking reasonable precautions to deal with it. Finally, there is the observation that hiding the taste of spoiled meat does not prevent the effects; a cook who routinely poisoned his employer and his guests would be unlikely to keep his position for long.

Two reference books that we have found helpful are the *Larousse Gastronomique* and the *Oxford English Dictionary*. The former is a dictionary of cooking, available in both English and French editions. The latter, which is also useful for many other sorts of SCA research, is the standard English scholar's dictionary; it contains a much more extensive range of obsolete words and meanings than an ordinary dictionary. Also, *Two Fifteenth Century Cookbooks* and *Curye on Inglysch* contain glossaries.

An approach to developing recipes that we have found both productive and entertaining is to hold cooking workshops. We select recipes that we would like to try or retry and invite anyone interested to come help us cook them. The workshop starts in the afternoon. As each person arrives, he chooses a recipe to do. We suggest that people who have not cooked from period recipes before do new recipes so that they can actually have the experience of working directly from an untouched original. The details of how the recipe is being prepared–quantities, temperatures, times and techniques–are written down as the dish is prepared. The afternoon and early evening are spent cooking, eating, and discussing how to modify the recipes next time; we offer anyone who wishes copies of the recipes to experiment with further at home. Many of the recipes in this book were developed at such sessions. We have never yet had to send out for pizza.

Tourney and War Food

Suppose you are going to a tournament and want to bring period food to eat and share during the day. Suppose you are going to a camping event, such as the Pennsic war, and expect to be encamped for something between a weekend and two weeks. What period foods are likely to prove useful?

For both one day events and wars, we have accumulated a small collection of period foods and drinks that can be made in advance and kept without refrigeration for an almost unlimited period of time. They include *Hulwa* (p. 121), *Hais* (p. 117), *Prince-Bisket* (p. 46), *Gingerbrede* (p. 46), *Excellent Cake* (p. 47; this is actually slightly out of period), *Khushkananaj* (p. 116), *Sekanjabin* (p. 125) and *Syrup of Pomegranate* (p. 125). The last two are drinks that are prepared as syrups and diluted (with cold water for sekanjabin and hot water for granatus) just before being served. The syrups are sufficiently concentrated so that, like honey or molasses, they keep indefinitely.

For a one day event we will often also bring a cold meat or cheese pie; *Spinach Tart* (p. 41) is one of our favorites. In addition, one can bring bread, cheese, sausage, nuts, dried fruit–all things which were eaten in period and can keep for a reasonable length of time.

A camping event, especially one more than two days long, raises a new set of challenges and opportunities–period cooking with period equipment. One of the associated problems is how to keep perishable ingredients long enough so that you can bring them at the beginning of the event and use them at the end. One could keep things in a cooler with lots of ice–especially at Pennsic, where ice is available to be bought. This is, however, a considerable nuisance–and besides, it is unlikely that either coolers or ice were available at a real medieval war.

Better solutions are to choose dishes that do not require perishable ingredients or to find period ways of preserving such ingredients. One of our future projects along these lines is to work out some good recipes for salted or dried fish, which was an important food in the Middle Ages and one that keeps indefinitely. Our most successful preserving technique so far is to pickle meat or fowl, using *Lord's Salt* (p. 74). The pickled meat is strongly flavored with vinegar and spices, so we pick a recipe to use it in that contains vinegar or verjuice in its list of ingredients. We wash most of the pickling solution off the meat and make up the recipe omitting the sour ingredient (and any spices that are already in the pickled meat). Two recipes that work well with pickled chicken are *Veal, Kid, or Hen in Bokenade* (p. 27) and *Conyng, Hen, or Mallard* (p. 29).

There is an Indian bread (p. 126) and two Islamic pastries, *Murakkaba* (p. 121) and *Musammana* (p. 121) which are made in a frying pan rather than an oven, and are therefore easy to make on site. There are also recipes for fritters and funnel cakes (pp 55-58), many of which are suitable for camping events.

There are many other possibilities for non-perishable period dishes. They include recipes using lentils and other dried beans (pp. 17-18, 99-100). They also include one very familiar dish–macaroni and cheese, known in the Middle Ages as *Macrows* (p. 70) or *Losyns* (p. 68).

If you have fresh meat available, there are many possible recipes; *Meat Roasted Over Coals* (p. 110) is good and very straightforward. If you roast a large amount of meat for one evening's dinner, *A Roast of Meat* (p. 98) is a good way of using up leftover roast meat for the next meal.

Creative Medieval Cooking

It is sometimes claimed that the dishes served at an SCA feast are medieval even though they do not come from any period cookbook. The idea is that the cook is producing original creations in a medieval style. After all, there is no reason to assume that all, or even very many, medieval cooks used cookbooks.

In principle, this is a legitimate argument–if it is made by an experienced medieval cook. Since we do not have the option of living in the Middle Ages, the only practical way to become an experienced medieval cook is by cooking from medieval cookbooks. In my experience, however, the people who make this argument have rarely done much, if any, cooking from period sources; their "original medieval creations" are usually either modern ethnic dishes or modified versions of standard modern recipes.

Even if "creative medieval cookery" is done by taking period recipes and modifying them, it is a risky business. Unless the cook has extensive experience cooking medieval recipes in their original form, he is likely to modify them in the direction of modern tastes–in order to make them fit better his ideas of what they should be like. But one of the attractions of medieval cooking is that it lets us discover things we do not expect–combinations of spices, or ways of preparing dishes, that seem strange to modern tastes yet turn out to be surprisingly good.

I would therefore advise anyone interested in medieval cooking to try to keep as closely as possible to the original recipe. There may, of course, be practical difficulties that prevent you from following the recipe exactly–ingredients you cannot obtain, cooking methods you cannot use ("hang it in a chimney where a fire is kept all the year"), or the like. But I do not think it is ever desirable, when first cooking a dish, to change it merely because you suspect that if you follow the recipe you will not like the result. The people who wrote the recipes down knew a great deal more about period cookery than we do; it is our job to be their students, not their teachers.

Period, Ethnic, and Traditional

There is some tendency for people in the Society to assume that all ethnic food is period. Thus, for example, "oriental" feasts often consist of dishes that one would find in a modern Chinese or Japanese restaurant and traditional or "peasant" cooking is sometimes included in feasts, even when there is no evidence that the particular dishes were made in period.

The assumption is a dangerous one; America is not the only place where things change over time. The fact that a dish was made by your grandmother, or even that she says she got it from her grandmother, may be evidence that the dish is a hundred years old; it is not evidence that it dates from before 1600. While traditional societies may appear very old-fashioned to us, there is ample evidence that such societies in general, and their cooking in particular, change over time. Potatoes are an important part of traditional cooking in Ireland, and tomatoes in Italy. Yet both are New World vegetables; they could not have been used before 1492 and were not in common use in Europe until a good deal later than that.

If we had no sources for medieval recipes, foreign or traditional dishes would be more suited to our feasts than hamburgers and french fries or Coke and pizza; even if they are not actually medieval, they at least help create the feeling that we are no longer in our normal Twentieth Century world. Similarly, if we had no sources for period dance, modern folk dances would fit into an event better than disco dancing. Since we do have sources for both period recipes and period dances, there seems no good reason to use out-of-period substitutes.

Late Period and Out of Period Foodstuffs

To do period cooking, it is desirable to avoid ingredients that were not available to period cooks. "Period," for the purposes of the SCA, is defined as pre-seventeenth century. Since most of the ingredients that are available now and were not available during the Middle Ages came into use between 1500 and 1700, it is not always easy to know which of them were available by the year 1600.

One solution is to avoid all of the new ingredients, thus, in effect, moving the cutoff date back to about 1492. This makes a good deal of sense as a way of learning what early cooking was like. We already know what a cuisine that includes the new foodstuffs is like–it is all around us. If we restrict ourselves to ingredients that were available throughout the Middle Ages and the Renaissance, we are likely to learn a good deal more about how period cooking differed from modern cooking than if we include in our cooking anything that might possibly have been in use somewhere in Europe by late December of 1600.

While there is much to be said for such a voluntary restriction, nothing in the rules or customs of the Society requires it of all cooks. Those who are willing to use late foodstuffs, providing they were in use by 1600, are left with the problem of determining which ones meet that requirement. This article is an attempt to do so.

Corn, potatoes, cocoa, vanilla, peppers –essentially the whole list of New World foods–were used in the New World long before Columbus. Since almost all Society personae are from the Old World, it seems reasonable to limit ourselves to foods that came into use in the Old World before 1600. A further argument in favor of doing so is that we have–so far as I know–no Aztec cookbooks, although there are descriptions by early travellers of what the natives of the New World ate and how they prepared it; references can be found in Finan and Coe. Although potatoes were eaten in South America during the fifteenth century, they were not eaten in the dishes for which we have fifteenth century recipes.

Most of our period feasts are based on the cooking of a very limited part of the Old World. Almost all period cookbooks used in the Society are either Western European or Islamic. For the purposes of this article I will therefore be mainly concerned with the availability of foods in Western Europe prior to the year 1600–more precisely, with the question of what foods were sufficiently well known so that they might plausibly have been served at a feast.

In trying to determine which foods were available in Western Europe before 1600, I have relied on a variety of sources. They include the *Oxford English Dictionary* (used primarily to determine when and in what context the English name of a food was first used–hereafter OED), cookbooks, and secondary sources including the *Larousse Gastronomique* (LG) and the *Encyclopedia Britannica,* 11th edition (EB).

Most of the new foodstuffs of the sixteenth and seventeenth century came from the New World, but there were some important exceptions. I will start with them.

Old World Foods

Coffee

The coffee plant is apparently native to Abyssinia. The use of coffee in Abyssinia was recorded in the fifteenth century and regarded at that time as an ancient practice (EB). I believe that there is a reference in one of the Greek historians to what sounds like coffee being drunk in what might well be Abyssinia, but I have not yet succeeded in tracking it down.

Coffee was apparently introduced into Yemen from Abyssinia in the middle of the 15th century. It reached Mecca in the last decade of the century and Cairo in the first decade of the 16th century (Hattox).

The use of coffee in Egypt is mentioned by a European resident near the end of the sixteenth century. It was brought to Italy in 1615 and to Paris in 1647 (LG). The first coffee house in England was opened in Oxford in 1650 (Wilson), and the first one in London in 1652 (EB). The earliest use of the word in English is in 1592, in a passage describing its use in Turkey (OED).

It appears that coffee is out of period for European feasts and late period for Islamic ones.

Tea

The use of tea in China and Ceylon goes back to prehistoric times. According to the *Larousse*, it was brought to Europe by the Dutch in 1610 and to England in 1644. According to the OED, it was first imported into Europe in the 17th century and first mentioned in a European language (Portuguese) in 1559. The first use of the word in English (in the form "Cha") is given as 1598; the passage seems to describe its use in China.

It appears that tea is out of period for European feasts and (since it was being brought from China by sea rather than overland) even further out of period for Islamic feasts. It is, of course, in period for Chinese and Japanese feasts. So far as I know, iced tea is a modern invention.

Bananas

The Four Seasons of the House of Cerruti, an Italian manuscript of the fourteenth century (based on an Arab work of the eleventh century) mentions bananas as something which "we know of .. only from texts or tales from merchants from Cyprus or pilgrims from the Holy Land. Sicilians ... know them well." It is clear from the accompanying picture that the artist had never seen a banana. The first bunch of bananas is said to have reached England in 1633 (Wilson).

Citrus Fruit

Citrus fruit are native to southern Asia and the Malay Archipelago, and cultivated citrus occur very early in China. In the West, the citron was known to classical antiquity. By the 10th c. the Arabs had sour oranges, and by the 12th century lemon, sour orange, citron, and pummelo had all made it as far as Spain and North Africa. By the 13th century lemon, sour orange, citron, and what is probably lime are described from northern Italy. The sweet orange is mentioned in a few documents from the second half of the 15th century as growing in Italy and southern France, and seems to have been fairly widely grown by the early 16th century. In 1520 or thereabouts the Portuguese brought a new and superior sweet orange variety from China, which then spread around the citrus-growing areas of Europe in the 16th and 17th centuries. Mandarin oranges do not seem to have made it to Europe until the early 19th century. The grapefruit seems to have developed out of the pummelo in the West Indies in the 18th c. (Batchelor and Webber). Sour oranges are still grown for use in marmalade; the usual variety is the Seville orange.

Artichokes and Cardoons

According to some sources, including McGee, the globe artichoke was known in classical antiquity; others describe it as bred out of the cardoon sometime in the later middle ages, probably in Muslim Spain. The latin word is "*cynara*;" our word "artichoke" comes from the Arabic "al kharshûf." Some modern sources describe the cardoon as a kind of artichoke, while others regard it as a different vegetable ancestral to the artichoke. My guess is that the classical "cynara" was the cardoon, making the globe artichoke familiar to us late period.

Molasses

Molasses is a residue from the process of refining sugar. Treacle was originally the name of a medical mixture one of whose ingredients was honey. It originated in classical antiquity and survived into the Middle Ages; at some point molasses or sugar syrup began to be used instead of honey for the base. "When the production of molasses in Britain's refineries out-stripped the needs of both apothecaries and distillers, it was sold off in its natural unmedicated state as a cheap sweetener. Its name of molasses was taken by the early settlers to America. But in Britain in the later seventeenth century the alternative term 'common treacle' came into circulation, and thereafter it was known simply as treacle." (Wilson).

Since, according to Wilson, England had its own sugar refineries by 1540, molasses might have been used as a sweetener in England before 1600. The word first appears in English in 1582 and all of the pre-1600 references are to its existence abroad. Molasses is, however, mentioned by Hugh Platt in the 1609 edition of *Delights for Ladies*; I have not been able to find a copy of an earlier edition. Presumably molasses would have been used earlier in areas where sugar was grown, such as Spain, Sicily and the Middle East.

Chemical Leavenings

So far as we can discover, both baking soda and baking powder are far out of period. According to the 1992 Old Farmer's Almanac, Saleratus (Potassium Bicarbonate) was patented as a chemical leavening in 1840. Hartshorn (Ammonium Carbonate) was used for stiffening jellies by about the end of the sixteenth century (Wilson) but we have found no reference to its use as a leavening agent prior to the late 18th century.

New World Foods
Potatoes

Sweet potatoes are described in 1555 as growing in the West Indies. By 1587 they are said to be "brought out of" Spain and Portugal, and described as venerous (aphrodisiacal). In 1599 Ben Johnson describes something as "above all your potatoes or oyster pies."

Ordinary potatoes, according to the OED, were described in 1553 and introduced into Spain shortly after 1580. They reached Italy about 1585 and were being grown in England by 1596. By 1678 the potato is described as "common in English gardens."

The *Larousse* gives somewhat earlier dates–1539 or 40 for the original importation into Spain, 1563 for the introduction into England ("but its cultivation was neglected there") and 1586 for the reintroduction by Sir Francis Drake. In 1593 several farmers were engaged to grow it in France, but in 1630 "the Parliament of Besançon, from fear of leprosy, forbade the cultivation of the potato." In 1619 "Potato figures among the foods to be served at the Royal table in England."

Both sorts of potatoes were being grown in parts of Europe before 1600, but it is not clear whether either was common enough to have been served at a feast. If served, potatoes would almost certainly have been regarded as a novelty. I know of no period recipes using potatoes. According to Crosby, the sweet potato arrived in China "at least as early as the 1560's."

Corn

"Corn," in British usage, refers to grains in general, most commonly wheat. The earliest reference in the OED to maize, the British name for the grain that Americans call corn, is from 1555. All of the pre-1600 references are to maize as a plant grown in the New World. Knowledge of maize seems to have spread rapidly; a picture of the plant appears in a Chinese book on botany from 1562. Pictures appear in European herbals from 1539 on. Finan concludes that they represent at least two distinct types of maize, one similar to Northern Flints, the other similar to some modern Caribbean varieties. Grains are variously described as red, black, brown, blue, white, yellow and purple.

How soon did maize become something more than a curiosity? Leonhard Fuchs, writing in Germany in 1542, described it as "now growing in all gardens" [*De historia stirpium*–cited in Finan]. That suggests that in at least one European country it was common enough before 1600 so that it could have been served at a feast–although I know of no evidence that it in fact was, and no period recipes for it. On the other hand, John Gerard wrote, in 1597: "We have as yet no certaine proofe or experience concerning the vertues of this kinde of Corne, although the barbarous Indians which know no better are constrained to make a vertue of necessitie, and think it a good food: whereas we may easily judge that it nourisheth but little, and is of a hard and euill digestion, a more convenient food for swine than for man" (Crosby). Gerard's conclusion is still widely accepted in Europe. In West Africa, however, maize was under cultivation "at least as early as the second half of the sixteenth century..." and in China in the sixteenth century (Crosby). There is also a reference to its being grown in the Middle East in the 1570's (Crosby).

Before leaving the subject of maize, I should mention that there have been occasional attempts to argue that it either had an Old World origin or spread to the Old World prior to Columbus. Mangelsdorf discusses the arguments at some length and concludes that they are mistaken.

I know of no evidence that either corn starch or corn syrup was used in period.

Tomatoes

The first European reference to the tomato is apparently one in a book published in Venice in 1544; it describes the tomato as having been brought to Italy "in our time" and eaten in Italy "fried in oil and with salt and pepper." It appears from later references that tomatoes were used as food in both Spain and Italy from the 1500's on. The first printed recipes using tomatoes appear in Italian at the end of the 17th century and are described as "alla Spagnuola." The first use of "Tomato" in English occurs in 1604 in a description of the West Indies (OED). As late as 1753, an English writer describes tomatoes as "a fruit...eaten either stewed or raw by the Spaniards and Italians and by the Jew families in England." But another writer, at about the same time, asserts that the tomato is "now much used in England," especially for soups and sauces. (Most of this is from Longone.)

It appears tomatoes are out of period for northern Europe and late period for southern Europe, but that no period recipes more elaborate than "fried in oil and with salt and pepper" are known.

Capsicum Peppers

The term "pepper" refers to two entirely different groups of plants. The spice pepper, both black and white, is the fruit of any of a group of related Old World trees, and is routinely mentioned in period cookbooks. The capsicum peppers, which include both hot peppers (chili, cayenne, paprika, etc.) and sweet or bell peppers, are New World. According to the OED, the first English use of the word "chili" is in 1662. According to Dewitt and Gerlach, there is a Spanish reference to hot peppers from the New World in 1493; apparently the seeds had been brought back by Columbus. They assert that peppers are mentioned in Italy in 1526 and in Hungary (in a list of foreign seeds planted in a noblewoman's garden–as "Turkish Red Pepper") in 1569. They also say that "according to Leonhard Fuchs, an early German professor of medicine, chiles were cultivated in Germany by 1542, in England by 1548, and in the Balkans by 1569." Assuming that both the dates they give and those they attribute to Fuchs are correct, it sounds as though chile peppers, at least, had spread through much of Europe by 1600. This does not, however, imply that they were in common use. We have not found any period recipes using capsicum peppers, nor period references to their being served at feasts.

Beans

Some beans are New World, some Old World. Crosby lists "lima, sieva, Rangoon, Madagascar, butter, Burma, pole, curry, kidney, French, navy, haricot, snap, string, common, and frijole bean" as American and mentions that soybeans are Old World. Broad beans, aka fava beans, are also Old World, as are lentils, chickpeas and the black-eyed bean (*Vigna unguiculata*). According to Crosby, the haricot bean "was in Europe by at least 1542, for in that year the botanists Tragus and Leonard Fuchs described and sketched it. It was probably grown in appreciable quantities in France by the end of the century; otherwise, why would the Englishman, Barnaby Googe, write of it as the 'French bean' in 1572?" There is also one reference to kidney beans and French beans being grown in the Middle East in the 1570's (Crosby). Some Old World beans were known in Asia but not, as far as we know, in Europe or the Middle East; these include soy beans in China and mung beans in India.

Peanuts

With peanuts as with corn, there has been some controversy over origin. The OED describes them as native to the New World and West Africa. Higgins discusses the evidence at some length and concludes that the peanut is a New World plant introduced into West Africa early in the sixteenth century, probably by the Portuguese, and into the East Indies at about the same time, probably by both the Portuguese and the Spanish. European explorers in Africa a century later observed peanuts, maize, cassava, and tobacco, and concluded that they all were native. He cites Chevalier, Auguste, "Histoire de L'Arachide.," *Rev. Bot. Appl. & d'Agr. Trop.* 13 (146 & 147): 722-752. According to Cosby, peanuts were grown in China in the sixteenth century.

There is some archeological evidence for peanuts in China at a much earlier date, briefly discussed by Simoon; my conclusion from his discussion is that the evidence is probably wrong.

The OED reports no uses of "peanut" (or "groundnut" as a synonym for "peanut") prior to the eighteenth century.

Pumpkin, Squash, Gourd

It seems to be well established that at least three of the four cultivated species of Cucurbita (*C. pepo, C. moschata* and *C. maxima*) existed in the New World long before Columbus; the fourth (*C. ficifolia*) is "ordinarily not thought of as a cultivated plant" (Whittaker), but apparently has been cultivated in the past. Whitaker argues, on the evidence of the absence of these species in the fifteenth century European herbals and their presence in the sixteenth century ones, that they were introduced into Europe from the New World. A variety of *C. pepo* similar to the squash now known as "Small Sugar" is illustrated in an herbal of 1542. What appears to be a field pumpkin is illustrated in 1560, with other varieties appearing in later herbals during the century. Whitaker concludes that "none of the cultivated species of Cucurbita were known to the botanists of the Western world before 1492." If so, all varieties of pumpkins, squash, and vegetable marrows are inappropriate before 1492; some were known in the sixteenth century, but may or may not have been sufficiently common to be used in feasts.

There is, however, a plant translated as "gourd" in both Italian and Islamic cookbooks before 1492. *The Four Seasons of the House of Cerruti*, which is 14th century, shows a "Cucurbite" that looks exactly like a green butternut squash–a fact of which Whitaker seems unaware when asserting the absence of all varieties of Cucurbita from pre-sixteenth century sources. It seems likely, however, that his conclusion was correct, and that what is shown in the picture and used in the recipes is not *C. pepo* but *Lagenaria sicereia*. For details see Paris et. al.

"The white-flowered gourd, *Lagenaria sicereia*," seems to "have been common to both Old and New Worlds" (Whitaker). I am told that the Italian Edible Gourd is a species of Lagenaria and available from, among others, J. L. Hudson, Seedman (www.jlhudsonseeds.net/). Simoons describes a *Lagenaria* still used in modern Chinese cooking. We have obtained what we think is the right gourd from a Chinese grocery store and used it in period recipes with satisfactory results. The taste and texture are somewhat similar to zucchini but less bitter. The Chinese, or perhaps Vietnamese, name for one variety, which the grower assured us had white flowers, is "opo."

Pineapple and Guava

These are New World fruits that were being grown in India in the 16th Century (Crosby).

Blueberry and Cranberry

It appears from comments by Simmons that the term "blueberry" describes a number of different New World species of the genus *Vaccinium*; the bilberry, which is a member of the same genus, is Old World. The blueberry produces "larger and better flavored berries than the European bilberry." According to McGee, "The cultivated blueberry, a native of the American east, north, and northwest, has been purposely bred only since about 1910 ... ."

According to McGee, cranberries are also species of *Vaccinium*. According to several earlier sources, there is disagreement as to whether they are members of *Vaccinium* or belong in a separate genus, *Oxycoccus*. There are both old world and new world cranberries, but "the commercial cranberry ... is an American native." (McGee) The word "cranberry" seems to have come into use with the new world variant of the berry.

It sounds, in both cases, as though a jelly made from modern berries would correspond pretty closely to something that might have been eaten in Europe in period, but individual berries would look noticeably different from their old world relatives. We do not know of any period recipes using either berry.

Spices

According to the OED, the word "allspice" is first used in 1621 and "vanilla" in 1662. Both are from the New World. They might have been used earlier in Spain or Italy, since South American foods seem to have reached those countries earlier than England.

Cocoa

A drink made from cocoa was drunk by the Aztecs; according to the *Larousse*, it was unsweetened, flavored with vanilla, and drunk cold. Cocoa was brought back by the Spaniards in the sixteenth century; they flavored it "with chillies and other hot spices" and made it "into a soup-like concoction." The first recorded use of chocolate in England was in 1650; Wadsworth published a recipe, apparently translated from Spanish, in 1652.

Black cites chocolate almonds being produced by 1670 and the use of chocolate "to flavour little light cakes called 'puffs'" and as a dinner dessert, with one recipe dating from 1681. Clotilde Vesco gives several recipes using chocolate which she dates to the fifteenth century (!) and attributes to documents in Florentine archives, if I correctly interpret the passage, but she gives little information about the originals and I suspect has either misdated or mistranslated them. Perhaps some reader whose Italian is better than mine can pursue the matter further.

The OED gives the first use of "Chocolate" in English as 1604, in a history of the Indies. References to drinking it start in the 1660's. The word "Cocoa" appears much later.

My conclusion is that a drink made from cocoa beans is in period, at least for Spanish personae, although the drink would be very different from modern cocoa, but that the use of chocolate as a food or an ingredient in foods is probably out of period.

Turkeys

The first reference to turkeys in the OED is in 1555. According to the *Larousse*, Brillat-Savarin says that turkeys came into use in Europe in the 17th century. There seems to have been some confusion initially with the guinea fowl, which is an Old World bird; it is therefore hard to be certain which early mentions of turkeys refer to what we now call turkeys. It seems likely, however, that turkeys were being eaten in Europe before 1600.

References

Batchelor, Leon D. and Webber, Herbert John, *The Citrus Industry*, 1946.
Black, Maggie, "Seventeenth Century Chocolate," in *Petits Propos Culinaires*, 14, June 1983.
Coe, Sophie, articles on Aztec and Inca food in *Petits Propos Culinaires*, 19, 20, 21, and 29.
Crosby, Alfred W. Jr., *The Columbian Exchange: Biological and Cultural Consequences of 1492*, Greenwood Publishing, Westport CT, 1972.
Dewitt, Dave and Gerlach, Nancy, *The Whole Chile Pepper Book,* Little, Brown Co., Boston 1990.
Finan, John J., *Maize in the Great Herbals.* Chronica Botanica Company, Waltham, Mass. 1950.
Hattox, Ralph S., *Coffee and Coffeehouses, The Origins of a Social Beverage in the Medieval Near East*, University of Washington Press, Seattle, 1985.
Higgins, B. B., "Origin and Early History of the Peanut" in *The Peanut–The Unpredictable Legume, A Symposium*, The National Fertilizer Association, Washington, D.C. 1951.
Longone, Jan, *From the Kitchen*, The American Magazine and Historical Chronicle Vol. 3 No. 2 1987-88. My principal source on tomatoes.

Mangelsdorf, Paul C., *Corn: Its Origin Evolution and Improvement*. Harvard University Press, Cambridge, Mass. 1974.

McGee, Harold, *On Food and Cooking: The Science and Lore of the Kitchen*, Consumer's Union, Mt. Vernon, N.Y. 1984.

Paris, Harry S. et al., "The Cucurbitaceae and Solanaceae illustrated in medieval manuscripts known as the *Tacuinum Sanitatis*," Annals of Botany Vol.103:8 (2009), webbed at http://www.hort.purdue.edu/newcrop/TS_aob.pdf

Simmons, Alan E., *Growing Unusual Fruit*, Walker and Company, N.Y. 1972.

Simoons, Frederick J., *Food in China,* CRC Press, Boca Raton 1991.

Spencer, Judith tr., *The Four Seasons of the House of Cerruti* (late fourteenth century Italian).

Vesco, Clotilde, *Cucina Fiorentina fra Medioevo e Rinascimento*, 1984.

Wadsworth, Capt. John, *Chocolate: or, An Indian Drinke*. London, 1652. Apparently translated from a book by Melchor de Lara, "Physitian General for the Kingdome of Spaine", 1631.

Whitaker, Thomas W., "American Origin of the Cultivated Cucurbits," *Annals of the Missouri Botanical Garden*, 1947.

Wilson, C. Anne, *Food and Drink in Britain: From the Stone Age to recent times*, Harper and Row 1974. This is an extraordinarily careful and detailed book.

This essay is still growing; if you come across relevant information, please write.

Scottish Oat Cakes: A Conjectural Reconstruction

"the only things they take with them [when riding to war] are a large flat stone placed between the saddle and the saddle-cloth and a bag of oatmeal strapped behind. When they have lived so long on half-cooked meat that their stomachs feel weak and hollow, they lay these stones on a fire and, mixing a little of their oatmeal with water, they sprinkle the thin paste on the hot stone and make a small cake, rather like a wafer, which they eat to help their digestion." (Froissart's Chronicles, Penguin Books translation.)

So far as I know, there are no surviving period recipes for oat cakes. This article is an attempt to reconstruct them, mainly on the basis of Froissart's brief comment.

Rolled oats—what we today call "oatmeal"—are a modern invention. I assume that "oat meal" in the middle ages meant the same thing as "meal" in other contexts—a coarse flour. The only other ingredient mentioned is water, but salt is frequently omitted in medieval recipes—Platina, for instance, explicitly says that he doesn't bother to mention it—so I have felt free to include it. The oat cakes Froissart describes are field rations, so unlikely to contain any perishable ingredients such as butter or lard, although they may possibly have been used in other contexts.

Consistent with these comments, the following is my conjectural recipe for oatcakes as they might have been made by Scottish troopers c. 1400:

½ c steel-cut oats   ¼ t salt   ¼ c water

Combine all ingredients and let the mixture stand for at least fifteen minutes. Make flat cakes ¼" to ⅜" in thickness, cook on a medium hot griddle, without oil, about 3-5 minutes. The result is a reasonably tasty flat bread, though inclined to be crumbly.

(An earlier version of this article was published in *Serve it Forth: A Periodical Forum for SCA Cooks*, Volume I, Number 2 (April 1996). Information on that publication, which unfortunately is no longer coming out, is at home.pcisys.net/~mem/sif_home.html.)

Hildegard von Bingen's Small Cakes

Some time ago I found on the web a fictitious—I am tempted to say fraudulent—recipe entitled "St. Hildegard's Cookies of Joy." I gather that versions can be found offline as well. It is a modern spice cookie recipe, including baking powder, sugar, butter and egg.

The original on which the recipe claims to be based, from a 12th century book on healing, consists of two sentences from the entry on "nutmeg." They read as follows:

"Take some nutmeg and an equal weight of cinnamon and a bit of cloves, and pulverise them. Then make small cakes with this and fine whole wheat flour and water. Eat them often. ..."

As you can see, this not only does not contain baking powder, which had not yet been invented, it does not contain sugar, butter, or egg either.

The following is an attempt to reconstruct what Hildegard actually intended. The only addition is salt—my justification for that being Platina's comment in his cookbook to the effect that he doesn't mention salt because everyone knows to add it.

1 t nutmeg	½ t cloves	¼ c water
1 t cinnamon	1 c whole wheat flour	¼ t salt

Mix the spices with the flour, stir in the water and knead until it is smooth. Divide into four equal portions, roll each into a ball, flatten it a little. Bake on a greased cookie sheet at 300° for 30 minutes, turning them over after the first fifteen.

It is clear from context that the cakes are intended mainly for medicinal purposes; as Hildegard writes:

"It will calm all bitterness of the heart and mind, open your heart and impaired senses, and make your mind cheerful. It purifies your senses and diminishes all harmful humors.

It doesn't taste bad, either.

Reference

Hildegard von Bingen's Physica, Priscilla Throop tr., Healing Arts Press, Rochester, VT 1998.

To Prepare a Most Honorable Feast

by Maistre Chiquart
translated by Elizabeth of Dendermonde

And first, God permitting to be held a most honorable feast at which are kings, queens, dukes, duchesses, counts, countesses, princes, princesses, marquis, marquises, barons, baronesses and lords of lower estate, and nobles also a great number, there are needed, for the ordinary cookery[1] and to make the feast honorably, to the honor of the lord who is giving the said feast, the things which follow.

And first: one hundred well-fattened cattle, one hundred and thirty sheep, also well fattened, one hundred and twenty pigs; and for each day during the feast, one hundred little piglets, both for roasting and for other needs, and sixty salted large well fattened pigs for larding and making soups.

And for this the butcher will be wise and well-advised if he is well supplied so that if it happens that the feast lasts longer than expected, one has promptly what is necessary; and also, if there are extras, do not butcher them so that nothing is wasted.

And there should be for each day of the feast two hundred kids and also lambs, one hundred calves, and two thousand head of poultry.

And you should have your poulterers, subtle, diligent, and wise, who have forty horses for going to various places to get venison, hares, conies, partridges, pheasants, small birds (those which they can get without number), river birds (those which one can obtain), pigeons, cranes, herons, and all wild birds – what one can find of whatever wild birds. And they should turn their attention to this two months or six weeks before the feast, and they should all have come or sent what they could obtain by three or four days before the said feast so that the said meat can be hung and each dealt with as it ought to be.

And they should provide for each day of the said feast six thousand eggs.

Again, for the said feast there should be provided two *charges* [about 320 pounds] of the major spices, that is white ginger, Mecca ginger, cinnamon, grains of paradise, and pepper.

The minor spices: of nutmeg six pounds, of cloves six pounds, of mace six pounds, and of galingale six pounds; again, 30 loaves of sugar, 25 pounds of saffron, 6 *charges* of almonds, one *charge* of rice, 30 pounds of amydon, 12 baskets of candied raisins, 12 baskets of good candied figs, 8 baskets of candied prunes, a quintal [about 110 pounds] of dates, 40 pounds of pine nuts, 18 pounds of turnsole, 18 pounds of alkanet, 18 pounds of gold leaf [!?], one pound of camphor, one hundred ells of good and fine tissue for straining; and these things are for nothing but the use of the kitchen. And again, there should be for the said feast two hundred boxes of sugar-spice pellets of all sorts and colors to put on potages. And if the feast lasts longer one will thus be provided with extra.

And for the profit of the lord who gives the feast, and in order to satisfy the need more promptly and quickly, one should grind to powder the aforesaid spices which are necessary for the said feast, and put each separately into large and good leather bags.

And in order to better prepare the said feast without reprehension or fault, the house-stewards, the kitchen masters, and the master cook should assemble and come together three or four months before the feast to put in order, visit, and find good and sufficient space to do the cooking, and this space should be so large and fine that large working sideboards can be set up in such fashion that between the serving sideboards and the others the kitchen masters can go with ease to pass out and receive the dishes.

And for this there should be provided large, fair, and proper cauldrons for cooking large meats, and other medium ones in great abundance for making potages and doing other things

---

[1] The phrase I translate "ordinary cookery" probably means the food prepared for the servants and the rest

necessary for cookery, and great hanging pans for cooking fish and other necessary things, and large common pots in great abundance for making soups and other things, and a dozen fair large mortars; and check the space for making sauces; and there should be twenty large frying pans, a dozen large casks, fifty small casks, sixty *cornues* [bowls with handles], one hundred wooden bowls, a dozen grills, six large graters, one hundred wooden spoons, twenty-five slotted spoons both large and small, six hooks, twenty iron shovels, twenty rotisseries, with turning mechanisms and irons for holding the spits. And one should definitely not trust wooden spits, because they will rot and you could lose all your meat, but you should have one hundred and twenty iron spits which are strong and are thirteen feet in length; and there should be other spits, three dozen which are of the aforesaid length but not so thick, to roast poultry, little piglets, and river fowl. And also, four dozen little spits to do endoring and act as skewers.

And there should be two casks of vinegar, one of white and one of claret, each of eight *sommes* [110 gallons], a good cask of fine verjuice of twenty *sommes* [275 gallons], and a cask of oil of ten *sommes* [137 ½ gallons].

And there should be one thousand cartloads of good dry firewood and a great storehouse full of coal, and you should always be sure of having more in case of there not being enough.

And so that the workers are not idle, and so that they do not lack for anything, there should be delivered funds in great abundance to the said kitchen masters to get salt, pot-vegetables and other necessary things which might be needed, which do not occur to me at present.

And in order to do things properly and cleanly, and in order to serve and accomplish it more quickly, there should be provided such a large quantity of vessels of gold, of silver, of pewter, and of wood, that is four thousand or more, that when one has served the first course one should have enough for serving the second and still have some left over, and in the mean time one can wash and clean the vessels used during the said first course.

And as at such a feast there could be some very high, puissant, noble, venerable and honorable lords and ladies who do not eat meat, for these there must be fish, marine and fresh-water, fresh and salt, in such manner as one can get them.

And as the sea-bream is king of the other sea fish, listed first is the sea-bream, conger-eel, grey mullet, hake, sole, red mullet, dorade, plaice, turbot, sea-crayfish, tuna, sturgeon, salmon, herrings, sardines, sea-urchin, mussels, eels, boops, ray, cuttle-fish, *arany marine*, anchovies, eels, both fresh and salted.

Concerning fresh-water fish: big trout, big eels, lampreys, filleted char, fillets of big pike, fillets of big carp, big perch, *ferrés, pallés*, graylings, burbot, crayfish, and all other fish.

And because at this feast there are some lords or ladies as was said above who have their own master cooks whom they command to prepare and make ready certain things, for such there should be given and made available to the said master cook quickly, amply, in great abundance and promptly everything for which he asks and which he needs for the said lord or lady or both so that he can serve them to his taste.

And also there should be 120 quintals of best cheese; of good and fine white cloth six hundred ells to cover the sideboards, fish, meats, and roasts; and sixty ells of linen cloth to make the colors of the jellies; and of white broadcloth to make the colors like the color of hyppocras, to make a dozen colors.

And there should be two large two-handed knives for dismembering cattle, and a dozen dressing knives for dressing; and also, two dozen knives to chop for potages and stuffings, and to prepare poultry and fish;

also, half a dozen scrubbers to clean the sideboards and the cutting boards, and a hundred baskets for carrying meat to the casks, both raw and cooked, which one brings to and from the sideboards, and also for bringing coal, for roasts and wherever it is needed and also for carrying and collecting serving vessels.

And if it happens that the feast is held in winter you will need for the kitchen for each night sixty torches, twenty pounds of wax candles, sixty pounds of tallow candles for visiting the butchers' place, the pastry-cooks' place, the place for the fish, and all the doings of the kitchen.

And for the making of pastry there should be a large and fair building close to the kitchen which can be made for two large and fair ovens for making meat and fish pastries, tarts, flans and *talmoses*,[2] *ratons*,[3] and all other things which are necessary for doing cooking.

And for this the said workers should be provided with 30 *sommes* [about 412 gallons] of best wheat flour for the aforesaid needs, and should be sure of getting more if the feast lasts longer.

And because, by the pleasure of the blessed and holy Trinity, the which without fail gives us amply of all good things, we have good and fair and great provisions for making our feast grandly, it is necessary for us to have master cooks and workers to make dishes and subtleties for the said feast; and if it happens that one is not provided with the said cooks and workers, one should send a summons to places where one can find them so that the said feast can be handled grandly and honorably.

Notes: Master Chiquart was chief cook to the Duke of Savoy and in 1420 composed *Du Fait de Cuisine,* from which the above is taken. He goes on to give both meat-day and fish-day menus for his feast, which is to last two days and consists of dinner and supper on both days, and he includes recipes for most of the dishes. These range from the simple to the extremely elaborate; his entremet consisting of a castle would take another article to describe.

It is often said that medieval food was highly spiced; since most medieval recipes do not give any quantities at all it is hard to tell if this is true or not. Chiquart, however, lists amount of meat for his whole feast by number of animals and amount of spices by weight. My lord, Cariadoc, has calculated the approximate amount of meat (on the assumption that Chiquart's animals were smaller than ours) to get a total of about 70,000 pounds of boneless meat, plus whatever amount of meat Chiquart got from game; this gives a ratio of spices to meat of about 1:100 by weight. This is not far from what he and I use for medieval dishes when we prepare them to our own taste, suggesting that the "heavily overspiced" theory is incorrect.

Reference:
Terence Scully. *Du Fait de Cuisine par Maistre Chiquart, 1420. (Ms. S 103 de la bibliotheque Supersaxo, a la Bibliotheque cantonale du Valais, a Sion.)*. Vallesia v. 40, pp. 101-231, 1985.

(Published in Tournaments Illuminated #84)

---

[2] A kind of cheese and egg pie.
[3] A sort of cake: see recipe for Rastons, p. 9.

To Make a Feast

The first step in planning a feast, even before choosing recipes, is to make a rough estimate of the available resources. How many people are willing to spend most of the event helping you cook? How many more are willing to spend a few hours chopping onions or rolling meatballs? How many ovens and burners does the kitchen have? Is your group–or the kitchen you are using–well provided with ten gallon pots and twelve inch frying pans? How much money will be available to spend on the feast and how many people should you expect to feed? The answers to questions like these will determine what sort of a feast it is practical to put on. If you are feeding a hundred people by yourself using one stove, you had better plan on something simple–perhaps a thick soup, bread, cheese, and fruit. With eight assistant cooks and a fair number of helpers, you can plan something a good deal more elaborate.

Once you have a rough estimate of resources, the next step is to work out a tentative menu. To do that you require a source of period recipes. There are two places to find them: primary sources (cookbooks written in period) and secondary sources, modern cookbooks giving worked-out versions of recipes from primary sources.

The problem with primary sources is that they rarely give information on details such as quantities, temperatures or times. That makes working out the recipes fun but time consuming; you will want to cook each dish several times, noting details of how you did it and modifying your instructions according to how it turns out, before serving it to a hall full of guests.

The problem with secondary sources is that they cannot always be trusted. If all you have is the modern version of the recipe, it is hard to tell if it is a careful and competent interpretation of the original, a careless and incompetent interpretation, or a modern recipe distantly inspired by something period. This applies to secondary sources produced within the SCA as well as to those produced elsewhere. It is not safe to assume that just because a cookbook has the name of a kingdom or barony on it, the recipes inside are from the Middle Ages; in our experience, the odds are that they are not. The same is true for recipes printed in T.I. or C.A. Sometimes they are period, sometimes they are not–and sometimes they say they are period and are not, which is the worst case. We therefore suggest that if you use secondary sources you restrict yourself to ones which include the original recipes as well as the worked out versions. Always remember that what the author has added to the original is simply his guess; you are free to substitute your own.

Suppose you have obtained a suitable number of recipes, directly from a primary or secondary source or indirectly through the local cooking guild or someone in your group who got them from such a source. Before definitely deciding to use one, cook it and try it. That will give you an idea both of how it tastes and of how much trouble it is to make.

In drawing up your menu, there are three points to consider. The first is the balance of flavors and textures. It is unlikely that you will want to cook a feast made up mainly of roast meats, or mainly of stews, or containing only spicy dishes or only bland dishes. Imagine eating the feast; if you think you would be bored half way through, you have the wrong menu. Avoid having any one ingredient in every dish; if there are eggs in everything, anyone allergic to eggs cannot eat. Try to include one or two substantial meatless dishes so that vegetarians will have something to eat. Also, remember that different people have different tastes. You will probably want some exotic dishes; there is little point in doing a genuine medieval feast and having it taste like something from Denny's. On the other hand, some of your guests will have plain tastes; there should be something for them too. My own policy is to put the more exotic dishes early in the feast, so that those who do not like them can fill up with the plainer dishes later. Besides, people are more likely to try something strange when they are hungry–and they might like it.

The second consideration is whether the feast you are planning is one you can cook. Do you have enough oven space for the number of pies you are planning? Are you doing more labor-intensive dishes than you have labor? How expensive are the ingredients? Once you have the menu worked out you will do detailed calculations to answer these questions, but it is useful to keep them in the back of your mind while designing the menu.

The third consideration is quantity. If you are serving eight main dishes, your guest does not have to make a full meal out of each of them. Our rule of thumb is to allow a total of half a pound of meat per person. That means that for every dish you estimate the total amount of meat, including fish and fowl and not counting fat, bones, or skin, add it up for all the dishes and divide by the number of people. If you have a lot of bulky non-meat dishes–soups or pies thickened with egg and cheese, for example–you might want to reduce the total to a third of a pound. If you are not certain how many guests will show up, you may want to make contingency plans—ways of expanding or contracting your feast at the last minute.

You now have a tentative menu. Next you will want to work out a set of detailed plans showing what is done when and how much it all costs. One convenient way of doing this is to use time lines. Make a list of all the fixed resources that you are afraid you may not have enough of– ovens, burners, large pots, electric frying pans. List them down the left side of a sheet of graph paper. Across the top of the sheet mark the time, starting whenever you plan to start cooking and ending when the last dish is served. Draw a horizontal line for each item. Mark on that line what the item is being used for at each time. The result (for a few items and a few dishes) will look something like:

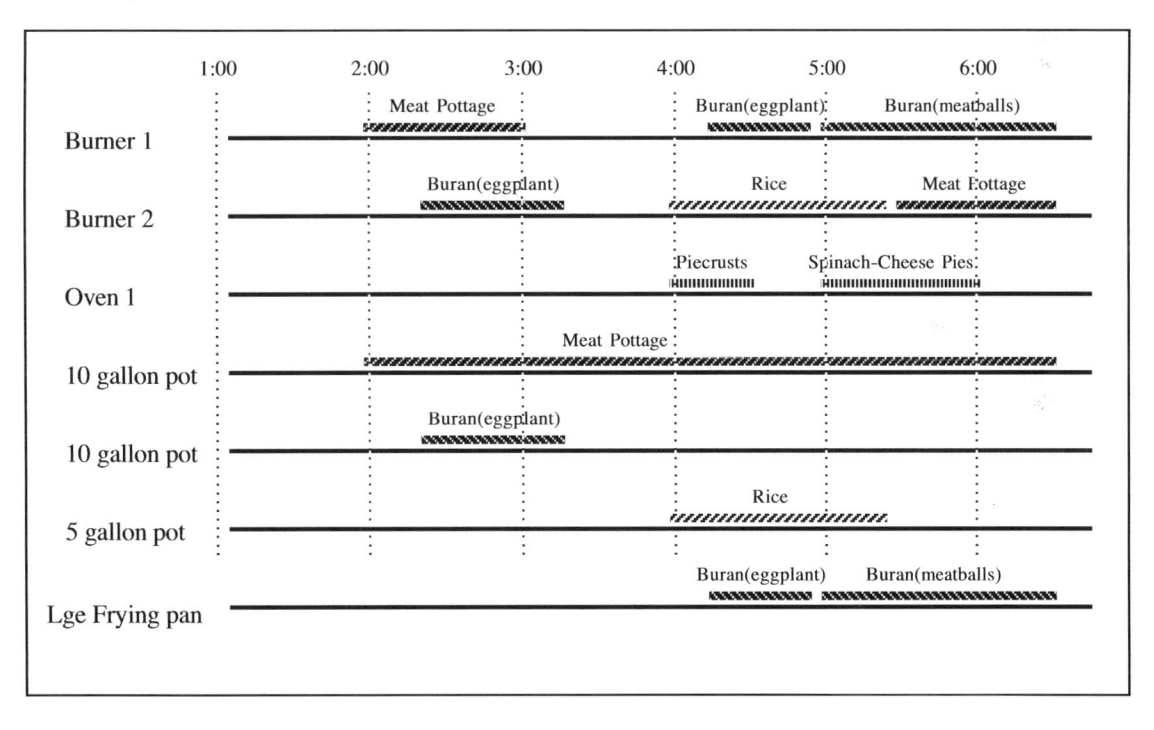

	1:00	2:00	3:00	4:00	5:00	6:00
Burner 1		Meat Pottage		Buran(eggplant)	Buran(meatballs)
Burner 2		Buran(eggplant)		Rice	Meat Pottage
Oven 1			Piecrusts	Spinach-Cheese Pies
10 gallon pot		Meat Pottage
10 gallon pot		Buran(eggplant)
5 gallon pot			Rice
Lge Frying pan			Buran(eggplant)	Buran(meatballs)

To make sense of the diagram, start with the meat pottage (recipe on p. 22). It occupies a 10 gallon pot from 2:00 until 6:30, when it will be served. The first stage in cooking it is to boil the meat; this is done on burner 1 from 2:00 to 3:00. The pottage is then taken off the burner, which is then free to be used for something else. The meat is taken out of the broth, cut up, and put back in along with beef broth, bread crumbs, and spices. At 5:30 the pot goes back on the stove, this time on burner 2 (burner 1 is by that time being used for something else) and is brought to a boil; the rest of the ingredients (chopped parsley, grated cheese, and eggs) are stirred in.

Starting at 2:20, the second 10 gallon pot is used on burner 2 to boil the eggplant which is one of the ingredients of buran, a medieval Islamic dish (p. 90). After that is finished, a 5 gallon pot of rice goes onto the burner. The rice is being cooked early because all the burners are needed for the last hour before the feast; a five gallon pot full of food should stay warm for a long time after it comes off the stove.

Starting about 4:15, the eggplant that was earlier boiled is fried in sesame oil, using the large frying pan on burner 1. When that is done the frying pan is rinsed out and used to fry the meatballs that are the other main ingredient in buran.

Obviously, lots of things are happening that are not shown on the chart. Meatballs and pie crusts must be made, pie filling mixed, and so forth. The chart was drawn on the assumption that none of those processes used scarce resources; there are plenty of plates to pile the meat balls on and rolling pins for rolling out pie crusts. Equally obviously, unless this is a very small and very oddly balanced feast, what is shown is only part of the chart; other resources are being used for other dishes.

The purpose of drawing up such a chart is not to figure out exactly what everything will be used for at every instant. That is not possible; something is certain to go wrong, and your plans will have to be revised on the spot. What the chart does is to show you whether or not it is possible to cook the feast you have planned in the kitchen you are using and where problems are likely to occur. If, after juggling alternative schedules, you discover that there is no way to produce the feast without using two more burners than you have, you can change your plans accordingly. Perhaps you should have one more baked dish and two fewer fried ones. Perhaps you should make an effort to get a couple of really large pots, thus allowing more food to cook on each burner. Perhaps you could shift the frying off the stove onto a couple of electric frying pans. Whatever the solution, it is better to discover the problem now than in the middle of cooking the feast.

In describing the time line, I have left out the most crucial resource of all–cooks. Ideally, for a large feast, each cook should be in charge of one dish–for a small feast, two. Some cooks may be able to do more than that, if there are dishes that can be completed early in the day and others that need not be started until fairly late, or if there are some very easy dishes. Cooking rice, for instance, is not a full time job, although cooking five gallons at once is trickier than you might expect. To decide which cooks do which dishes, the simplest procedure is to show them the recipes and let them choose for themselves. Once a cook has chosen a recipe, he should arrange to cook it for himself at home at least once.

The number of cooks puts a limit on how many dishes you can prepare on the day of the feast. One way around that limit is to do some of your cooking earlier. That is fine, as long as you restrict yourself to dishes which taste just as good the second day as the first. Too much pre-cooking of too many things and you end up spending a lot of time and effort to produce the sort of meal you expect to get in a college cafeteria.

Your time lines tell you whether you can cook the feast you plan; you still need to find out whether you can pay for it. Make up a shopping list, showing how much of every ingredient you will need. Then check out a couple of supermarkets to find out how much everything will cost. Add it all up and you have a rough estimate of the cost of the feast. With luck the real cost will be lower, since you will do a more careful job of shopping when you are actually buying the food.

You now have a reasonable idea of what you need to do the feast. If it is consistent with what you have, you are ready for the next stage. If not, revise your menu, change your plans, or find additional resources.

Once your plans are made, the next thing to do is to arrange a practice dinner. This is a dinner party for and by the cooks; you may also want to invite the autocrat of the event. Each cook prepares the dish or dishes he will be making for the feast, in a quantity appropriately scaled down for the number present. The dishes are served in the order in which they will be served in the feast.

The practice dinner serves several purposes. The most important is to test out the feast as a whole. Does the balance of the dishes seem satisfactory? Is there enough food to fill everyone up, but not enough to provide vast quantities of left-overs? Should there be more of some dishes and less of others? You get much better answers to such questions by cooking the feast and eating it than by staring at recipes.

A second purpose of the practice feast is to get more precise information on what will be needed to produce the real feast. As each dish is prepared, the cook should note down what tools are required, how large a pot was needed for the amount made, and about how much time each step took. If rolling enough meatballs for eight people takes one cook five minutes, then rolling enough for 240 people will take about two and a half man-hours; that is useful information. If enough gharibah to serve eight people fills a quart pot, then enough for 240 will require about an eight gallon pot. After the practice feast, you can use the information to redo your time lines more precisely. If you decide that you should have more or less of some dishes, you can alter the shopping list accordingly. At this point you should also make a list of all the tools you will need. It is possible to roll out pie crust with a wine bottle, but a rolling pin works better.

In estimating how long things will take, remember that five gallons of water takes a great deal longer to come to a boil than does a quart. That is why, on the sample time line, I allowed an hour and a half for cooking rice, a task that normally takes about half an hour. If you have a chance, you may want to actually measure how long it takes a very large pot of water to come to a boil on the stove you will be using to cook the feast. That will help you decide how much extra time to allow for cooking large quantities.

A third purpose is to spot unexpected problems. You should have discovered all such problems already in the process of drawing up the time lines, but don't count on it.

A fourth and last purpose of the practice feast is to let the cooks get to know each other, in a more relaxed context than cooking a real feast.

After the practice feast is over and you and the other cooks have finished discussing its implications, you are ready for the final stage of planning. Give the autocrat and the chief server a list of dishes and ingredients so that they can answer questions from people with allergies or religious restrictions. Make sure that everything on your list of necessary equipment is being brought by someone. Redo your time lines, taking account of what you have learned and of any changes you have decided on. If possible, leave some margin for error. Try to schedule a couple of hours free for yourself, sometime in the afternoon; that way you will be available to help with any crisis that develops. If the crisis does not develop until later, you can always spend the two hours helping to roll meatballs.

Now you are ready to start shopping. Decide what has to be bought the day before the feast and what can be bought early; this depends in part on the availability of refrigerator and freezer space. Check supermarket ads during the week before the feast; someone may have chicken leg quarters on sale for $.29/lb. Investigate bulk food sources and see how their prices compare. In Chicago, there is an area called the Water Market where onions are sold in fifty pound bags and squash in forty pound boxes. If the prices are good enough, it may be worth buying forty pounds of squash and giving fifteen away. To locate bulk sources in your area, you might try the business-to-business phone book, if there is one. Or ask someone friendly at a local restaurant where they get their food. Perhaps the chief cook for the last event your group did can tell you the best place for bulk eggs or meat.

Remember that, while the cost in money of producing the feast is important, so is the cost in time. Boned lamb shoulders may cost a little more per pound of meat than unboned ones, but they save a lot of time. What is sold as washed spinach will have to be rewashed, but the process will take a lot less time than if you start with unwashed spinach. You do not want to be penny wise and hour foolish.

In addition to the food, you will also want to buy things such as dishwashing soap, wax paper for rolling out piecrusts, plastic wrap for covering things, paper towels, sponges and scrubbies, scouring powder, and whatever else you expect to need. Don't forget to bring dish towels and one oven thermometer for each oven.

Another thing to do at this stage, if you have not already done it, is to locate a good grocery store near the event site. I have still not figured out why I ended up short ten pounds of eggplants for the Tregirtse Twelfth Night feast–but I am glad I knew where to send someone to get them.

The cooking of the feast will probably begin before the event; if you are making mead, it may be a week, a month, or a year before. If you are baking bread, you probably want to do it the day before the event, so it will be fresh. Some stews are just as good the second day as the first, although if the stew is thickened you have to be very careful to keep it from scorching when you warm it up. Cold nibbles, such as hais, hulwa, prince biscuit, currant cakes, and the like keep well for a long time; they can be made whenever convenient. Arrange to have a reasonable number of helpers at this stage of things. Rolling hais is a simple process, but if you are doing it by yourself for two hundred people in the intervals between kneading bread, putting bread in ovens, and taking bread out of ovens, you may not get much sleep.

It is now the day of the event; you, the food, the pots, the rolling pins, and three boxes of assorted odds and ends have arrived in the kitchen. You have marked all of your pots and tools, and told everyone else to mark theirs. Some of them will have forgotten, so be sure you have tape and a waterproof pen. It may be a good idea to make a list of what everyone has brought, to make it more likely that everything will get back to where it belongs.

Your assistant cooks arrive. Make sure they know what is happening. Show them where the time line is and where you have the equipment and food. The idea of having each cook in charge of a dish is to minimize the degree to which everything depends on you.

As things start happening, try to keep track of what is happening. See who needs help, who has help to offer. When it turns out that necessary ingredients are missing, make up a shopping list and arrange a grocery store run. Arrange to set one of your volunteer workers to washing things; that way clean pots and utensils will be available when needed. Check the oven temperatures with your thermometers; their thermostats may not be accurate. As you get close to the time the feast is scheduled to be served, check with the autocrat on timing. If the event is running an hour late, there is no point in delivering the feast on time and having it all eaten cold; you may have to alter your plans accordingly. When the feast actually starts, coordinate the delivery of the dishes with whomever is in charge of serving. Dishes stay warm better in large pots on the stove than sitting in bowls for half an hour waiting for servers who are doing something else.

After the feast is done, the next stage is cleanup. When you agreed to be head cook, you made it clear to the autocrat that neither you nor the other cooks intended, after spending the first nine hours of the event cooking the feast, to spend the next three cleaning up, so someone else is in charge of that. Your job is to notify whomever that is that you are now finished with the kitchen. After everything has been washed, it is your job to make sure that everything borrowed gets back to its owner; you are the one who borrowed it. You may also want to make sure that the leftover meat pottage goes home with you, one of the other cooks, or someone else who will appreciate it, instead of being dumped.

You are now done. If nothing went catastrophically wrong, you have done a good job. Note down the problems for next time, thank everyone who helped you, especially the lady who showed up in the kitchen at noon and washed dishes for six hours, go home and go to bed.

[by Cariadoc and Elizabeth]

An Islamic Dinner

Islamic feasts in the Society are only occasionally cooked from recipes from period sources; yet Islam was a literate culture early in our period, with the result that there are a number of surviving cookbooks from the 10th to the 15th century. My lord Cariadoc and I have been cooking from the cookbooks available in English for some years and now have a large stock of tested Islamic recipes, so I decided to cook a dinner for the Grey Gargoyles' Spring Tournament completely from medieval Islamic recipes. I had three objectives in designing the menu, in addition to making a good dinner that my friends would enjoy: I wanted to show something of the range of medieval Islamic food; I wanted to make it a very low-work feast, so that more of us could enjoy the tourney; and I wanted to reduce the cost as much as possible. Other considerations included balance of flavors, allowing for allergies, and limited kitchen space.

Menu

There are a number of recipes for relishes or dips in the period Islamic cookbooks. The feast started with one of these, Badinjan Muhassa (p. 111), served with bread. Unfortunately, I knew very little about medieval Islamic bread other than the fact that it existed, but I assumed that modern pita bread would be a reasonable guess. Badinjan Muhassa is based on eggplant, ground and toasted walnut, and raw onion; eggplant is probably the most common vegetable in medieval Islamic cookbooks. This version of the recipe is from a 10th century collection; another version is in the 13th-century cookbook of al-Bagdadi.

The main course consisted of Tabâhajah from the manuscript of Yahya b. Khalid (p. 97), a Cooked Dish of Lentils (p. 99), and Andalusian Chicken (p. 77), served with rice. The Tabâhajah is from another of the cookbooks in the 10th-century collection. It is one of those rare period recipes which gives exact quantities for most of the ingredients. It consists of meat (we used lamb) marinated, cooked in oil, and topped with chopped greens. The marinade is based on *murri*, a condiment widely used in medieval Islamic cooking. Real *murri* was made by a lengthy process involving fermentation; so far as we know it has not been used since the 15th century. However, there exists a period recipe for quick and cheap imitation *murri,* and we made up a supply of that for the marinade. Judging by comments, and by the limited amount left over, the Tabâhajah was the real hit of the feast.

The Cooked Dish of Lentils consists of lentils cooked with onions and spices, with eggs cooked on top at the end. It is one of the easiest dishes I know of, the only real work being chopping the onions, and is a favorite with our after fighter practice crowd. It also provides a main dish for vegetarians (at least those who eat eggs and dairy products). Both this and the Andalusian Chicken are from an Andalusian (Moorish Spanish) cookbook of the 13th century by al-Andalusi.

The original title on the recipe for Andalusian Chicken was just "Another Dish," so I gave it a more descriptive name. It is made by frying the chicken with oil and some seasonings "until it is gilded," simmering it in the juice of onion and green coriander (cilantro), and finally thickening the sauce with breadcrumb and egg.

Of the three main dishes, the lentil dish has neither meat nor wheat, the Tabâhajah has neither eggs nor dairy products, and the chicken has neither onions nor dairy products, so that someone with any single one of these common food allergies would be able to eat at least one dish. With only three main dishes, I could not allow for multiple allergies. In order that our guests could find out what was in the food, the servers, both kitchens, and the autocrat were provided with a list of all ingredients in each dish, including drinks and desserts.

We served two drinks in addition to water: sekanjabin (a sweet mint drink, p. 125) and a lemon drink (p. 125). Both of these are made by making a flavored sugar syrup, which keeps without refrigeration, and diluting it to prepare the drink. Sekanjabin is mentioned by al-Nadim in the 10th century and still survives today; we used a modern Middle-Eastern recipe. The lemon drink comes from an anonymous 13th-century Andalusian cookbook which has a great many recipes for syrup drinks of this sort.

For dessert we served a plate of several pastries and sweets. Khushkananaj (p. 116) is a pastry made with flour and sesame oil with a filling of almonds, sugar, and rosewater. Hais (p. 117) are little balls made of dates, ground nuts, breadcrumbs, and butter. They are a fair amount of work, but as they keep well (the original recipe recommends them as travelers' food) they were made a week in advance. Both of these come from the 13th-century eastern Islamic cookbook of al-Bagdadi. Hulwa is a general term for sweets or candy. There is a recipe (p. 121) for several kinds of hulwa in the 15th-century eastern Islamic cookbook of Ibn al-Mabrad. One kind is rather like modern divinity and can be made with either sugar or honey; we made it for the feast with sugar. A second kind of candy we made is Makshufa (p. 122), from al-Bagdadi's cookbook, made with sugar, honey, almonds, and sesame oil.

Serving

In the anonymous Andalusian cookbook there is a discussion of whether food should be served with each kind on a separate dish or with everything on one platter: "Many of the great figures and their companions order that the separate dishes be placed on each table before the diners, one after another; and by my life, this is more beautiful than putting an uneaten mound all on the table, and it is more elegant, better-bred, and modern"[p. 24 verso-25 recto in the Arabic original]. In spite of his strong words, I decided on the inelegant version. We served each table a large platter with rice on top of which were the chicken, the lamb and the lentils next to each other. The Badinjan Muhassa and the bread were served first in small bowls, and all the desserts for each table on one plate.

Practical Considerations

Cost: It is usually worth checking out wholesale prices for the most expensive and largest quantity items in a feast; for meats, it is worth figuring out the cheapest cut that will work for the dishes you are cooking. We bought boneless lamb shoulders and chicken leg quarters from a wholesale butcher who happens to be our seneschal. If the butcher had not been a member of the group we would have had to cut up the lamb and cut the chicken legs and thighs apart ourselves rather than getting it done for us, but we still would have gotten a much better price than at the local grocery. Often ethnic or health food stores will have some foods in bulk that would be available in your local grocery only in small quantities at high prices; we got nuts and some of the spices in bulk at an Indian grocery store. Serving one meatless main dish (the lentils) also helped to keep the cost down. The total cost of the food was about $475 for almost 250 people. *[This would have been in about 1990.]*

Quantity: My usual rule for estimating quantities is that all dishes put together should add up to about half a pound of boneless meat per person, a little less if there are a lot of hefty meatless dishes or if you don't expect people to be very hungry. Given that this was a tournament, I expected people to be hungry. I allowed a quarter pound of lamb per person and 7 ounces of chicken with bone, which comes to about another quarter pound of boneless meat. How much of the other dishes we wanted I estimated by experience. I checked these estimates by serving a "practice feast" a few weeks before the event: the whole feast done in miniature for 8 people. (This also helps to spot other potential problems with a feast.)

What fed the whole crowd, with a few main dish leftovers and a moderate amount of dessert leftovers, was: 25 recipes of Badinjan Muhassa, 64 recipes of Tabâhajah, 21 recipes of Cooked Dish of Lentils, 32 recipes of Andalusian Chicken, 3 recipes of Hais, 8 recipes of Khushkananaj, 5 recipes of Hulwa, 6.5 recipes of Makshufa, 5 recipes of sekanjabin, and about 3 gallons of lemon syrup.

Work: I deliberately chose low-work dishes, and ones where some of the work could be done in advance. The walnut for the Badinjan Muhassa was ground and toasted a few days before the feast, and the Badinjan Muhassa was mixed up the day before the feast. The murri for the Tabâhajah was made the week before. The hardest part of making Andalusian chicken is turning onions and green coriander into juice. We did that in advance with the help of an unmedieval blender and food processor, turning the kitchen green in the process, and froze the juice. The onions for the lentil dish were chopped the day before, and the desserts were made anywhere from a week to a day in advance, depending on how well they keep. The use of only one platter per table for the main dishes and rice reduced the amount of washing-up to be done.

Kitchens: Our site has two small kitchens, the smaller one with a four-burner stove and the larger with a six-burner stove. Since the food was cooking in very large pots, only two pots could fit onto the smaller stove, and four onto the larger stove. Both the rice and the lentils could start cooking on the stove and then be removed to finish cooking by their own heat; five gallons of lentils or nine gallons of rice will stay hot enough to cook for a long time. (By the same token, leftovers should be put in small containers before being refrigerated after the feast: that much food in one mass will stay warm enough to spoil for a long time even in the refrigerator.) We therefore cooked the rice and lentils first and the lamb and chicken afterward on the same stoves.

[by Elizabeth; originally published in *Tournaments Illuminated* #105]

How to Make Arrack

Sugarcane is also used for the preparation of intoxicating liquor, but brown sugar is better for this purpose. There are various ways of preparing it. They pound *Babul* bark mixing it at the rate of ten sers to one man of sugarcane, and put three times as much water over it. Then they take large jars, fill them with the mixture, and put them into the ground, surrounding them with dry horse dung. From seven to ten days are required to produce fermentation. It is a sign of perfection, when it has a sweet, but astringent taste. ... This beverage, when strained, may be used, but it is mostly employed for the preparation of arrack.

They have several methods of distilling it; *first*, they put the above liquor into brass vessels, in the interior of which a cup is put, so as not to shake, nor must the liquid flow into it. The vessels are then covered with inverted lids which are fastened with clay. After pouring cold water on the lids, they kindle the fire, changing the water as often as it gets warm. As soon as the vapour inside reaches the cold lid, it condenses, and falls as arrack into the cup.

The *Ain-i-Akbari*, 16th c. Indian

Making this is probably illegal in the U.S. The method of distillation is one I first encountered in a modern survival manual.

A Dinner at Pennsic

My lord and I have the custom of cooking dinner for our entire encampment one evening at Pennsic, working from period recipes. On this occasion we were cooking for 25 people. Our constraints are that there are only two of us, although we usually get some help; we have a fairly good kitchen set-up, but it does not so far include an oven; we do not keep a cooler at Pennsic; and we wanted to do something simple enough that we could be assured of being able to wash the dishes in daylight.

The easiest sorts of food to cook over a campfire are spit-roasted meat and dishes in a large pot or frying pan. As no one in our camp was making a grocery store run that day, we decided against meat. Greens, eggs, and butter were the most perishable foodstuffs we were using, and all will keep for a day or two without refrigeration as long as you do not leave them out in the sun; also, eggs are available on site. As we make them, two of the recipes have meat broth. They could, however, be made suitable for a medieval fast day out of Lent (or for a modern vegetarian) by using vegetable broth instead, as the original recipes merely say "good broth." I figured that to feed that number of people we would probably need three large pots of food, so we might as well make three different dishes as well as dessert.

There are several medieval versions of noodles and cheese, both English and Italian. We chose Losyns (p. 68) as it specifies that the noodles be made in advance and dried, allowing us to do so at our leisure before we came. The name of the dish is presumably related to lasagna, so one could make long flat noodles, but we interpret it as the losenges of heraldry and make diamond-shaped noodles. We generally use a mixture of whole wheat and white flour, on the theory that most medieval flour would not be as fine as our modern white flour. "Poudre douce" (sweet powder) is a spice mixture used in both this and the following recipe; we do not know exactly what is in it, but our guess is sugar, cinnamon, and ginger. We mixed it up before we came.

The Carrots in Potage (p. 22) recipe is originally for turnips in potage, with "pastunakes" (carrots or parsnips) or skirrets (a root vegetable we have been unable to find) given as alternatives. It works fine with all three of the vegetables we have tried, but carrots are the easiest to be sure of finding in a modern grocery store. For the Fried Broad Beans (p. 17), we bought dried fava beans in advance at a specialty food store. The greens we used (cabbage, parsley, and spinach) were period ones which we could buy locally; other times we have used turnip, mustard, or dandelion greens.

For a dessert, the most obvious choices are fruit, sweets one can make in advance and bring, such as Islamic candies and pastries or late-period English cakes, and things you can do in a frying pan. Since we were eating fruit and nibbles we had brought with us for most of our breakfasts and lunches, we decided on Murakkaba (p. 121), an interesting solution to the problem of how to make a thick cake without an oven. There are also English recipes for fritters we could have made, but the murakkaba was such a hit the previous year that we decided to repeat it.

Equipment needed:
Two large pots (1 ½ to 2 gallon) with lids, plus a third to heat wash water; two large frying pans for broad beans, one of which gets re-used for murrakkaba; about four bowls, one quite large; a cutting board; a sharp knife or two; several big spoons and ladles; a measuring cup and spoons (if you don't want modern-looking ones, take a period-looking mug and spoons and measure how much they will hold at home); and a cooking set-up which allows two large pots and two frying pans on the fire at once.

Quantities
What we made, which fed our 25 people almost exactly, was: 4 recipes of Losyns, 4 recipes of Carrots in Potage, 4 recipes of Fried Broad Beans and 3 recipes of Murakkaba, done as 2 cakes.

[by Elizabeth; originally published in *Tournaments Illuminated* #113]

Printed in Great Britain
by Amazon